Education and Power in Nigeria

Paul Beckett and James O'Connell

AFRICANA PUBLISHING COMPANY
NEW YORK

A division of Holmes and Meier Publishers, Inc.

First published in the United States of America 1978 by
Africana Publishing Company
A division of Holmes and Meier Publishers, Inc.
101 Fifth Avenue
New York, N.Y. 10003

© 1977 Paul Beckett and James O'Connell

ALL RIGHTS RESERVED

Library of Congress Cataloging in Publication Data

O'Connell, James, 1925–
   Education and power in Nigeria

   1. Education and state—Nigeria. 2. Higher education and state—Nigeria. 3. Students—Nigerial—Political activity. I. Beckett, Paul Louis, 1913– joint author. II. Title.
LC95.N55027   379.669   77–15452
ISBN 0-8419-0346-8

Printed in Great Britain

Contents

1 Introduction
2 Social Background: an Elite-In-Formation
3 Social Origins and Identity
4 Career and Happiness: Perspectives on the Future
5 General Political Values: Order and Unity
6 Participation and Democracy: The Dynamics of Politics in Nigeria
7 University Students and the Nigerian Future
Appendix 1: Information on the Samples
Appendix 2: The Questionnaires

Acknowledgements

Robert Gavin, Festus Ogunlade and Otto Marenin, all at that time of Ahmadu Bello University, read the whole or part of the draft of this book and helped to improve it with their suggestions. We want to thank as well the following who contributed in a variety of ways to the project: Ishaya Audu, Hadiza Audu, Pauline Baker, Kathleen Beckett, Jo Bostock, John Collins, Paul Collins, Ibrahim Dapchi, Billy Dudley, Mary Halloway, Katherine Hoomkwop, John Hughes, Pauline Hughes, Ken Lupton, Stephen Malgwi, Ignatius Musa, Kola Ogungbesan, Michael Olisa, Russell Parkes, Margaret Peil, James Polhemus, Bitrus Sawa, Joseph Schyler, Emmy Simmons, Ian Woods and Ali Yahaya. But we also have in mind a much longer list—much too long for inclusion here—of other persons who have helped us in our study through their contributions of time, knowledge and skill. We are grateful to all these people. Finally, we wish to express our gratitude to the nearly 3,000 university students who good humouredly contributed their time and permitted us to invade their privacy with our questionnaires.

P.B.
J.O'C.

1 Introduction

1. THE EDUCATED ELITE IN NIGERIAN SOCIETY

Professor Ayandele, a member of Nigeria's highly educated elite, has remarked:

> Ever self-centred since the middle of the 19th century the educated elite have all along commented upon themselves, presenting themselves as the class around whom history has been revolving in modern Nigeria; as clairvoyant modernists and modernisers, who were to create, build and integrate Nigeria in the developed zone of the world; as the oppressed nationalist crusaders who used their brain, pen and tongue to expel the British colonial exploiters; as the wizards of nation-building, who were to erect a virile, sphinx-like Nigerian nation upon the ashes of British Nigeria.[1]

British Nigeria, after the Second World War, was preparing itself for the termination of the colonial era. The "revolution from above" represented by political decolonization bypassed the traditional authority holders even in the strongholds of indirect rule. The well-known hostility expressed by colonialists toward the educated elite[2] was reversed, on the surface at least, as the colonial rulers moved hastily to develop substitute 'high level manpower'. The educated elite had from the earliest colonial years shown a peculiar faith that there would be a succession, and that they would be the successors. This early faith, running originally, as Ayandele remarks, 'against every evidence',[3] did in fact gain its reward as a system of electoral politics was hastily engineered, and as the more deeply-rooted roles of politico-administrative power in the public services were opened up to 'indigenisation'. The educated elite were recognised as the heirs.

Viewed from the standpoint of elite groups, the colonial society as it developed and existed through the first half of the 20th century, Nigeria's formative years, was an artificially simple one. A set of bureaucratic organisations, modern in organisation and aim, ruled over a politically-defined collectivity which was pre-modern in terms of material culture and organisation, parochial in terms of political culture and socially unintegrated. Electoral politics were a feature not of true colonialism but of terminal colonialism. Such large-scale economic organisation as developed was mainly under the auspices of the state (the railroads, especially) or foreign enterprise (United Africa Company, etc.). Except in the largest southern commercial centres, power, status and wealth in the colonial society remained throughout most of the colonial period rooted in the structures of government: in the colonial administration proper and in the various 'traditional' bodies that formed part of the system of colonial rule.[4] The first half of the century modified the early simpler colonial order. In saying 'seek ye first the political kingdom' Nkrumah expressed recognition of one of the basic characteristics of the colonial situation. But it was not until the 1940's and 1950's that in Nigeria, as well as in the other territories of British West Africa, an indigenous educated elite emerged to challenge the colonial possession of power and wealth. They quickly filled the new positions of power in electoral politics, and gradually took over a larger and larger proportion of the old positions of power, the administrative roles, from the colonial expatriates. Two sections of this 'successor elite'—the politicians, and the civil servants and technicians—must therefore be distinguished. The main defining common denominator of the successor elite taken as a whole is education, i.e. formal education of the type generally if awkwardly called 'modern' or 'Western'. Some of the men who came forward as political leaders had high traditional status; a few had prior economic power; but *all* of those in the first wave and the first rank had some degree of modern education.[5] This was still more true of those who filled the senior posts in the administration that heretofore had been the preserve of the white colonial expatriates.

In contemporary Nigeria entry to the administrative class of the public service normally requires university education. Rapid Nigerianization during the 1950's, however, meant in many cases replacing graduate white administrators by non-graduate Nigerians, often with only secondary level education, who received further training in short courses. This was because not enough university graduates were available. As graduates have become available recruitment to the lower ranks of the administrative class in the Federal and State public services has been dominantly from the ranks of the new university graduates, and in the States where their numbers are adequate, almost exclusively so. While there is not as rigid a separation between the executive and administrative classes in the Nigerian public service system as in the original British one, it is clear that in fact the great majority of those who reach the high ranks will enter directly (as opposed to working their way up from the executive class), and that the great majority of the direct entrants will be holders of university or professional degrees.[6] A sharply-defined adminstrative upper class exists, therefore, and it will be increasingly the preserve of university graduates.

The suspension of civilian political rule in Nigeria, as in so many other African countries, has had the effect of increasing the significance of the administrative class of the public service. The alliance of military officers, themselves mainly graduates of post-secondary military schools and in some cases of universities, and high level civil servants which is inevitably at the heart of 'military' rule means that representatives of the highest educated stratum of society are in control. For the present, the less uniformly well-educated 'class' of politicians are eliminated from the scene. In the sense of being an administrative state resting on a foundation of potential military force, the post-political military regime displays a striking affinity to the situation during most of the colonial period.

This demonstrates the extraordinary significance in Nigeria of the highly educated (mainly, university educated) elite. It is the educated elite, and not traditional or economic elites, who have succeeded to the control of the institutions of state which have themselves become of greater significance in setting the main patterns of continuity and change in the post-colonial society. It is ironic but far from surprising that the group most thoroughly initiated into the culture of the colonizers should be the group that in a general way presides over the period and process of decolonization.

The significance of the highly educated elite, so much noted, as Ayandele asserts, by its own historians, has also been noted by non-African scholars and commentators. The best known frankly normative interpretations of the post colonial African countries, those of Fanon, Dumont, and First,[7] regard the 'national bourgeoisie' (mainly a bourgeoisie of the civil service, as Fanon explains) as having stepped into the shoes of the departing colonial masters; and as creating a 'black parody' of the white colonial system (First) in the process of acting as intermediaries in Africa's exploitation by Europe. Such interpretations represent the most emphatic acknowledgement of the significance of the highly educated elite in shaping (or in the critics' view, misshaping) independence.

The highly educated elite is in fact very small in proportion to the total population. Taking for the moment Harbison's functional definition of the 'senior' elite category and his estimate of numbers,[8] the number of Nigerians qualified for senior positions (mainly but not exclusively in the public sector) could be put at roughly 15,000 at the time of independence. As Harbison notes, by the time of independence a university degree or advanced teacher's college degree (or its equivalent) was increasingly being considered requisite for entrance into this 'senior' stratum.[9] If we estimate the country's population at the time of independence as 50 million, Harbison's figure suggests that the senior elite's proportion in the society as a whole might approximate 0.03 per cent.

In the 17 years since independence, employment in the large-scale modern organizations, both public and private, has grown tremendously. The present paucity in Nigeria of reliable economic and demographic statistics makes it impossible to give firm figures on numbers of high-level jobs, but it may be worthwhile to indulge in some 'guesstimates', so long as the highly tentative nature of the resulting figures is kept in mind. A major study conducted by the Public Service Review Commission and reported in September, 1974 estimates public sector employment (excluding the military) at more than 600,000, composed as follows:

Table 1.

Public Sector Categories*	Number of Employees (in thousands)
Federal Civil Service (including police)	102†
State Civil Services	140
Education Services	160
Parastatals	230
	632

*Excludes local government, judiciary and unestablished staff.
†Established positions less an estimate on vacancies.
(Source: Public Service Review Commission, *Report on Grading and Pay,* Vol. 1 (Lagos, 1974). Adapted from Table 5-1, p.13).

The Commission does not provide data on the number of employees at senior levels of the public sector as a whole; but deriving from their data a proportion (7.6 percent) representing the maximum number of positions within the Federal civil service requiring university degrees or roughly equivalent training (and recognizing that not all persons in such positions would in fact have such backgrounds), we can apply that percentage to the public sector as a whole and suggest that the public sector senior elite might be estimated at about 50,000. Another 10,000 might be added as a rather generous estimate of the number of jobs in comparable senior categories in the private sector.[10] Estimating the population at between 60 and 65 million, this suggests that the senior elite might represent 0.1 percent of the total population. Small as this group is, it is many times greater in number than the British staff of colonial Nigeria ever was. Its influence is also greater than that of the British colonial elite not only because of its larger numbers but also as a result of its more extensive connections with the rest of society.

The artificial social simplicity (in the urban, modern sector) of the colonial period is passing. Since independence vast numbers of men and women have come to the cities. Nearly 400,000 pupils emerge annually from primary school; more than 60,000 emerge annually from the secondary schools. The ranks of urban labourers and clerks, the two other 'estates' of the urban modern sector, have swollen. In addition, the tertiary sector that serves the mass of urban citizens, the small traders, food cookers, mechanics, bicycle repairers, printers, etc., literally teems with men and women of these professions and their children and apprentices. The Nigerian cities have acquired much of the turmoil, complexity, confusion, richness and squalor of Dickens' London.

In a number of commercial centres very rich men, by the standards of any modern country, are emerging, many of whom have never gone far in formal education and who have never held political or administrative posts. The highly educated elite enjoys a less isolated splendour than in the years of terminal colonialism and the time of independence. There is increasing evidence of discontent on the part of the other 'estates' with the distribution of rewards which favours the heirs of colonialism, the highly educated.[11] Members of the highly educated elite, preoccupied historically with ethnic division,[12] are becoming more conscious of the potential dangers of the horizontal class divisions and antagonisms within the society. While in most of the African countries it was essentially the highly educated elite that succeeded the colonialists, more recent developments in a few countries suggest the possibility of revolution among clerks and sergeants, the 'second estate' of the urban sector. Pressure from the literate and politically informed members of this sector seems at the moment a more serious threat to the dominance of the highly educated elite than working-class or peasant revolt, although both the latter may periodically disrupt the existing order and force limited redistribution.

In a situation of increasing complexity, however, the highly educated elite seems generally secure within the large-scale organizations of the society. The statist heritage of colonialism remains strong and the institutions of government directly or indirectly afford a large measure of control over the general framework of the national social life, government itself, the economy, communications and information, and education.

2. THE DEVELOPMENT OF THE NIGERIAN UNIVERSITY SYSTEM

To understand the role of the university-educated elite in Nigeria we need to be aware of the main features of university education, its development and its present status.

As early as the 1860's the educated elite in British West Africa began to demand the establishment of some form of university system to serve West Africans. By the 1920's and 1930's numerous Africans trained abroad advocated the establishment of university education in one or another of the British West African territories. [13] In Nigeria the general re-evaluation of educational policy in the 1920's resulted in the establishment of Yaba Higher College in 1934[14] which provided several hundred pupils with post-secondary professional training, not intended to be of full university standard.

During the 1930's and 1940's increasing numbers of students—first from the Yoruba areas of western Nigeria and later from Iboland and other areas of the mid-west and east—were finding their way overseas for university education. University education within Nigeria itself was a post-war phenomenon, reflecting the changing rhythm of British colonialism and incipient decolonization. The University College, Ibadan, offering a programme culminating in university degrees from the University of London, was established in 1948. The slow growth of its student numbers, however, indicates how little urgency was attached to internal production of university-trained manpower during the 1950's. In this period more

Table 2.

Numbers of degree recipients, Ibadan University (University College, Ibadan), 1950-1960

1950	2	1956	46	
1951	18	1957	66	
1952	32	1958	54	
1953	31	1959	103	
1954	33	1960	182	
1955	48	Total, 1950-1960: 615		

(Source: Tabulated from listing by name of all Ibadan graduates, 1950-1973, Appendix, J. F. Ajayi and T.N. Tamuno, (editors), *The University of Ibadan 1948-73* (Ibadan University Press, 1973), pp. 293-497.

Nigerians studied at universities abroad than in the Ibadan University College. Even by the year of independence, 1960, the total number of graduates produced annually at home or abroad was estimated at less than 1,000.[15] In the Northern Region, which includes more than half the country's population, the situation was particularly serious. The total number of graduates of northern origin was not more than a few dozen annually at the time of independence. At the same time, however, the three regional governments and the Federal government were rapidly phasing out expatriates from the top level of the administration.

The report of the Ashby Commission on higher education[16] combined with the exigencies of rapid transition toward self-government and independence to give a sense of urgency to the development of university institutions in Nigeria. The Eastern Region of Nigeria had been in the process of establishing a university since the mid-1950's. The University of Nigeria at Nsukka (referred to hereafter as Nsukka University) opened in October 1960. In 1962 Lagos and Ife Universities opened, as well as Ahmadu Bello University (ABU) in the Northern Region. Pressures continued for more universities and in 1970 the University of Benin was established in the Mid-West (now Bendel) State. Since 1975 the Federal Government has established seven more universities: at Jus, Maidugur, Kano, Sokoto, Calabar, Port Harcourt and Ilorin. A confirmation of the significance of graduates in the society was the extreme interest that focussed on the founding of the new university institutions and their location.

Expansion of the universities has been extremely rapid; an indication of growth and present size is provided by the data in Table 3. Total enrolment in all the universities together has passed the 20,000 mark. In

Table 3.

Enrolment in Nigerian Universities

University	Date Opened	Student Enrolment 1962-63* Session	Student Enrolment 1964-65† Session	Student Enrolment 1972-73* Session
Ibadan University	1948	1,689	2,284	4,110
Nsukka University	1960	1,257	2,482	3,891
Ahmadu Bello University	1962	425	719	5,086
Ife University	1962	244	659	3,632
Lagos University	1962	131	563	2,605
Benin University	1970	— —	— —	417

*(Source: 'Memorandum by the Committee of Vice-Chancellors of Nigerian Universities to the Public Service Review Commission,' 1973. Figures include certain non-degree diploma and pre-degree courses, which significantly affect Ahmadu Bello University enrolments in the 1972-73 column.)
†(Source: N. Okafor, op.cit., Table 14, p.200.)

June, 1972, 3,174 students received university degrees from the universities taken together, and about 7,000 students are expected to receive degrees in June 1975. The existing universities are continuing to grow rapidly. Of the five older universities, ABU and Nsukka University (which is still recovering from the impact of the 1967-70 civil war) are growing fastest. Taking into account the political pressure for expanding enrolments and the creation of more universities, no levelling off of the growth of the university system can be foreseen within the decade of the 1970's. Enrolment of Nigerians in overseas first degree courses remains significant in absolute numbers, but has fallen greatly in proportion to enrolment in Nigeria's own universities.

The rapid growth since independence of Nigeria's university system has had a revolutionary impact on the country's high-level manpower situation.[17] Approximately the same number of students graduate annually from Nigerian universities as graduated both at home and overseas during all the years of British colonial rule. The main 'consumers' of the product, the State and Federal governments, the large private enterprises and the secondary school systems, have all undergone rapid expansion in the years since independence. The universities have expanded even faster, and while data on manpower needs and supply are weak, it can be said that supply is coming much closer to meeting demand, with the probability that within a few years the universities will be overproducing graduates in relation to the number of jobs traditionally regarded as suitable for graduates.

It is important to note, however, that production of graduates is not distributed evenly throughout the country. The colonial heritage of differential development, particularly between the north and the south, remains acute in education at every level. A study of student recruitment to the University of Ibadan shows that over the years 1948-66 students from the Northern Region accounted for only a little more than five percent of the total enrolment of the university (which, over most of that period, was the only university in the country). When the mainly Yoruba students from Ilorin and Kabba Provinces are omitted, northern students accounted for only 1.9 percent of total enrolments.[18] Yet more than half the country's total population live in the north.

Since the beginning of electoral politics in about 1950 this massive differential in the production of high-level manpower has provided one of the main sources of regional and ethnic distrust and competition. The following chapter includes an analysis of differentials in university student recruitment. The imbalance between north and south (deeply rooted in similar differentials in primary and secondary school enrolments) has been only partially redressed by the establishment of ABU in 1962 to serve the northern peoples. Differentials also exist *within* as well as *between* the major regions. University education is a highly politicized issue because its significance in determining access to society's most strategic posts is universally recognized. To illustrate the problem it can be roughly estimated that on the basis of their earlier start in 'Western' education, the southern ethnic groups presently control more than 90 percent of posts in the Federal civil service, even though they account for less than half the population. In a post-colonial society in which the Federal government controls so much of the modern sector, such a disproportion is of high political significance.

3. THE SCOPE OF THE SURVEY

The survey reported in this study is comprehensive in scope and goes beyond even a broad conception of 'politics' to embrace those social, economic and personal issues that form the background to politics and that seem to us significant in themselves for an understanding of Nigerian society. Certain theoretical and practical considerations combined to guide us in shaping the scope of the research.

The most important theoretical consideration was our desire to discover the fundamental attitudes and values of the students. We wanted to be able to make generalizations and predictions of longer term significance about this particular elite group. We decided to look for some of the general values that condition specific choices and those that were likely to endure through particular forms of change. We were also anxious to avoid the time-trap method represented by a focus on the topical, i.e., in eliciting reactions to policies and persons that were mainly significant within a topical situation at a particular point in time.

Underlying the first theoretical consideration was a second, namely the belief that Nigerian university students have greater significance as part of the broader social and political system than as actors or audience in a more narrowly defined concept of politics. We think that this elite group is less significant in terms of what its members are now (viz., students) than in terms of where they have come from (their relations with their families and home communities) and where they are going to (the vast majority into governmental service and the rest mostly into large-scale private enterprise). By virtue of being a group in transition (the university period itself being the final stage) they reflect the aspirations of groups they have come from as well as the values of those they hope soon to join. In this connexion we have dealt with them principally as elites in formation (potential, presumptive, aspiring elites).

The most important practical consideration was that during the entire duration of our research (1970-75) formal politics, in the sense of electoral competition and parliamentary government, were legally suspended and officially non-existent in Nigeria. Hence, it was impossible to buttress the attitudinal side of the survey with an investigation of participational elements—such as politicization, activism, partisanship and radicalism—that have received much attention elsewhere.[19] We regret the loss of elements of this dimension, but we do not think that the loss is ultimately a serious one for two reasons. First, many of the activities students participate in they indulge in as *students only;* they drop them as soon as they graduate and have to face up to the problems of family and livelihood. Second, Nigerian students have not had—and did not have in the civilian days except in one or two isolated instances—an important impact on national politics;[20] on the campuses themselves students have treated student electoral politics as irrelevant, even to themselves. Where students have played a role in Nigerian politics they have done so at local level and not as students but as educated members of their local communities.

Another practical consideration was the lack of previous information and theoretical work on which to ground our research on students and their attitudes in Nigeria. Basic statistical data on highly educated persons is weak (as is demographic information on the country as a whole)[21]. Very little work has been done on university students from a political standpoint, either in terms of political activity or culture[22]. From the beginning, therefore we had to accept that our work was of an exploratory nature. At the same time we decided that our questions must be relevant to Nigerian circumstances, even if the results would not be immediately comparable with work done elsewhere, particularly in the Western democracies. We felt that this approach was preferable to the danger of producing misleading results (given the paucity of previous work) by simply adopting items used elsewhere.

An indication of the range of topics covered can best be provided by a review of the structure of the chapters which follow. The material presented is organized in five substantive chapters. Chapter 2 focuses on the social characteristics of university students, and the political and social significance of the patterns discovered. Chapter 3 examines in more depth the personal backgrounds of students and their relations with their families and home communities, and relates the findings to general questions of 'deracination' and social identity. Chapter 4 considers the students' future in terms of outlooks or careers and happiness. Chapter 5 adopts a more specifically political focus, examining basic political values and outlooks on government. Chapter 6 again deals specifically with the political dimension, moving closer to the dynamics of political interaction in

Nigeria and focusing on the problem of democracy. Chapter 7 offers several general perspectives on the results.

4. SOURCES OF DATA: PARTICIPATION, OBSERVATION AND SURVEY

This work is based primarily on formal questionnaire surveys, but a word should be said about less formal and structured sources of information on the students. The roots of this study lie in the considerable fund of 'observation' we have gained in years of close contact with students both as teachers and sometimes as friends. (One author, O'Connell, has taught for 17 years, first at Ibadan and then at ABU. The other author, Beckett, has taught for six years at ABU.) Our experience provided the main starting points in terms of the hypotheses underlying the survey, and inevitably acted as a lens through which the results were viewed and interpreted.

Our roles at ABU brought obvious advantages, especially in terms of relations with colleagues throughout the Nigerian universities going back many years. These advantages were perhaps partially offset by the fact that the project was a part-time one, and by the fact that we may have been more sensitive than an 'outsider' to the danger of giving offence to any part of the university community. (In fact, this latter problem had little importance since for the reasons already discussed we were not interested in doing the sort of survey which is 'sensitive' in terms of being highly 'political' and topical.) Another advantage offered by our relatively permanent roles was that the study could be a long-term one, allowing time to consider the results produced by three questionnaires before going to the final stage.

We believe that the weakness inevitably associated with the use of structured questionnaires, particularly with close-ended questions, have been compensated for to a considerable extent by our lengthy 'participant observation' and, more formally, by analysis of student essays, both biographical sketches commissioned as part of our study, and essays on topics such as 'modernization' in the students' home community (a subject designed to give maximum freedom of expression to the students' own social perspectives). During the study, we have also had oral discussions with students (individually and in groups) both about questions we used and about the results we obtained.

However, the major results of the formal questionnaire survey form the basis of this study. We have tried to make it clear when the discussion extends beyond the context of the questionnaire results or direct inference from them. We have been cautious in putting forward the opinions formed in so many years of teaching experience. On this point, it is worth remarking that the value of formal study is borne out by the fact that we have ourselves gained considerable knowledge about the university students, and have at a number of points been surprised by the data.[23]

5. *THE QUESTIONNAIRE SURVEY*

We decided at the beginning that the major instrument of data-gathering would be written questionnaires filled in by the students (self-administration).

Three distinct questionnaires were used in what was, in effect, a study with four phases. Each successive questionnaire was designed both to supplement and to deepen the results of the preceding one. In the final stage, composite questionnaires were formulated including what experience had shown were the most fruitful questions on the three distinct questionnaires. These composite questionnaires were administered at Nigeria's three most important (and regionally distinctive) universities: ABU in the north; Ibadan in the west; and Nsukka in the eastern part of the country. The texts of the questionnaires are presented in Appendix 2. A variety of question formats were employed, including, in the first questionnaire, some open-ended (fill-in) questions. Based on experience, the open-ended format questions were eliminated from the later questionnaires, and the 'number-in-order' ranking questions which were used a great deal in the first two questionnaires were replaced by the more precise 'pairs' format in which a series of paired alternatives are placed in two-way competition. .

Our main source of information was a probability sample representative of the ABU main-campus degree-programme student body in the 1973-74 session. The sampling frame used was a list by name, year in university and major of all ABU students. The sample was produced by 'systematic sampling' by an interval technique. Application of the interval technique made it unnecessary to use stratification to ensure representation of disciplines and academic years. The names drawn were assigned at random to paid student assistants who were responsible for delivering and collecting the questionnaires. A good return rate (83.6 percent) was obtained; the number of completed questionnaires obtained (286) represents a sample ratio (to the main campus degree-programme student body at that time) of about 1:10. Further information on this sample is provided in Appendix 1.

Associated with the probability sample are some 11 non-probability samples done at various times at ABU, Ibadan, Nsukka, Lagos and Ife universities. Our first two ABU questionnaires utilized non-probability samples. We used the university's structure of courses of study to select classes for administration of the questionnaires. After an initial and unsatisfactory experiment with a handout-and-voluntary-return method, the questionnaires were completed in class. In this way, samples of 495 and 419 completed questionnaires were constructed using questionnaire I and II, respectively. (Further discussion of these samples will be found in Appendix 1.) A third questionnaire was designed and administered to 215 ABU students. Finally, the composite questionnaire drawing questions from the first, second and third questionnaires was constructed and was used in the probability sample survey discussed above. The probability sample survey, the results of which could be checked against the results of the earlier surveys, confirmed what analysis of the earlier results had already led us to believe: that except for the effect of known and controllable biases (such as over-representation of certain courses of study, or certain years in university) the non-probability samples were producing reliable results.

The main focus of our study within the Nigerian university system was ABU, where we ourselves were teachers. We also asked colleagues at other Nigerian universities to carry out administrations of our questionnaires when the opportunity arose. Given the strongly regionalist pattern of recruitment to the various universities, and the sharp regional differences in terms of social and economic development and various aspects of political history, we were interested to see whether systematic differences would be apparent between the ABU results and those from other universities. In addition to the four ABU samples, eight separate administrations of one or another of the questionnaires were made at four of the other five universities (Ibadan, Nsukka, Lagos and Ife). With one exception (Nsukka, 1973) the samples at universities other than ABU were relatively small, and were non-probability samples consisting of blocks of students found within particular courses. The numbers ranged from about 100 (the smallest samples that we report) to about 200, except for the large sample (N=566) of the final composite questionnaire at Nsukka University in November, 1973. (See Appendix 1.)

Analysis of the results of these relatively small and originally experimental samples at the other universities put us in something of a quandary. The results are striking for their general uniformity and consistency, which suggests, if not proves, the general reliability of the results. The uniformity and consistency also suggest that variability of student opinions both within and between universities, is, on most issues, less than might have been predicted. In the light of this we felt that the results from the other universities should be presented, weak as their technical basis may be, and the reader is encouraged to form his own judgement. We urge, however, that the nature of the data be kept in mind, and we emphatically do not wish to claim a technical solidity that they do not possess. In strict technical terms the samples from the other universities cannot positively be extended beyond themselves.

The decision to put forward the material from other universities posed a less important problem, namely the question of presentation of results. Like all authors reporting laboriously garnered quantitative data, we wanted to make available to the reader as much of it as possible. At the same time, we wished the tables to be simple enough to be readily readable—and presenting up to six columns of only slightly varying data from separate samples was judged not likely, for most readers, to enhance readability. Consequently, we decided, where possible, to present results from ABU, Ibadan and Nsukka, Nigeria's three largest universities, each placed in, and drawing students principally from, one of Nigeria's three main geographical (and formerly political) regions.

6. *ANALYSIS OF DATA AND PRESENTATION OF RESULTS*

There has been some criticism of the use in social research in Africa of quantitative analytical techniques which go beyond the strength of the basic data and the interpretative power of surrounding theory. In our opinion, this criticism has generally been well-founded. It is in these terms that we assert as a virtue what admittedly came naturally to two researchers whose backgrounds and previous experience were not "quantitative". In our own analysis we have not constructed indices, nor translated specific questions or combinations of them into measures of abstract concepts such as 'ethos' or 'social efficacy'. In our presentation, similarly, the aim is to involve the reader in the primary level of analysis and interpretation and to facilitate judgements of the work at that level. Our main tools of analysis have been two and three variable crosstabulations, using programmes developed by staff of the Ahmadu Bello University Computer Centre.

Even at this relatively simple level our long and rather complex questionnaires resulted in a range of data far too great for presentation in a relatively short work. We thought it more important, and more in keeping with the exploratory nature of the work, to emphasize breadth rather than more specific and complex treatment of a narrower range of questions. Hence our presentation remains for the most part at the level of simple tabulations of results (with the inter-university comparisons referred to earlier). The results of cross-tabulations are referred to only when they cast special light on questions being discussed. We hope in later shorter reports to present more detailed analysis of selected topics.

In keeping with the general emphasis on simplicity of presentation, percentages are computed to omit 'no answers' from the tables; numbers on which the percentages in tables are based are not shown in the text tables; and chi square values are not presented. 'No answer' rates were low in most administrations (and in all of those on which the text tables are based). The numbers of each sample (on which the text tables are based) are indicated in Appendix 1. Finally, it should be mentioned that we have used all of the questions which we consider to be significant to the topics discussed; but a few questions which either seemed to perform badly in use or are irrelevant to the subjects covered here are omitted from presentation and discussion in the following chapters. Appendix 2 presents the full text of the questionnaires.

A minor question of presentation must also be discussed. A question format of which we made considerable use in our first two questionnaires called for students to rank ('number in order') a number of alternatives. Thus, for instance, in our first questionnaire students were asked the following:

'In what order would you list the qualities you look for in a job? *(Number in order)*'.
— Security
— High salary
— Status in the community
— Personal fulfilment and maximum use of talents
— Usefulness to the community

Generally four to six alternatives were provided in questions with this format; in a few cases (e.g., questions 11 and 12 on Questionnaire I) up to eight alternatives were provided. In coding, the number given by each respondent to each alternative was recorded. In computer processing, each alternative was treated as an item and tabulation indicated for each the number and percentage of first rankings, second rankings and so on down to lowest ranking. Questions with this format present a problem in the text tables since the data is complex. We have simplified the presentations, first, by giving the results from only one university sample (where possible, ABU, 1973). To further simplify, we have given 'percentage of first rankings' and 'percentage of lowest rankings' received by each alternative. As a further indication of the overall pattern (and, especially, the omitted middle rankings) we have also included the 'modal ranking' received by the alternative in question—i.e., the rank assigned to an alternative by more students than any other rank. Use of the modal measure will provide the interested reader with an approximate picture of the overall pattern of results when taken together with first and last place rankings received by each alternative.

As a result of the considerations discussed, the reader may find a blend of simplicity and complexity which is initially somewhat unnerving. On the one hand, our analysis and presentation of results may seem unexpectedly simple in terms of current practice in survey research. On the other hand, some of our question formats may initially seem complex and difficult to follow. The appearance of complexity, the reader will quickly find, is deceptive. The appearance of simplicity is more genuine and we hope will be accepted by the reader as an invitation to participate in an exploration.

FOOTNOTES

1. E. A. Ayandele, *The Educated Elite in the Nigerian Society* (Ibadan: Ibadan University Press, 1974), p.3.
2. *Ibid.* See Ayandele's survey of disparaging remarks, pp.21-23 and *passim.*
3. *Ibid.*, p.41.
4. This generalization can be illustrated with particularly stark simplicity by figures on incomes in the northern cities in the middle 1920's—nearly midway in the colonial period. In Maiduguri, centre of government and commerce within a large province (and the modern capital of one of Africa's oldest empires), in 1925 the wealthiest trader's income was estimated at £100 per annum, while district heads (a step below the top rank in the native authority system) earned incomes of up to six times that figure. (R. J. Gavin, 'The Borno Economy in the 1920's', unpublished paper, Borno Seminar, ABU, 1973. pp.9-10.) In Kano, northern Nigeria's largest commercial centre, average annual incomes of the wealthiest category of traders were put at £80 (1926 Assessment, Kano) while the Emir of Kano's salary with £8,500 and those of his five top administrators ranged from £720 to £1,200. See J. N. Paden, *Religion and Political Culture in Kano* (Berkeley and Los Angeles: University of California Press, 1973), Table 1, pp.24-25. Paden shows that more than three quarters of the Kano population had incomes 100 or even 200 times smaller than those of the administrative elite.
5. There were a few men in all of the various Nigerian assemblies who were semi-illiterate and who had little ability to communicate in English. They were local notables, often men of high traditional status, who were coopted by the first-rank leaders, and who had little impact on the overall direction of political events.
6. The class structure of the civil service was based on the Gorsuch Report (1952). There were four broad classes: sub-clerical and manipulative, clerical and technical, executive and higher technical, and administrative and professional. The Udoji Commission (Public Service Review Commission, Lagos, 1974, *Main Report,* Chapter 5) recommended the introduction of a 'unified grade structure'. The government's White Paper accepted 'the principle of unified salary structures . . . for the entire public sector.' *The Public Service of Nigeria: Government Views on the Report of the Public Service Commission,* Lagos, 1974, p.5. This is unlikely to affect significantly the dominance by the graduates of the higher levels.
7. See Frantz Fanon, *Les damnés de la terre* (Paris: Maspero, 1974 edit.); René Dumont, *L'Afrique noire est mal partie* (Editions du Seuil: Paris, 1966 edit.); Ruth First, *The Barrel of a Gun: Political Power in Africa and the Coup d'Etat* (Penguin: Harmondsworth, 1970).
8. See F. Harbison, 'Human Resources and Economic Development in Nigeria' in R. O. Tilman and Taylor Cole (editors), *The Nigerian Political Scene* (Durham, North Carolina: Duke University Press, 1962), pp.198-219. Definition of categories and estimates are found in pp.204-209. Harbison's figures, prepared in connection with the

INTRODUCTION 21

work of the Ashby Commission on Higher Education in Nigeria, necessarily reflect the extreme weakness of demographic and economic data in Nigeria. Harbison's exact figure including post-primary teachers with university degree qualifications, is 15,375. While this figure is the best available, it undoubtedly represents an under-estimate.

9. *Ibid.*
10. In order to deal with the problem of comparability of remuneration between the public and private sectors the Public Service Review Commission surveyed enterprises in the private sector accounting for 173,230 jobs. Of this total, 7,661 would appear to be positions for which university or other advanced education would be appropriate. (See Public Service Review Commission, *Report on Grading and Pay,* Vol. IV, Table 4-3; pp.38-41.) We round this up to 10,000 to take (generous) account of the portion of the private sector not covered by the Commission's survey.
11. Comparisons of earnings and standards of living of different groups run through the trade union document presented by the United Committee of the Central Labour Organisation to the Adebo Salaries and Wages Review Commission: *Equitable Demand for Economic Growth and National Prosperity,* Lagos-Ibadan, 1970. Comparisons, words like 'relativities', 'parities', 'differentials', have entered widely into Nigerian discussion and are being more acutely and bitterly made since the government's decisions on the Udoji salary recommendations in 1974.
12. Dr. K. O. Dike, the first Nigerian Vice-Chancellor of the University of Ibadan, said in a Convocation address in 1966: 'It must be said to our shame that the Nigerian intellectual, far from being an influence for national integration, is the greatest exploiter of parochial and clannish sentiment . . . As you leave us, you are going into a Nigeria torn by tribal strife, a country in which deep suspicions exist between the different sections. You will be no credit to this university if you leave us to join the band of educated advocates of tribal division and strife and worshippers of tribal gods.' Cited in P. L. van den Berghe, *Power and Privilege at an African University,* (Cambridge, Mass: Schenkman, 1973) p.224.
13. The small but articulate highly educated elite in British West Africa had made establishment of a university system to serve West Africa one of their demands. In particular, J. Horton, in his *West African Countries and Peoples . . .,* published in 1868, called for a University for Western Africa, using the Church Missionary Society's Fourah Bay College as the nucleus. On early demands for access to university education (with particular emphasis on Nigeria) see N. Okafor, *The Development of Universities in Nigeria* (London: Longman Group, Ltd., 1971), especially Chapter 3, 'Nationalism and the Demand for Universities in Nigeria'.
14. The various course programmes of the college were commenced at different intervals from 1930; the college did not open formally until 1934. See F. O. Ogunlade, *'Yaba Higher College and the Formation of an Intellectual Elite',* unpublished M.A. thesis, Ibadan University, 1970.
15. Studies of Nigeria's manpower resources and needs and of the country's system of higher education were made just prior to independence. For a convenient summary on high-level manpower see F. Harbison, *op. cit.,* pp.198-219. Harbison (p.210) estimates (in the absence of solid data) the number of Nigerian graduates returning annually from overseas universities at the time of independence at something like 800, with slightly under 200 being produced internally. According to his analysis, Nigeria's annual need for graduates was at least twice as large as overseas and internal graduates together. On the educational system the influential recommendations of the "Ashby Commission" on higher education can be found in E. Ashby, *Investment in Education: The Report of the Commission on Post-School Certificate and Higher Education in Nigeria* (Lagos, 1960).
16. *Ibid.*
17. Publications of the National Manpower Board, in existence from 1962, may be consulted. These laudable efforts have been hampered by the weakness of basic data and the difficulty of instituting adequate reporting even within the public sector.

18. P. L. van den Berghe and C. M. Nuttney, 'Some Social Characteristics of University of Ibadan Students' *Nigerian Journal of Economic and Social Studies*, Vol. 11, No. 3 (November, 1969), pp.355-377; see pp.360-3 on recruitment of students from regions and provinces; percentages in text above are computed from data in Table IV.
19. Useful and representative collections of work done on students and politics are S. M. Lipset (editor), *Student Politics* (New York and London: Basic Books, 1967) and D. K. Emmerson (editor), *Students and Politics in Developing Nations* (New York: Praeger, 1968).
20. We want to make a reference in passing to the violent clashes that have taken place on Nigerian campuses since 1971 between students and government forces culminating in 1975 in the closure of the universities of Ibadan, Ife and Lagos for several weeks. These clashes give the impression that recent student generations are more politicized than their predecessors because students appear to be questionning government policy more than in the past. With some exceptions, such as the excursion from Ibadan to Lagos about the Anglo-Nigerian Defence Pact, earlier student demonstrations were mainly about food and material conditions (even the incident at Ibadan in 1971 in which a student was killed arose out of a food protest). In the civilian era the students disliked the political class but never moved directly against them; and they nearly all supported the political parties that had their bases in their regions of origin. There seem to us several factors involved in the recent change of orientation in student demonstrations. First, with the enormous growth in student numbers students give the impression that for the first time they are conscious of themselves as *students*—and movements of student power elsewhere have suggested a fuller political role to Nigerian students. Second, the students give the impression that they feel less immediately than in the past that they are about to become part of the ruling intelligentsia. The increase in the number of younger students as well as the consolidation of the hold on upper civil service posts by previous generations of graduates almost certainly contributes to this feeling, yet it is probably shared only by a small section of the undergraduates. In so far as it exists, however, it is consolidated by the introduction of the compulsory youth service year which places a gap between the end of university and a career post. The students resent this service year and it is an embittering factor in their relations with the military government. Finally, the students dislike the autocratic character of the government. But when all these things have been said, we think that the present student disturbances do not represent a radical break with previous student attitudes. One suspects that once civilian politics with strong ethnic and communal bases returns, students will divide along lines similar to those of the past and will probably be more apathetic in politics as students and much more active as local and ethnic partisans.
21. Nigeria carried out a nation-wide census in November, 1973, but its results were disputed and have been annulled. Nigeria's 1963 Census figures were also widely disputed. At certain points (especially in Chapter II) we have made reference to the 1952 census, not in terms of absolute figures (which are badly out of date) but in terms of proportions of various demographic categories.
22. Relatively little survey research has been done in Nigeria with any segment of the population, and only a few political studies of university students are available. See W. J. Hanna, 'Students', in J. S. Coleman and C. G. Rosberg (editors), *Political Parties and National Integration in Tropical Africa* (Berkeley and Los Angeles, California, University of California Press, 1966), pp.413-433; C. S. Rooks, 'University Students and Politics in Nigeria', unpublished paper for Conference on Students and Politics, Harvard University and University of Puerto Rico, San Juan, March 27-31, 1967; O. Klineberg and M. Zavalloni *Nationalism and Tribalism Among African Students: A Study of Social Identity* (The Hague: Mouton, 1969), which includes survey data on Nigerian students abroad; M. O. Shoremi and F. Mott, 'Aspirations and Attitudes of University of Lagos Undergraduates' in *Research Bulletin No. 6/001, University of Lagos Human Resources Research Unit*, 1974; P. Baker, 'Seeds of Radicalism Among

an Aspirant Elite' in U. G. Damachi and H. D. Seibel (editors), *Social Change and Economic Development in NIgeria* (New York: Praeger, 1973), pp.185-205; P. Day, 'An Opinion Survey of the Students in the University of Ife: 1962-1963' in *Nigerian Journal of Economics and Social Studies*, Vol. 7, No. 3, November, 1965. Important social data on the Ibadan University student body is provided in P. L. van den Berghe and C. M. Nuttney, *op. cit.*, pp.355-377. An earlier study of the Nigerian high elite is H. H. Smythe and M. M. Smythe, *The New Nigerian Elite*, (Stanford University Press, 1960).

23. Our experience thus does not support van den Berghe's assertion that 'the best a survey can do . . . is to confirm and quantify what the researcher already knows.' See P. L. van den Berghe 'Social Science in Africa: Epistemological Problems' in O'Barr, Spain and Tessler, (editors) *Survey Research in Africa: Its Applications and Limits*, (Northwestern University Press, 1973), p.33.

2 Social Background: an Elite-in-Formation

This chapter is an essay on social background characteristics of Nigerian university students. Our main source of information is data from ABU[1] which is stronger than the data from other universities, and also illustrates the eneven development of education in Nigeria, since ABU was for long the only full university serving the northern States of Nigeria. Data from other universities are also included. We draw on work done by van den Berghe and Nuttney on social characteristics of the Ibadan student body,[2] and we also relate the Nigerian data to comparable data from other West African countries. Finally, we raise questions about the directions which access to higher education—and social class formation—are likely to take in Nigeria and elsewhere in West Africa.

1. AGE, SEX, RELIGION AND TYPE OF PRE-UNIVERSITY EDUCATION

Before we consider certain features of our samples such as ethnicity and social class which are of basic importance, it will be useful to summarize other characteristics of the student bodies: age, sex, religion and previous education.

By comparison with most university student bodies in Britain and the United States, Nigerian students tend to be older (see Table 4).
About two-thirds or more of all of our samples, even those biased heavily toward the first year in university, were 22 years or older, i.e., older than the approximate normal minimum age of completion of university studies in Western countries. Between 20 and 35 percent of Nigerian students were older than 25. The higher age of the students compared with university students in Western countries is in part a reflection of the fact that many students enter primary school later than the age of five or six. Many also have to interrupt progress towards the university level with several years of employment. Students' age is an indication of social class: the children of the poorer and rural parents are more likely to have entered school at a later age and to have dropped out of school to work for

Table 4.

Age of Students: Three University Samples

Age Categories	ABU 1973	Ibadan 1973	Nsukka 1973
18-21	21.4%	33.7%	36.5%
22-25	48.8%	36.2%	41.0%
26-29	21.7%	20.9%	15.4%
30 and more	8.2%	9.2%	7.1%
	100.1%	100.0%	100.0%

extended periods. Age also tends to be associated with field of study, students in the sciences and medicine being younger, and students in the arts, social sciences and education older; this association is particularly strong at Ibadan. In terms of sex, male students are very greatly overrepresented; only about 12 percent of the ABU and 17 percent of the Nsukka sample were women. Van den Berghe and Nuttney show that over the period 1948-1966 female students accounted for 11 percent of all students at Ibadan.[3] In the ABU samples comparison by class year (as well as other evidence) indicates that the proportion of female students at ABU is rising steadily. There was a gradual increase at Ibadan from less than five percent in the early 1950's to slightly more than 20 percent in 1966, but enrolment statistics for 1973-74 at Ibadan indicate the proportion of women has again dropped; in that year only a little under 17 percent of the students were female.[4] It is clear that in all the universities women students will be very much in the minority for the foreseeable future. Table 5 on students' religion shows that Christians are greatly over-represented. In the northern States, from which most of the ABU

Table 5. Students' Religion

	ABU 1973	Ibadan* 1973	Nsukka 1973
Christian	71.9%	85.8%	96.8%
Muslim	24.9%	7.6%	1.2%
Other (or none)	3.2%	6.6%	2.0%

*P. L. van den Berghe and C. M. Nuttney, *op. cit.*, p.357 indicate that over the period 1948-66, 91.9 percent of Ibadan students gave their religion as Christians; 5.7 percent as Muslim; 0.1 percent as traditionalists.

students are drawn, less than 10 percent of the population is Christian. Yet in 1973 more than two-thirds of the ABU student body was Christian. Within the Yoruba ethnic group which accounts for about half of Ibadan's students, there are as many Muslims as there are Christians (about one third each), yet Muslims in the Ibadan sample accounted for only 7.6 percent (Table 5)[5]. Most underrepresented of all are the 'animists' or adherents of traditional religion in Nigeria's population. Very few of the students declared agnosticism or atheism, even when the question format offered the opportunity to do so.

The Christian overrepresentation demonstrates the profound influence of the missions which offered education as well as religion. Muslim underrepresentation is the reverse side of this historical factor: the colonial government did not provide government-supported education in Muslim communities on the same scale as the missions did in many non-Muslim communities. Several factors contribute to the underrepresentation of Muslims among Yoruba students at Ibadan (as at Ife and Lagos): primary schools managed by the missions were inevitably more open to Christians than to Muslims; attendance at Christian schools led some Yoruba Muslims whose traditional roots in Islam were shallow to abandon their religion; and many communities (Ibadan is a notable example), that for various reasons only reluctantly accepted modern schooling, became Muslim rather than Christian, and thus contributed to this statistical pattern.

2. ETHNICITY AND HOME STATE: PATTERNS OF OVER AND UNDERREPRESENTATION

No aspect of education is politically more divisive than the inter-related problems of regional and ethnic under and overrepresentation. The most important feature of areal representation at Nigerian universities is the disproportion between the northern and the southern States. We have noted already that this disproportion is deeply rooted in the political, social and economic history of Nigeria under colonial rule. The northern fears of southern 'domination' which were so important in shaping the politics of the 1950's and Nigeria's constitution on independence, were based largely on the south's disproportionate possession of the modern skills derived from education which qualified candidates for jobs. There was, and still is, a sharp differential in educational development at all educational levels from the primary level upwards. At the university level the uneven development up to 1966 is illustrated by data provided by van den Berghe and Nuttney (Table 6). From 1948 to 1960 Ibadan was the

SOCIAL BACKGROUND: AN ELITE-IN-FORMATION 27

Table 6. Percentages of Ibadan Students coming from the Main Regions of Nigeria (1948-1966)

Main Regions:	1948-52	1953-57	1958-62	1963-66	All Years
Lagos, West and Mid-West	49.9%	53.4%	53.2%	64.6%	53.3%
East	47.1%	41.6%	35.8%*	33.0%	38.6%
North	3.0%	5.0%	11.1%	2.4%†	6.1%
Total	100.0% (N=499)	100.0% (N=813)	100.1% (N=1001)	100.0% (N=702)	100.0%‡ (N=3015)

* Part of this drop is attributable to the opening of the University of Nigeria at Nsukka in 1960.
† Most of this drop is due to the opening of Ahmadu Bello University at Zaria in 1962.
‡ "No answers" were not included in the computation of percentages.

(Source: This table (together with notes) is drawn from P. L. van den Berghe and C. M. Nuttney, *op. cit.*, p. 360, (Table III).)

only university in the country. The creation of Nsukka University in 1960 accounts for the drop in eastern students at Ibadan after that date. Similarly, the creation of ABU in 1962 accounts for the sharp drop in the percentage of northern students at Ibadan. During the 1960's four additional universities were created; and in the 1970's seven more university institutions have been added. Statistics on origin of students by state at the five universities, while illustrating northern growth at ABU, confirm the continuing overall imbalance between the regions and, in fact, indicate that the north-south gap is widening in terms of absolute numbers (see Table 7). ABU was created as a regional university, but a greater percentage of its students come from outside its regional catchment area than is true of southern universities. According to the figures in Table 7, more than half of the northern students attending southern universities came from Kwara State, the most southerly of the northern States, and were mostly Yoruba. Many of the rest came from Benue Plateau State in the north. The far northern States (North West, Kano, North Central and North East) were scarcely represented outside ABU (and, as we shall see, they are underrepresented there).

Southern groups are also unevenly represented in the student bodies of southern universities. The Mid-West State was the best represented in our samples in terms of the relation of university students to total population. In the years shown in Table 7 its students formed 15 percent of Ibadan students, 21 percent of Lagos University students, and seven percent of students at Nsukka University. At ABU students from the Mid-West State amounted to 3.6 per cent of the total but at Benin they constituted 60 per cent. Yet by any account the population of the Mid-

28 SOCIAL BACKGROUND: AN ELITE-IN-FORMATION

Table 7. Enrolment of Universities by Students' State of Origin*

States	Ahmadu Bello† 1974-75	Benin‡ 1971-72	Ibadan 1973-74	Lagos 1973-74	Nsukka¶ 1974-75	Ife¶ 1974-75
Northern States:	%	%	%	%	%	%
Benue Plateau	15.3	1.2	2.0	0.4	0.4	1.1
Kano	8.0	0.4	0.0	0.06	0.1	0.1
Kwara	20.5	2.8	4.2	2.6	0.4	4.3
North Central	12.0	0.0	0.1	0.03	0.01	0.5
North East	17.9	0.0	0.2	0.1	0.01	0.5
North West	10.0	0.0	0.07	0.0	0.01	0.3
Sub-total:	(83.7)	(4.4)	(6.6)	(3.3)	(1.2)	(6.8)
Southern States:						
East Central	2.2	12.4	17.6	15.7	75.0	9.1
Lagos	0.8	3.2	3.1	6.0	0.3	1.8
Mid-West	3.6	60.8	14.9	21.1	6.6	10.2
Rivers	2.1	2.8	2.3	2.2	1.3	2.0
South East	1.9	4.0	3.9	3.0	9.6	2.2
West	3.3	2.0	49.2	46.8	5.4	66.9
Sub-total:	(13.9)	(95.2)	(91.0)	(94.8)	(98.2)	(92.2)
Non-Nigerian	2.5	0.4	2.5	1.9	0.5	0.9
Total:	100.1	100.0	100.1	100.0	99.9	99.9
(Total Enrolment)	(4655)	(250)	(4615)	(3402)	(5799)	(4600)

* Table is compiled from statistics of the universities concerned. Data not received from the University of Benin.
† ABU figures omit the pre-degree Basic Studies programmes (equivalent to secondary sixth form) and diploma courses.
‡ The University of Benin was newly opened at this time, with only 250 students.
¶ Includes degree, diploma and post-graduate students.

West State is not more than five percent of the Nigerian total. The Western State was extremely well represented (and with much larger absolute population figures than the Mid West State) at Ife, Lagos and Ibadan universities where its 'indigenes' formed slightly more or slightly less than half the student bodies. East Central State students formed almost seventy-five percent of Nsukka students and 12 percent of Benin students. The South East State's representation was reduced by the educational backwardness of Ogoja province. Rivers State was poorly represented in comparison with the other southern States. Thus, proportions of student numbers by State of origin are uneven. The extreme inequality is best illustrated by the fact that the three main southern States—East Central, Mid-West and West—account for some 70 per cent of university students, while the three dominantly Hausa northern States which have about the same population as the three main southern States account for only some seven percent of the students.

When these geographical patterns are translated into ethnic terms attention is drawn to the predominance of Yoruba and Ibo students in the Nigerian university system as a whole. Data compiled by van den Berghe and Nuttney at Ibadan, by Shoremi and Mott at Lagos[6] and by us in samples at the various universities indicates that slightly more than 50 percent of the students at Ibadan and Lagos, about 75 percent at Ife, and about 20 percent at ABU are Yoruba. The extent and significance of this overrepresentation is demonstrated by the fact that the Yoruba ethnic group, representing approximately 17 percent of the total Nigerian population, provides approximately 40 percent of all the university students in the country. Ibo proportions in the universities were considerably reduced by the crisis and civil war, and at universities other than Nsukka they are still growing in number. Upwards of 75 percent of the Nsukka students, about 25 percent of Lagos students, between 20 and 25 percent of students at Ibadan and about six per cent of ABU students are Ibo; probably nearly 30 percent of the country's university students are Ibo. Yoruba and Ibo students together probably account for more than two-thirds of Nigeria's university student population, yet their share of the country's total population is not much more than 30 percent. Other imbalances are dwarfed by these disproportions.

It is worth pausing briefly to suggest the social and political implications of the material that has been summarized. For northerners in general and far northerners in particular educational inequality has serious implications. First, they will continue to be extremely poorly represented in the Federal administrative and technical services—and this in a country where the personal origin of public servants is considered a matter of great significance. Second, they will almost certainly be unable to fill many technical and teaching posts in their own States, and will have to call on southern (or expatriate) skills. Finally, the social developments that have given the southerners their present lead in university entrance have also given them the edge in commercial and industrial development. Southerners, and particularly Yoruba, are best placed strategically with capital and skills to make use of the opportunities arising from the government policy of indigenization of ownership and management of economic enterprises. Nor will they easily lose their lead in the next generation or two. Pressure from the north for redress of the imbalance (as skilled northerners become available in greater numbers) is likely to be offset by pressure from the much larger volume of southern applicants emerging from educational institutions.[7]

3. THE SOCIAL CLASS BACKGROUND OF THE STUDENTS

Universities in Nigeria (as elsewhere) function as instruments of class formation and they can be expected to function as instruments of perpetuation of established class structures. Data was collected on the primary occupations of students' fathers. Some three-quarters of men in Nigeria presently engage in farming as a primary occupation.[8] To find out whether civil servants, professionals and other high status occupations were over-represented data was also collected on fathers' average annual income. According to the conventional statistics, annual average per capital income in Nigeria as a whole is about $120. Finally, data was collected on fathers' and mothers' education to discover whether the parents were representative of the population in general.

Data on students' fathers' income and occupation are summarized in Table 8. The most striking feature of the data shown is the large proportion of students' fathers in the farming and low income categories. This was true among all our university samples, including the Lagos, Ife and the other Ibadan samples not shown. The largest other category was that of the 'trader/businessmen', more than half of whom (see Table 8: C) were in the middle to lower income categories in the ABU data. Teachers were less well represented than one might have expected. Civil servants

Table 8. Data on Students' Fathers' Occupations and Incomes

A. *Fathers' Occupation: University Comparisons*

Father's Occupation	University Samples ABU, 1973	Ibadan, 1973	Nsukka, 1973
	%	%	%
Farmer	51.6	49.2	30.1
Civil Servant	6.1	12.3	13.1
Professions	2.9	4.6	5.2
Teacher	6.1	5.1	7.3
Trader/Businessman	14.1	14.4	19.3
Chief	0.7	0.0	0.4
Artisan	1.5	1.0	1.3
Labourer	1.8	2.6	2.0
Other	15.2	10.8	21.4
	100.0	100.0	100.0

SOCIAL BACKGROUND: AN ELITE-IN-FORMATION   31

B. *Father's Income: University Comparisons*

Income (in Naira*)	ABU, 1973	Ibadan, 1973	Nsukka, 1973
	%	%	%
Subsistence farmer	33.1	24.9	18.7
Less than N400	17.3	21.6	22.4
N400-800	20.6	20.4	22.8
N800-2000	15.8	18.8	19.7
N2000-4000	6.3	6.6	11.5
N4000+	7.0	7.7	4.9
	100.0	100.0	100.0

C. *Father's Occupation and Income: Income Categories as a percentage of Occupations*

	ABU, 1970 and 1971†					
	Subsistence and Less than N100	N100-400	Incomes Categories N400-1200	N1200-2000	N2000+	All incomes
Occupations						
	%	%	%	%	%	%
Farmer	62.0	28.0	9.1	0.4	0.4	99.9 (N=450)
Civil Servant	0.0	7.8	21.9	29.7	40.6	100.0 (N=64)
Professions	0.0	0.0	37.5	37.5	25.0	100.0 (N=24)
Teacher	0.0	35.1	48.7	5.4	10.8	100.0 (N=37)
Trader/Businessman	5.9	20.0	28.2	18.8	27.1	100.0 (N=85)
Chief	0.0	33.3	55.6	0.0	11.1	100.0 (N=9)
Other	12.9	25.9	35.3	12.1	13.8	100.0 (N=116)
All Occupations	38.1	24.7	19.4	7.9	9.9	100.0 (N=785)

* The Naira, Nigeria's currency unit since 1973, equals ½ the former Nigerian pound, and approximately $1.50.
† The ABU 1970 and 1971 samples are combined for the purpose of this analysis, providing a sample of 785 students who gave information on *both* father's income and occupation. This information was elicited in terms of Nigerian pounds and is here converted to Naira for consistency with the later data.

in the higher income categories and highly educated professionals, the social strata to which the students will be going, were numerically weak in the ABU sample and did not account for a much larger proportion in the Ibadan and Nsukka samples. Labourers and industrial workers also accounted for a very small proportion of students' parents. Van den Berghe remarks with reference to his Ibadan data: 'As a rough estimate, something like half of the students come from "common" Nigerian families, i.e. are the children of illiterate or barely literate parents with a social background of small-scale farming, petty trade or manual work'.[9] Our data strongly supports this generalization, and suggests in fact that 'something like half' is a conservative estimate. To date natural tendencies toward greater class selectivity have been offset all over Nigeria by the rapid growth of the universities' enrolments, meaning that the system as a whole has actually become more open in recruiting from among the poorer, rural areas. Parental occupation (like the related variable of father's income and education) is also associated with area of study in the university (though more so at Ibadan than ABU). Students in the sciences and technology tend generally to come from more well-to-do families than do humanities students.

The data on father's income (Table 8B) confirm the general pattern of data on father's occupation. 50 percent of the ABU students and about 40 percent of those in the Ibadan and Nsukka samples assessed their father's annual income at less than N400 annually. In an urban setting an income of N400 amounts to poverty. Even in a village setting where such an income might well be above average, school fees and other cash outlays would account for a large proportion of it. Only a little more or less than 15 per cent of the fathers of the students in the samples could be considered 'rich' by the standards of Nigeria's modern community (where, at the time of these surveys, N2000 might be taken as an approximate threshold of car-owning elite status). Well under ten percent in these samples could be considered really 'rich', earning more than N4000 annually.

The modifying effect of other variables, such as student's ethnicity and home area, on the occupation and income data will be noted later. The general pattern indicated by the data on father's income and occupation demonstrates, on the one hand, that higher incomes are greatly over-represented among fathers of students *in relation to the population as a whole*; the same is true for the higher status occupations. On the other hand, however, a very sizeable proportion of the students at all the universities come from groups, particularly farmers, that are extremely poor. Only in the Nsukka sample shown in Table 8B did the lowest income category not account for more of the respondents than any other.

Data on parental education add to and modify the picture represented by the income and occupation data (see Table 9). The low level of **parental education** disguises the remarkably **high** level of formal schooling and the concomitantly low level of illiteracy. The samples from Ibadan and Lagos university were biased heavily toward the social sciences and, therefore, show a somewhat lower level of educational attainment than would be true were the samples more representative in terms of fields of study. The ABU data, for example, may be compared

Table 9. Education of Students' Parents: Contrasting Samples

Educational Level	ABU, 1970, 1971*		Ibadan, 1970, 1972*		Lagos, 1971, 1972‡	
	Father	Mother	Father	Mother	Father	Mother
	%	%	%	%	%	%
Illiterate	37.1	62.5	51.0	72.3	50.7	67.3
Literate	15.9	10.8	5.4	4.9	1.3	2.6
Koranic	8.6	9.2	0.0	0.4	0.0	0.0
Primary	23.3	12.0	29.0	16.7	27.4	17.9
T.T.C.†	5.3	1.4	3.1	1.5	5.9	5.2
Secondary	6.8	3.7	7.7	4.2	8.1	5.2
University	3.0	0.4	3.9	0.0	6.7	1.8
	100.0	100.0	100.1	100.0	100.1	100.0
	(N=811)	(N=841)	(N=259)	(N=264)	(N=223)	(N=229)

* Samples referred to are combined for the purposes of this analysis, producing the 'N's shown. 'No answers' are omitted from computation of percentages.
† TTC = Teachers Training College (in most cases designed to provide training up to 'O' level standard).
‡ Data presented here from our Lagos samples (combined) can be compared with data from the Shoremi and Mott study, shown in Table 15 below. See note * to Table 15. Contrasts are explained by the fact that our Lagos samples consisted mainly of social science students.

with data available from the 1952 census statistics. These statistics are not only the only ones with a firm basis, but are also an appropriate point in time for comparison with students' parents. According to the 1952 census, only 1.9 percent of the Northern Region's population were literate in Roman script, and another 5.4 percent were literate in Arabic (Ajami) script.[10] The rest (92.7 percent) of the population aged seven or over was classified as illiterate. Yet only 37 percent of the ABU students' fathers were reported as illiterate. Nearly 25 percent had primary education and 15.1 percent had secondary, TTC or university education. Mothers' educational levels were lower, but their rate of illiteracy (63 percent) was very much lower than the rate for the general population, especially for the mothers' generation.

The highly significant conclusion, then, would seem to be that *these parents are less typical of the relevant general population in terms of education than in terms of occupation and income.* Similar comparisons could be made between the parents of students at the southern universities and the general population there, where the universal primary education schemes date only from the middle 1950's. Southern parents are less atypical of their populations than northern parents, but still noticeably more educated and literate than the average.

The data on parents' education and income can be related as in Table 10 (for the ABU sample only). The result is a strong pattern of association between the two variables.

SOCIAL BACKGROUND: AN ELITE-IN-FORMATION

Table 10. Fathers' Education and Fathers' Income

	ABU 1970, 1971*			
Father's Education	Father's Income†			
	Under N400	N400-1200	More than N1200	Total
	%	%	%	%
Illiterate	90.6	7.1	2.3	100 (N=267)
Primary‡	55.8	29.7	14.5	100 (N=172)
Secondary‡	4.6	31.8	63.6	100 (N=44)
University	0.0	0.0	100.0	100 (N=24)

* For the purpose of this analysis, ABU 1970 and 1971 samples are combined, producing the 'N's shown. 'No answers' are omitted.
† Income amounts, recorded originally in Nigerian pounds, are translated into Naira (1N=$1.50) for consistency with later data.
‡ Full or partial.

But the figures also lend strength to the conclusion drawn above: that students' fathers are more unusual in terms of education than in terms of income and occupation. A significant proportion of the fathers corresponded to the norm in terms of occupation (farmers) and income (under N400) yet had at least primary education. Overall, cross tabulation shows that only 56 percent of the fathers who were farmers were illiterate; 20 percent of them had primary education. Alternatively, of those who had full or partial primary education, 43 percent were farmers. The suggestion is that it is at the *secondary* level of education that there is a sharp differentiation from the masses in terms of occupation and income (all but five per cent of the fathers with secondary education had middle or higher incomes) and that men with primary education are more likely than might be supposed to remain in farming occupations, usually within the home community. At the same time, the data suggests that the offspring of parents who have had formal education are much more likely to reach the university level of education.

4. THE INTERPLAY OF SOCIAL FACTORS

It has become clear that a number of the variables discussed above are closely interrelated. Treating the ABU data as a case study, we can show in more detail the interplay of social factors, indicating in the process the complexity of the patterns.

The parental class variables have a marked effect on sex and age proportions. Female students at ABU had a notably higher class background than males. For instance, the women were less than half as likely to have fathers who were farmers than the men and five times as likely to have fathers who were civil servants. The relation between class and age is illustrated by the fact that students whose fathers were in the higher *income* categories were twice as likely to be found in the lowest *age* categories than students whose fathers were in the lowest *income* categories. There is a weaker relationship between class and type of primary and secondary education (government or voluntary agency), those with the higher class backgrounds being a little more likely to have attended government schools.

Region and religion both modify the class findings. Table 11 provides comparisons of ABU students coming from northern and southern States, and likewise compares the two States which are entirely Middle Belt (see Table 13 below) with the three northern States which were, historically, dominated by Hausa-Fulani emirates. In terms of the major north-south division there are clear differences in the patterns of family background. The fathers of ABU's southern students were about half as likely to be farmers, twice as likely to be civil servants, less than half as likely to have

Table 11. Comparisons of Students' Fathers by Regions

	*ABU 1970, 1971**			
Percentage of Fathers:	*Northern States†*	*Southern States‡*	*Kano, North Central, North West States¶*	*Benue Plateau Kwara States*
	%	%	%	%
Farmers:	61.2	37.5	48.2	71.4
Civil servants:	7.8	14.8	12.3	3.4
Incomes under N100:	39.0	14.7	31.9	45.6
Incomes over N2000:	10.3	13.7	21.0	4.9
Illiterate:	32.6	24.2	18.5	44.5
Primary or secondary education:#	20.4	40.0	19.3	20.3
	N=361-377	N=88-95	N=114-119	N=175-182

(Variations in numbers result from varying 'no answers'.)

* ABU 1970 and 1971 samples are combined for the purpose of this analysis.
† Includes Benue Plateau, Kano, Kwara, North Central, North East and North West States.
‡ Includes East Central, Lagos, Mid-West, Rivers, South East and Western States.
¶ North East State is omitted from this group because its ABU student contingent is drawn very heavily from Middle Belt groups, while its centre at Maiduguri has more in common with the "far north" States that likewise have their capitals in the capitals of former great emirates. North Central and North West States have their strong Middle Belt elements as well.
# Full or partial.

very low incomes (but only slightly more likely to have very high incomes), less likely to be illiterate and twice as likely to have formal (primary or secondary) schooling.

This is to say that the southern students tend to come from higher "class" backgrounds as the term has been used here. This is largely a reflection of more widespread education and the higher frequency of non-farming occupations in the south, as the comparative data from the other universities suggests.

The table also indicates the considerable patterns of variation that exist between the northern States. Thus fathers of students from what may loosely be called far northern States were "higher" in terms of occupation, income and education, suggesting that students from more privileged families form a considerably more important (though far from dominant) proportion of the contingents from the far northern States, following a "modernizing aristocracy" pattern. The table also indicates, however, the weakness of analysis by region in Nigeria. Thus more detailed analysis reveals sharp differences *within* the northern areas; a more detailed analysis within the groupings of States and within the individual States (with Kano largely excepted) would also show further systematic, cross-cutting variation. The key factor is ethnicity. Significant variations are generally found until one comes down to the level of language groups (though, obviously, numerous cases exist of areas of differentiation within language groups). While there are important

Table 12. Comparisons of Students' Fathers by Religion

	ABU 1970, 1971*			
Percentage of Fathers:	Muslims	All Christians	Protestants	Roman Catholics
	%	%	%	%
Farmers:	41.1	63.6	60.6	70.4
Civil servants:	10.1	6.5	6.6	6.3
Incomes under N100:	26.4	41.5	39.4	47.9
Incomes over N2000:	17.8	9.7	8.7	13.1
Primary or secondary education:†	27.6	28.9	32.4	18.2
	(N=293)	(N=573)	(N=431)	(N=142)

* ABU 1970 and 1971 samples are combined for the purpose of this analysis.
† Full or partial.

uniformities in historical experience at the level of region and sub-region, the uniformities along ethnic lines seem more important.

The same generalization can be made about variations along religious lines (see Table 12). The data suggests that Muslims are in general "higher" on the indices treated than Christians, and that in general Roman Catholics are still "lower" than Protestants. Once again, however, we must emphasize that in the Nigerian context in general, and in our sample in particular, religion as a variable factor should for most purposes be accorded dependent rather than independent status. To understand why Catholic students' fathers are more likely to be farmers and to make less than N100 than are Protestants, one should examine not contrasting religious belief and practice, but rather the ethnic groups and areas from which students come, and cultural and historical features of each.

The interplay of social factors should, therefore, be considered from the standpoint of ethnicity (see Table 13). In general, these variations by ethnicity are sharper than those produced by the regional and religious comparisons above (Tables 11 and 12) and serve to explain the patterns encountered there. To illustrate, one is better able to understand the variations from the average of Muslim students, if one realizes that 50 percent of Muslim students were Hausa. It thus becomes clear that the Hausa, rather than Muslim students, were less likely to have fathers who were farmers with incomes under N100.

A number of significant points emerge from the data. The underrepresentation of female students was more closely related to ethnicity than to religion. Sharp contrasts are apparent with respect to age, pre-university employment, and the parental variables, particularly between the Hausa and Yoruba. Hausa were much younger and less likely to have held full-time jobs than the Yoruba. Their fathers were more likely to be rich, and far less (three times) likely to be illiterate. The rate of primary and secondary education for Yoruba fathers was the same as for Hausa, but the much earlier development of schools in the Yoruba areas should be taken into account. The parental data thus indicates that Yoruba students come from much less privileged households; their own age and work experience, furthermore, indicate that their personal routes to the university have tended to be slower and harder.

The two composite groups, on the parental variables, diverge still more from the Hausa pattern. Particularly in the case of the Upper Middle Belt groups, the fathers were overwhelmingly poor farmers, and almost half were illiterate. Both Hausa and Yoruba societies are traditionally more hierarchical and more occupationally diverse than most other Nigerian groups, including those listed in the Middle Belt groups (with the possible

SOCIAL BACKGROUND: AN ELITE-IN-FORMATION

Table 13. Variations by Ethnicity

	\multicolumn{5}{c}{ABU 1970, 1971*}
	Hausa	Yoruba	Lower Middle Belt†	Upper Middle Belt†	All Students
Sex:	%	%	%	%	%
Female	4.9	9.5	6.0	6.4	8.2
Male	95.9	90.5	94.0	93.6	91.8
Age:					
18-22	45.5	27.0	40.5	40.5	42.8
23-25	37.0	40.0	42.7	37.9	37.2
26+	17.5	33.0	16.8	22.1	20.0
Religion:					
Muslim	90.6	17.8	29.1	11.4	33.5
Protestant	8.2	72.0	37.4	67.8	47.5
Roman Catholic	0.0	6.2	26.9	17.9	14.1
Pre-University Employment:					
Have held full-time job	51.2	73.9	57.6	62.1	62.7
Father's Occupation:					
Farmer	33.8	53.6	67.7	82.1	56.4
Civil Servant	14.9	6.6	3.9	1.5	9.7
Father's Income:					
Less than N100	20.9	30.5	48.8	59.3	37.2
More than N2000	18.9	11.8	7.4	0.0	12.8
Father's Education:					
Illiterate	12.7	40.2	49.2	47.1	31.9
Primary or Secondary‡	31.8	31.2	21.1	23.5	28.9

* ABU 1970 and 1971 samples are combined for the purpose of this analysis. The numbers on which the calculations are based are Hausa, 160; Yoruba, 194; Lower Middle Belt, 133; and Upper Middle Belt, 141. 628 students are thus accounted for, the remaining students falling into language groups not within these categories. The "All Students" column, however, refers to the total sample of 914 students. (ABU 1970 and 1971).
† With the exception of Hausa and Yoruba, the numbers of students within individual language groups were too small for valid comparison with other variables. To give further indications on variations by ethnicity, we constructed two composite groups, referred to here as "Upper Middle Belt" and "Lower Middle Belt." The composition of each group is as shown below.
Lower Middle Belt: Idoma, Igala, Igbirra, Nupe, Basa-Nge.
Upper Middle Belt: Angas, Bata, Bolewa, Bura, Higi, Jaba, Jukun, Kaje, Kilba, Mbula, Ninzam, Nzanki, Sura, Tangale, Tera, Warjawa, Chala, Buazza, Jengo, Cham, Kagoro, Eggon, Cheka, Chamba, Gudo, Jen, Afo, Ankwe, Birom, Bachama, Wurkum, Saya, Pyem, Babur, Kagoma, Rukuba, Ikulu and Bankal.
We put the peoples together on the basis of geographical contiguity and similarities of culture and historical experience. Strictly speaking, these should be called ethno-linguistic-regional groups. The Lower Middle Belt (LMB) groups belong to the Kwa language category and are located in the southern area of the former Northern Region (all are located in the present Kwara, North West and Benue Plateau States). The Upper Middle Belt (UMB) groups are located in the more northern areas of the former Region (in the present North East, North Central, and Benue Plateau States) and belong to either the Chadic or Benue-Congo language groups.
‡ Full or partial.

exception of the Nupe). Both (especially the Yoruba) have been longer and more widely exposed to processes of educational, commercial and political development which have widened income and status differentials. It is to be expected, therefore, that the Middle Belt groups would be characterized by less occupational diversity (among the fathers), higher rates of illiteracy and somewhat lower incomes than either the Yoruba or Hausa. Among the Upper Middle Belt groups, in fact, nearly half of the fathers were subsistence farmers. These patterns reflect general historical patterns. Educational development, cash crops and commercial growth came later to the Lower Middle Belt groups than to the Yoruba, and still later to the Upper Middle Belt. Our figures on proportions of farmer fathers reflect the historical progression. It is worth noticing that relatively poor Middle Belt communities which were often politically alienated within the former Northern Region have profited more from the educational facilities made possible by regional revenues than have the dominant Hausa and Kanuri[11] groups.

5. *SOME WEST AFRICAN COMPARISONS*

Other West African countries have little data comparable to those discussed above. What is available, however, suggests the probability of similar trends in recruitment to higher education. This can be illustrated by relating some of the Nigerian material to material on Ghana and the Ivory Coast, drawing on Clignet and Foster's work on secondary students in Ghana and the Ivory Coast and on material available on the social background of Ghanaian university students.[12]

The Nigerian data indicates striking inequalities in recruitment to advanced education and thus to potential-elite status. The factors referred to above may be grouped under ethnicity and region, parental 'class' (as indicated by father's occupation and education), and students' own sex and religion. In terms of region the most important pattern of inequality in recruitment is that between the north and south of Nigeria. It is interesting that similar patterns are evident in Ghana and the Ivory Coast. Clignet and Foster found that in the Ivory Coast secondary school students from the south were overrepresented by a factor of 1.6 while northern students were underrepresented by a factor of 1.7.[13] In Ghana, they found that regional differentials in secondary school recruitment were more striking still with the south and central areas overrepresented by a factor of 1.4 and the north five times underrepresented. In all three countries these regional inequalities have historical explanations; above all 'they have arisen largely as the result of the historical pattern of

SOCIAL BACKGROUND: AN ELITE-IN-FORMATION

European penetration into various areas and concomitant variations in the rate of internal socio-economic change.'[14] It is probable that in all the countries close analysis would show (as was illustrated by the case study presentation of ABU data above) that within the broad pattern of north-south cleavages a myriad of more particular inequalities exists reflecting more localized historical factors, in particular, decisions made by mission organizations and local reactions to new opportunities.

Regional and ethnic inequalities are closely related: our case study analysis of the ABU data indicates that ethnic differentials are sharper than regional ones, and that variations by ethnic group are in general of primary significance and are reflected more or less clearly by regional variations. It is interesting that Clignet and Foster's Ivory Coast data seems to be characterized by the same pattern; whereas regional variations spread from factors of 1.6 overrepresentation to 1.7 under-representation, their comparison of major ethnic groups ranges from overrepresentation by a factor of 2.9 (Agni) to underrepresentation by a factor of 3.0 (Senuofo-Lobi).

The data available from Nigeria, Ghana and the Ivory Coast on fathers' occupation follows a similar pattern as indicated in Table 14.

Table 14. Students' Fathers' Occupations, Nigeria, Ghana, Ivory Coast

Student's Father's Occupation	ABU Students 1970-71	Nigeria Ibadan Students 1948-66*	Lagos Students 1974‡	Ghana 6th Form 1964†	Legon Univ. 1964†	Ivory Coast Secondary Students 1963¶
	%	%	%	%	%	%
Farmer, Fisherman	56.6	30.8	30.5	23.3	37.7	66.8
Administrative, Clerical and Professional	23.6	40.0	34.8	55.0	45.6	18.1
Trader, Businessman	11.8	16.4	25.4	7.8	3.5	5.6
Workers	—	8.1	?	6.5	6.1	6.9
Other	8.0	4.8	9.2	7.4	7.1	2.6
Totals	100.0	100.1	99.9	100.0	100.0	100.0

* *Source:* P. L. van den Berghe and C. M. Nuttney, *op. cit.*, Table VII. For consistency with other data we have combined their "clerical and sales", "semi-professional", and "professional" into our "administrative, clerical, professional" group; and we have combined their "artisans" and "unskilled workers" groups.
† *Source:* W. Birmingham, I. Neustadt, E. N. Omaboe (editors), *A Study of Contemporary Ghana* (London, Allen & Unwin, 1967), Vol. 2, p.236, Table 6.10.
‡ *Source:* M. O. Shoremi and F. Mott, *op. cit.*, Table 4. Their occupational categories do not provide for workers. 'Other' includes 'none' or 'not available'.
¶ *Source:* R. P. Clignet and P. Foster, *The Fortunate Few*, Table 11 (p.57). Their "uniformed services" appears in the "other" group above. The other categories are the same, though the titles used differ slightly.

SOCIAL BACKGROUND: AN ELITE-IN-FORMATION 41

A number of common features are apparent. Farmers and fishermen are very much underrepresented among students' fathers in relation to their numbers in the population as a whole, whereas administrative and clerical occupations and, to a somewhat lesser extent, traders and businessmen are overrepresented.

On the other hand, the proportion of students' fathers who *are* farmers or in other low income occupations may be more surprising. The data on Ghana and the Ivory Coast, like that on Nigeria, suggest a remarkably open pattern of recruitment to higher education compared with that in many non-African countries.

An important question is the extent to which this relative accessibility will prove to be temporary, as larger proportions of second and third generation elites compete for places in the institutions of higher education. At first sight, a comparison of the Ibadan, Lagos and Ghana data, where occupational diversification and average incomes are higher, with that from northern Nigeria (ABU) and the Ivory Coast, suggests that as development progresses, the proportions of 'farmer fathers' are likely to diminish from between half and two-thirds of students' fathers to around one-third. However, diachronic data available from Ibadan and Ghana (Legon University) does not bear out such a hypothesis. Van den Berghe and Nuttney's Ibadan data show an *increase* in the proportion of farmers among students' fathers from a little less than 30 percent in the first decade to 38 percent in the 1962-66 period. Data compiled by Finlay, Koplin and Ballard at Legon University in Ghana show a similar increase in the proportion of 'farmer fathers' from 25.8 percent in 1953 to 41.8 percent in a 1966 survey.[15] The data are inadequate to pursue this question further, but they suggest that two contrary forces are at work in West Africa. On the one hand, students who are children of middle and higher elites (especially in government employment) and, to a lesser extent, children of trading and business groups, are reaching institutions of higher education in much larger numbers. Their numbers can be expected to continue to increase at an accelerating rate in the next decade. On the other hand, this factor has been largely offset by generally expanding systems of education at the secondary and university level which have increased recruitment from the rural areas, with the effect of maintaining or even increasing the proportion of fathers who are farmers.

Another significant feature of the data on fathers' occupation is the extreme underrepresentation of the urban working classes among fathers of the students. These groups account for considerably larger proportions in the general population than the administrative, professional and clerical groups. The workers, moreover, are at least as urban as the white collar classes; they share high access to educational institutions and are presumably subject to an intense demonstration effect of the significance of education. Yet they are very much underrepresented among the fathers of the students. In the data supplied by Clignet and Foster for both Ivory Coast and Ghana, the unskilled or semi-skilled workers are considerably more underrepresented even than farmers and fishermen.[16] The Ibadan data provided by van den Berghe and Nuttney show that from 1948 to 1966 the proportion of unskilled workers among the fathers of the Ibadan student population grew only as follows:[17]

1948-52	1952-57	1958-62	1962-66	1948-66
0.2%	0.5%	0,8%	1.3%	0.7%

While the comparative data available is as yet incomplete and much too tentative to be regarded as more than suggestive, the possibility is that whereas the class structure remains relatively fluid and open with regard to recruitment from rural areas and farming backgrounds, *within the urban sector* the beginnings of a more rigid, closed and permanent class system may be visible as the children of the middle and upper elites are disproportionately drawn to higher education (and another generation of privilege) and the children of workers, for whatever reasons, are largely excluded.

Some comparative data on the education of fathers of university and secondary students are presented in Table 15. At first sight these data seem remarkable for the contrasts. The low proportion of illiteracy among fathers of ABU students (accounted for in large part by Koranic

Table 15. Father's Education: Nigeria, Ivory Coast, Ghana

Father's Education	Nigeria		Ivory Coast	Ghana
	ABU 1970, 1971	Lagos* 1974	Secondary† 1963	Legon Univ. ‡ 1966
	%	%	%	%
None (illiterate)	35.1	29.8	69.1	30.6
Primary (full or partial)	22.1	34.1	20.2	38.1
Above primary	14.2	36.1	10.7	31.4
Other and no answer	28.6	—	—	—
	100.0 (N=857)	100.0 (N=353)	100.0 (N=2,074)	100.1 (N=371)

* Adapted from M. O. Shoremi and F. Mott, *op. cit.*, Table 2 (1974 data, fathers of male students only). We have not used the total Shoremi and Mott sample because it is heavily biased by having a much greater proportion of female students than exists at the university, 33.5 percent of their sample is female, while the university registry figures record women students as only 16.6 percent of the student body.
† Adapted from R. P. Clignet and P. Foster, *The Fortunate Few*, Table 12. Categories 'some primary' and 'full primary' have been combined.
‡ Adapted from D. J. Finlay, R. E. Koplin and C. A. Ballard, *op. cit.*, Table 4, p.79.

education and adult literacy programmes) and the fathers of Lagos and Legon students is striking in contrast with fathers of Ivory Coast students. The level of post-primary education among Lagos and Legon fathers contrasts with the much lower proportions among ABU and Ivory Coast fathers.

The common feature which lies beneath these apparent contrasts is perhaps more significant: in all three countries persons with formal education are enormously overrepresented among the fathers of students. With reference to Ghana and the Ivory Coast, Clignet and Foster make the following points:

> We know that, in Ghana, the education of the fathers of our students is very much higher than that prevailing among the adult male population. Indeed, the gradient among selectivity ratios is far steeper than it is for either urban/rural or occupational characteristics, indicating the rather greater importance of paternal education in influencing secondary school access. We have little doubt that the situation is much the same in the Ivory Coast... We should hazard that the selectivity gradients by level of paternal education are probably even steeper than those for Ghana.[18]

The Nigerian data presents the same pattern, and we can elaborate the point from the ABU data which is more extensive. According to the 1952 census, 83.1 percent of adult males in the then Northern Region of Nigeria engaged in farming or fishing as their primary occupation (the proportion of fishermen in northern Nigeria is negligible). If (bearing in mind the weakness of the census data) one employs this figure, then the proportion of farmers among fathers of the ABU students in our sample (57 percent) constitutes underrepresentation by a factor of 1.5. But if one assumes that some 85 percent of northern males old enough to have university-aged children are illiterate (a conservative guess) then illiterate fathers in the sample (35 percent) are underrepresented *by a factor of 2.4*. Using the same census data, formally educated fathers in our sample would seem to be *over*represented by at least 15 times. Our evidence, then, supports Clignet and Foster's suggestion: the father's education is considerably more relevant to a child's chances of reaching a high level of education than the father's occupation or income. This suggests that there may frequently be a time-lag of one generation before the impact of education is fully felt in the mobilization of masses of people to nontraditional ways of life outside home villages.

Finally, two variables relating to the students themselves should be considered: the students' sex and their religion. If we have, until now, given relatively little space to differentials in recruitment to university according to sex, it is not because the patterns are not significant, but because they are so obvious. First, at ABU as in the other educational contexts about which we have information, female students are vastly underrepresented (accounting for only about 12 percent of our 1973 sample). At Ibadan the percentage of female students encountered in records covering 2,699 students over 18 years was 11 percent. In the Ivory Coast secondary system, Clignet and Foster's sample of 2,074 included 11.4 percent women.

Second, there is a very strong association of the sex variable with parental background. Some available comparative data are shown in Table 16. The main features of this comparison are quickly summarized.

Table 16. Comparisons of Fathers by Sex of Student

Student's Father's Occupation	ABU Male	Female	Ibadan* Male	Female	Lagos† Male	Female	Ivory Coast‡ (Secondary Students) Male	Female
	%	%	%	%	%	%	%	%
Farmer	59.2	25.0	32.4	11.3	30.5	6.9	71.6	29.5
Administrative, Clerical, Professional	21.5	48.5	37.9	63.2	34.8	59.5	14.3	48.1
Chiefs	0.9	2.9	1.9	2.4	?	?	—	—
Workers, Artisans	—	—	8.5	4.8	?	?	6.6	9.7
Traders	11.6	13.2	16.9	11.3	25.4	17.9	5.0	9.7
Other	6.8	10.4	2.6	7.1	9.2	15.6	2.5¶	3.0¶
	100.0	100.0	100.2	100.1	99.9	99.9	100.0	100.0
	(N=817)	(N=68)	(N=2487)	(N=212)	(N=353)	(N=175)	(N=1837)	(N=237)

* Adapted from P. L. van den Berghe and C. M. Nuttney, op. cit., Table X.
† Adapted from M. O. Shoremi and P. Mott, op. cit. No categories are provided to correspond to 'chiefs' and 'workers, artisans'.
‡ Source: adapted from R. P. Clignet and P. Foster, The Fortunate Few, Table 11.
¶ Consists of "uniformed services".

Variations in father's occupation by sex follow in the same direction; the female students are far more likely to come from families of higher income and status, and far less likely to come from farming families. This pattern of differentiation is to be expected; as van den Berghe and Nuttney remark:

> ... in developing countries, the incentive and the means to educate girls as well as boys are much more restricted to the upper strata than in the developed countries. ... The few women who make it to university come overwhelmingly from the more privileged ethnic, religious and class groups.[19]

This brings us to the final factor of inequality to be discussed, which is

SOCIAL BACKGROUND: AN ELITE-IN-FORMATION   45

that of religion. In the ABU and Ibadan student bodies, as among Ivory Coast secondary students, Muslim students are very much underrepresented in relation to the proportions of Muslims in the population. As with female students the Muslim students tend to be drawn from higher family backgrounds in terms of education and income than the general student population, and particularly atypical backgrounds in relation to the Muslim segment of the general population. Table 17 compares the

Table 17. Comparisons between Fathers of Christians and Muslims

	ABU 1973	
	Muslims	Christians
	(N=71)	(N=205)
N400 or less:	34.4%	56.1%
Farmers:	36.8%	57.8%

occupations and incomes of fathers of Christian and Muslim students, using data from the ABU 1973 sample.

Three popular notions about the effect of Islam continue to find expression both by non-African commentators and by non-Muslim Africans: that Muslims generally reject "Western" education because of religious hostility to it; that in the more stratified Muslim African societies, it is the higher status groups only that get advanced education; and that education of females will be more retarded among Muslim groups because of religious hostility to educated and emancipated women. Superficially, these stereotypes are supported to some extent by most of the data available on recruitment to advanced education. This support is, however, only of a superficial nature. With reference to the first stereotype, historical factors, especially colonial policies, help to explain to a considerable extent the educational 'backwardness' in the Muslim areas of northern Nigeria. The considerable difference in representation at university between the various Muslim ethnic groups in our ABU sample also serves to argue against the operation of a religious constant in these differentials, as does the eagerness of most far northern areas to increase as rapidly as possible their educational enrolment at all levels.

The second stereotype comes closer to finding confirmation in the available data. Muslim fathers (like fathers of female students and fathers of students in other underrepresented categories) are less likely than the average to be poor or to be farmers. It is perhaps more important, however, to recognize the converse of this association, (as Table 17 shows) that more than one third of the ABU Muslim students' fathers *were* poor and *were* farmers. The picture of a 'modernizing aristocracy' can easily be overdrawn.

Our data offer very little support to the third stereotype. In the ABU 1973 sample the proportion of Muslims among the female students was actually higher than the proportion of the Muslims among the student body as a whole. Alternatively, the proportion of women among the Muslim students was slightly more than the proportion of women in the sample as a whole.[20]

6. CONCLUSION

Once we analyse differentials and inequalities among the students we are faced with two cross-cutting aspects. On the one hand, children of already established elites, above all, public servants, business and professional men, who have had access to modern-type education, are overrepresented, while the vast bulk of the population engaged in farming (and fishing) is underrepresented. On the other hand, all the findings are remarkable for the evidence of continuing open recruitment in terms of social background. This is particularly striking in the case of the ABU data where half of the fathers were farmers earning less than N400 annually. Even in Ghana the fathers of more than one-third of the Legon students were farmers. This situation contrasts with that in many developing countries in other continents: to take an extreme example, a survey of 1,250 university-level students in Brazil showed that less than one percent had fathers who were illiterate, though 46 percent of adult male Brazilians are illiterate.[21] Nigerian and other West African institutions of advanced education are in the process of creating elites which seem to be solidifying into classes. But these elites are as yet broad-based. The great majority of those who are now graduates are connected by family and personal experience to the village and farm life of the majority.

It is important to realise however that the educational systems which we have been looking at have been in a state of rapid expansion. Children of elites that moved into senior posts after the Second World War, and especially during the rapid Africanization of the 1950's, have begun to reach the university level of education in significant numbers. Our data indicates that the children of the bureaucratic and business elites *are* far more likely to attend university than children of other occupational groups, especially farmers. Perpetuation and consolidation of privilege definitely occurs, but the rapid expansion of the educational systems has thus far permitted continued expansion of recruitment from poorer families to continue, and even to broaden into new groups and areas. It is the rapid expansion of the systems which has permitted the coexistence of contrary tendencies which otherwise would be in clear conflict.

The important question now is how a levelling off of expansion of higher educational institutions will affect patterns of selection, and thus elite recruitment. The competition from the well-to-do in Nigeria, for example, is only now developing significantly as the children of the large groups of senior administrators, professionals and others, who benefited from the indigenisation policies of the period before independence, reach university age.

FOOTNOTES

1. It has, however, not been possible to utilize all our relevant ABU material in this chapter. More detailed analyses of the ABU data are available in P. Beckett and J. O'Connell, "Social Characteristics of an Elite-in-Formation: Nigerian University Students", *British Journal of Sociology*, September, 1975; and P. Beckett and J. O'Connell, "A Problem of Political Socialization: Differential Impacts of Secondary Education", *Savanna*, Vol. 1, No. 2 (December, 1972), pp. 199-212. The present chapter represents a revised and reduced version of our "Social Characteristics...." article.
2. P. L. van den Berghe and C. M. Nuttney, *op. cit.*, pp. 355-377. See also P. L. van den Berghe "Pluralism at a Nigerian University: A Case Study", *Race*, Vol: XII, No. 4 (1971), pp. 429-41; and P. L. van den Berghe, *Power and Privilege*.
3. *Ibid.*, p. 152.
4. Our Ibadan statistics were supplied by Mr. O. Fatodu, Acting Deputy Registrar; our Lagos statistics by Mrs. M. E. Eke, Assistant Registrar (Academic); our Ife statistics by Mr. 'Biddun Banwo; our Nsukka statistics by Mrs. Ngozi Anyakora; and our ABU statistics by Mr. Bitrus Sawa— to all of whom we are grateful.
5. On religious proportions among the Yoruba, see J. D. J. Peel, *Aladura: A Religious Movement Among the Yoruba* (London: Oxford University Press, 1968), pp. 52-53.
6. M. O. Shoremi and F. Mott, *op. cit.*
7. The National Manpower Board provides a register of professional manpower in 1964. The following table gives the numbers and proportions of such manpower by region of origin:

	No.	Percentage
Federal Territory	79	6.3%
Northern Region	54	4.3%
Eastern Region	468	37.0%
Western Region	499	39.5%
Mid-Western Region	162	12.8%
	1,264	100.0%

National Manpower Board, Federation of Nigeria, *A Study of Nigerian Professional Manpower in Selected Occupations 1964* (Lagos, 1964), pp. 2,8. It is significant that the percentages given in these two tables reflect similar imbalances to those that we currently estimate for university students.

8. No reliable data on proportions of occupations in the total populations is available. The 1952 census, which purported to provide exact occupational data, put "Agriculture, Forestry, Fishing, Hunting" occupations at 83.1 percent of the total for northern

SOCIAL BACKGROUND: AN ELITE-IN-FORMATION

Nigeria and 78.6 percent for Nigeria as a whole. (See Table 17, "Primary Occupations of Populations of Nigeria by Sex and Regions, 1952-1952 Census", Northern Nigeria *Statistical Yearbook 1966).* Difficulties of classification are well known. A large proportion of males in the northern States farm full-time during the wet season, and carry on crafts or trading, or sell their labour during the dry season. Most of their cash income may come from the dry season activity, while their farming may remain the most important source of their actual subsistence. It becomes difficult to say which is "primary". We suspect that the 1952 figures understate the proportion whose primary source of subsistence is farming.

9. P. L. van den Berghe, *Power and Privilege,* p. 153.
10. Literacy in Roman script (language unspecified) was classified in terms of four years of primary education or more (0.9 percent) and "others" (1.0 percent). Literacy in Arabic script varied from 8.1 percent in Kano Province to 0.4 percent in what became Sardauna Province. Table 24, "Literacy of Population of 7 years of Age and Over in Northern Nigeria by Province, 1952 Census", in northern Nigeria *Statistical Yearbook 1966,* p. 18. The same caution expressed earlier regarding the census data applies here.
11. The Kanuri are the dominant group in Borno State (formerly in the North Eastern State). They share with the Hausa the oldest established attachment to Islam in northern Nigeria as well as a long court and recorded history.
12. R. P. Clignet and P. Foster, "Potential Elites in Ghana and the Ivory Coast: A Preliminary Comparison", *American Journal of Sociology,* Vol. LXX, No. 3 (1964), pp. 349-362; reprinted in M. E. Doro and N. M. Stultz (editors), *Governing in Black Africa* (New Jersey, Prentice-Hall, 1970), pp. 190-205. Our comparisons with the Ivory Coast are drawn mainly from this article, and from R. P. Clignet and P. Foster, *The Fortunate Few: A Study of Secondary Schools and Students in the Ivory Coast* (Chicago, Northwestern University Press, 1966). See also P. Foster, "Ethnicity and the Schools in Ghana," *Comparative Education Review,* VI (October, 1962), p. 127-135.
13. The "selectivity ratio" method used by Clignet and Foster expresses underrepresentation by means of fractions (tenths) rather than negative number. For consistency with our own presentations we have taken the liberty of recomputing their "selectivity ratios" on the same basis as our own. Thus underrepresentation by a factor of 1.7 is, in their system, a selectivity ratio of 0.6
14. R. P. Clignet and P. Foster, *The Fortunate Few,* p. 5.
15. D. J. Finlay, R. E. Koplin and C. A. Ballard, Jnr. "Ghana" in D. K. Emmerson (editor), *Students and Politics in Developing Nations,* (New York, Praeger, 1968), pp. 64-102.
16. R. P. Clignet and P. Foster, "Potential Elites in Ghana and the Ivory Coast," Table 3.
17. Drawn from P. L. van den Berghe and C. M. Nuttney, *op. cit,* Table IX.
18. R. P. Clignet and P. Foster, "Potential Elites in Ghana and the Ivory Coast", pp. 198-99. In connection with their more extensive survey of secondary students in the Ivory Coast they remark: "the variable most systematically related to differential ethnic enrolment would appear to be the father's level of education." See R. P. Clignet and P. Foster, *The Fortunate Few,* p. 71.
19. P. L. van den Berghe and C. M. Nuttney, *op. cit.,* p. 370.
20. We find ourselves heartily in agreement with Clignet and Foster who make the following comments on the basis of their study of secondary students in the Ivory Coast: "The negative stance of Islam vis-à-vis educational development has perhaps been exaggerated . . . . Moslem girls seem to do just as well as their Christian counterparts in obtaining secondary education . . . . This fact alone should make us wary of attributing variable recruitment patterns to religious differences." R. P. Clignet and P. Foster, *The Fortunate Few,* p. 160.
21. L. Scheman, "The Brazilian Law Student: Background, Habits, Attitudes," *Journal of Inter-American Studies,* V (July, 1963), cited in R. O. Myhr, "Brazil", in D. K. Emmerson, (editor), *Students and Politics in Developing Nations* (New York, Praeger, 1968), p.257.

3 Social Origins and Identity

Perhaps the single most important characteristic of the members of Nigeria's new urban population is that most come from the village. Technological extremes are more pronounced in a country like Nigeria than they are in the U.S.A., for instance, where far reaching technological changes have been spread over most of this century. In Nigeria change is concentrated in the lives of university graduates and students. The preceding chapter includes some evidence that university students are drawn disproportionately from the more progressive elements of rural communities (and beyond that, that the non-rural occupations are somewhat overrepresented among the students' fathers). We now explore the human implications of these facts. We must emphasize again that farming is the full time occupation of almost half the students' fathers (and that undoubtedly a considerable proportion of fathers who are listed under other occupational headings engage in farming as well). If educated parents are overrepresented in relation to the population as a whole, the fact remains that between one-third and one-half of fathers and between two-thirds and three-quarters of mothers are absolutely illiterate; only half or less of fathers and one-third or less of mothers have had any formal modern education; only a very small minority of parents of either sex have education to university level. Some four-fifths of the university students will attain a higher income level than their fathers in their first year of work after graduation (omitting from consideration the compulsory post-graduation National Youth Service Corps year).[1] About half of the students will earn between twice and four (or more) times as much as their fathers in the first year of work.

In the descriptions that follow we concentrate on the background of students who come from rural areas. Such descriptions are only applicable in modified form to the minority of students who come from the modern cities and from non-farming families.[2]

1. GETTING TO UNIVERSITY: 'ALLAH SAYS, "GET UP AND I WILL HELP YOU'."[3]

To communicate the human dimension of our survey in more concrete terms, we draw where possible on autobiographical statements prepared for us by a number of ABU students.[4] Any one of the ABU students is most likely to have been born (probably without benefit of modern medicine) in a small one-room mud house within a family compound of small mud houses. Much of the life of compound and village is in fact, not 'traditional' in strict historical terms, for the 20th century has brought enormous social change throughout rural Nigeria. Yet this background of a simple material culture, relative insulation from literate culture, and an agricultural economy with its heavy reliance on human labour, could scarcely be more remote from the situation of the Nigerian graduate civil servant whose material culture (in terms of house, car, appliances, TV, clothes, etc.) does not differ appreciably from that of the well-educated administrative middle classes in the developed countries.

If a university student is now in his 20s, he has probably taken 16 or 17 years to move from that maternal hut and paternal compound to his dormitory room at the university. Many students are much older, and it has taken much longer. For most it has been a period of struggle. In many cases there is a near epic quality: finding the way to university for some seems almost as complex as Odysseus' journey home. For very few of the students is the route to university as easy, automatic, and unconscious as it is for large numbers of university students in the U.S.A. and Great Britain. The students we deal with are by definition a chosen few. We can take ABU students as an example. In 1962, the year of ABU's foundation, when a large proportion of the present university students were in primary school, there were in the Northern Region some 360,000 primary students.[5] By 1974 when that group was in their twenties, there were only a few more than 4,000 degree students at ABU (and very much smaller numbers of students of northern origin at other Nigerian universities or abroad). University students are those who have passed a number of prior examinations; they have been chosen and then chosen from among the chosen.[6] The students often seem to be characterized as much by their determination as by superior intelligence. A woman student, asked to describe herself, listed eight things about herself. Asked which was most important to her, she had no hesitation in selecting: "I am a strong-willed person". ("If not for my strong will, . . . I would not have been in the university . . .").

The first step, and the first division among age peers is in actually beginning school. For some, in communities where primary education is already well-established, the choice is fairly automatic. Some are forced to school by foresighted fathers or other relatives. A surprising proportion, however, judging by case histories we have collected, make the decision themselves while still under the age of ten and in the face of opposition from at least part of their families.[7] This is not infrequent among Muslim children whose parents may prefer Koranic education and regard the new schools as Christian. One boy, born to Muslim parents in a predominantly pagan (and subsequently Christian) society, writes:

> Tula was and still is a predominantly Christian/Pagan society, as a result most of the children go to school. Owing to the influence of the children and my personal conviction, I resolved to go to the primary school. My father was not willing to let me go because he wanted me to remain in the Quranic school (which the writer had begun 'at a very early age'). I went to Tula Primary School in 1954. At the time I entered the Tula Primary School, my senior brother was with one of the itinerant mallams and when he came home he stood head and toe that I should be withdrawn from the primary school. I refused to yield.

However, other patterns are also found among Muslim university students. Another boy also began in Koranic school, from where he was sent to a primary school 'in the town' (i.e., outside his own aristocratic residential quarter) by his father:

> Both my grandmother, my Koranic teacher and even myself objected (to) this. The prevailing tendency by then of Fulani Muslims was utter rejection of anything to do with Nasara (Europeans) and all their ethics and innovation. There was especially at that time no dichotomy between Christianity and Western education. Hence I went to the primary school against my wish and with convictions that I would end up a Joseph.

Not only Muslim students, however, have had to contend with local prejudice against new education. A student from the present Rivers State in southern Nigeria writes:

> My community, Ikwerre Division, had early contact with Europeans . . . [but] the first generation of school children were the sons of slaves. Later it was discovered that they were quite lucky when they secured employment, and remitted some part of their earnings home. [But] whatever might be the quantity of wealth accumulated by these immigrants, people at home were not moved to emulate them because as descendants of slaves, they had no full rights according to native law and customs. . .
> My great grandmother was one of the daughters of the famous

Mgboh (ruling dynasty) in all the eight villages that make up my town, Emohua. My mother came from the principal family.... And my present family is one of the principal houses of my village....
I started going to school after the death of my grandmother. An indication that if she had survived longer, I would no doubt have been an illiterate. The general opinion at that time was that those who were sent to school were regarded as slaves or families which were unable to feed their children well....
I went to school without instruction from my parents. It all occured one morning when I saw a cousin of mine going to school, and I asked him to hold on for me. When I came back home and my parents were told about it, none of them scolded me for it.

Surprisingly frequently it seems, in fact, to be the child who decides that school is a good thing, often emulating peers. A student writes:

I can still remember vividly that my father never formally sent me to school....[The] circumstances which sent me to school arose out of pride of my playmates who were then attending the village school. Whether what they were saying had any meaning or not [probably referring to the children's English], I did feel isolated whenever they started writing figures or the alphabet with their fingers in the sand each time we met to play.

The entrance into primary school marks the beginning of a long period of formalized acculturation which increasingly distances the student both culturally and physically from the home. It is not necessarily fun; primary schools in Nigeria tend to feature a certain amount of manual labour and also corporal punishment.[8] The students who reached university level were almost always the best students in their classes. A Muslim Hausa boy remarks:

I remember that in the mission school where I started my education I always answered most of the questions other people . . . found difficult to answer. Although a Moslem by birth, I had often led in reciting any religious stories we were taught by our lady [christian missionary] teacher.

One of the most significant factors of this educational experience is the extent to which students are taken away from the home village and the village culture. Many students are able to attend the first years of primary school in their home village, or within walking distance of their parents' compound. Others, however, are sent to larger towns to live with relatives or friends of their parents. At the age of seven or eight, such a child may find himself very much on his own, in an environment which may not be so comfortable:

> I did not actually like [want] to go to Gombe for schooling as I did not recognize the advantages then . . . I did not want to stay away from my people and especially I never liked to stay in my new master's house in Gombe [a friend of his father's] which was a large compound with so many women and children, because of the hostility shown to small boys, who come from outside and who were, consequently, treated as strangers. . . . Innocent children who were just brought in from distant villages were often beaten by the man's wives. In truth, this is one of the common things in Africa. . . .

The English tradition of boarding schools has found fertile soil in Nigeria.[9] In northern Nigeria, boarding school begins for many with 'Senior Primary School' (following four years of Junior Primary School, usually in the village of birth). For the student quoted above, boarding school was a blessed escape from an unfortunate compound situation. But far more commonly, Senior Primary School is the first experience (at the age of 11 or 12 perhaps) of living away from the family compound and the home village. Apart from frequently being traumatic for such young children,[10] this first boarding school experience is the beginning of the process of introducing the children into wider cultural and social systems. A boy who came from one of the richest families in a poor area writes:

> My stay at the Boarding School was the first time I moved away from my family. Because of the under-privileged condition of most of the pupils I stayed with in the primary school, I tended to look at them with contempt. But my stay in the Boarding School began to help me in shedding part of the contempt I had for my counterparts because at the Boarding School, we were treated as equal—housed in the dormitory, ate in the same dining hall—in fact shared everything in common.

The beginning of secondary school, at the age of 14 or more, marks a more definitive exile from the native village and culture. Only a minority have secondary schools close to their homes. For the vast majority, attending secondary school involves going to a district or provincial capital which may be 100 miles or more from home. It is important to note that for a great many students this exile from family and home community is an exile from 'nation', in the sense of language group, as well. Often the student is able to speak his first or mother language only with small numbers of fellow 'exiles'. This necessitates the use of English as a medium of communication with peers (not only as a classroom language) and also often results in acquiring or perfecting knowledge of one of Nigeria's major *lingua franca* languages. A Fulani student, who has previously explained his aversion to Hausa and English in primary school (where he refused to use them outside the classroom) arrived at a secondary school several hundred miles from his home:

> I found that I could not survive short of speaking English or Hausa . . . (I) made a lot of Hausa friends which indirectly elevated my Hausa vocabulary and language.

The student normally spends five years on the regular secondary course, and may do two more years of 'sixth form' work at the same or a different secondary school to obtain advanced level ('A-level') qualifications for university entrance. Alternatively, the student may study on his own, often while working full time in a teaching or clerical job, to attain A-level qualifications. During secondary school the student is likely to visit his family during holidays, but as his secondary education progresses he is less likely to be reintegrated into the family economy (where it is based on farming) except in occasional, mainly symbolic ways. He is likely to spend much of his time in the company of 'mates' of comparable educational status; visits to fellow students in other towns and meetings between boy and girl students seem to be the major events that punctuate these periods of holiday. While we have no direct knowledge of the situation, it is probable that there is a certain separation between these returning students and their age peers (the great majority, by this time) who have never been to school or have dropped out at an earlier stage.

During this period of 12 or 14 years of formal education, the student is brought further and further within the world culture that is primarily Western European in origin. All primary and secondary students are invited to become as proficient in English, mathematics and so forth, as their counterparts in, say, Great Britain and the U.S.A. Nigerian university students are, by definition, those who have succeeded. It goes without saying that there is a heavier cost for such people than for students in developed countries whose home culture coincides more closely with the school culture, and similarly, that there are also compensations. Some of the passages by students which have already been quoted indicate the extent to which formal education is regarded as Christian and European. In addition to learning in a language of alien origin, there are deeper implications, in terms of separation (alienation is too strong a word) from one's native culture. Fortunately, education which initially separates, may, as it proceeds, provide its own basis for reintegration, as the following passage indicates:

> Since I started schooling or embraced Christianity, and up to very recently, I regarded many . . . Igala customs as 'uncivilized' and out of date. I should not be entirely blamed for this . . . Christian

teachings paved the way for this attitude. For example we were taught that it was bad and sinful to take part in traditional burial ceremonies, take part in traditional dances, songs and plays. But when I started acquiring good tools for analysis I discovered that there is nothing bad or sinful in these customs... Once I was able to discover for myself that most of what were regarded as being bad in Igala by Christian teachings were not really so, I started identifying myself more and more with my home community. In this way I became interested in what their problems and needs are and tried to contribute my quota towards solving these problems.

Our research indicates that frequently students feel that their long separation from their community of origin has robbed them of complete mastery of their first language, while at the same time their relatively late start in English and the rest of school-taught culture leaves them inevitably less than perfect there also. In the words of a student:

I started getting my education in English from the age of eight. But the background was not such as to enable me actually (to) appreciate the nature of learning the language. Consequently my use of the language throughout... primary school was poor. English then, was looked on as something to be used for fun. The result of this background is that I have a better command of my dialect [first language] than English. However, my command of my language dialect is not as good as those of my contemporaries who hadn't the opportunity of attending school or of learning English. I am consequently neither fluent in Ishan nor fluent in English. It is a paradox.

These introductory comments, and especially the students' own words, contribute to a better understanding of the subject and will add some flavour and hopefully some warmth to the necessarily dry results produced by a questionnaire survey. The personal determination with which most of the students have made their way upward to the university level should be emphasised. Many, through bad advice or lack of alternatives, find themselves in the stream of students officially destined not for university but for teaching at the primary level. It is remarkable (and the despair of educational planners) how many refuse to accept this handicap.[11] A student remarks that after finishing his primary education in 1961:

I had two offers, and I was the only person with the two offers, either to go to Bauchi Secondary School or Bauchi Teachers College. The headmaster of the school who had all along been friendly to me, advised me to go to the T.C.... But I later on began to regret my going to the T.C. because I felt that I had limited opportunity of furthering my education compared with the boys in the secondary school. My frustration was to be more when I finished the Grade II course and started teaching while my mates in the Primary School who went to the Secondary School were doing the H.S.C. course which was preparatory to coming to the university. The most annoying part of it was that none of them was better than me when we were in the Primary School. I started teaching in January, 1967 with the Tangale-Waja L.A. I made a determined effort that year to get to the Advanced Teachers College [which brings people up to A-level standard, and which although designed to provide Teachers College teachers, functions as a backdoor into the universities]. But my effort was fruitless because of the crisis over my Grade II results which were wrongly gazetted. I therefore had to wait for another year and in October 1968 I was admitted into Kano Advanced Teachers College ... I finished my three years N.C.E. course [at the A.T.C.] in June 1971 and in July I took up a teaching appointment with [my State government]... Before I left the A.T.C. I had applied for admission to this University (ABU) and two southern universities... I taught for three months before I got my letter of admission and therefore left...

This student is fairly typical. Although after primary education he had to pass through Teachers College, then teach, then do a three year Advanced Teachers' Course, and then teach briefly before even beginning his university education, he remarks in summing up:

> My educational pursuit has been faster and more consistent compared to most of my mates right from the primary school level.

A more extreme (but not a-typical or unusual) case is that of an older student, born "between 1929 and 1930". After a late start in primary school, he spent two years at a Teachers Training College at Benin which qualified him for a Teachers Grade III Certificate. While holding a full-time job as a teacher, he read first for O-level and then A-level examinations at home. After teaching "in many schools" in the former Eastern Region of Nigeria he joined the Regional Public Service in 1958. His struggle to get university education was now entering the final phase, but that phase was a long one:

> ... in 1962, I applied to do M.A. Degree in Cooperatives in Western Germany through the head of my department... Unfortunately the head of my department deliberately refused to recommend me. I was not alone as regards this ugly experience where I was working. This has been the fate of (many) people who had worked under this selfish boss...

In 1964, I was given direct entry to University of Nigeria, Nsukka to

SOCIAL ORIGINS AND IDENTITY 57

do B.Sc. (Psychology) degree. Also I applied for the Federal Scholarship, but failed the interview. This opportunity slipped from my grips because I had no money to foot the bill. It was later I realized that if I had contacted my village meeting, I could have been sponsored.

In 1966, I was awarded a Commonwealth Scholarship to do a course in Community Development, but the civil war intervened, and dashed my hopes again to pieces. I suffered terribly during the war—was conscripted many times, but managed to 'buy' my freedom.

Fortunately, I got admission to Ahmadu Bello University, Zaria, in 1971/72 Session. I am first grateful to God and the University for this golden opportunity which I had struggled for over a decade.

This student graduated with a B.Sc. from the Department of Government in June, 1974, at the age of (approximately) 44.

This illustrates the determination to advance and the faith in education as the supreme means of advancement which is characteristic of the chosen few in the university. It is little wonder if, having surmounted so many obstacles, and having left so many of their fellows behind, that students tend to think of themselves as superior in intelligence and character. Another student volunteers the following:

Out of about two hundred of us who competed for admission into Kaltungo Boarding School I was among the lucky thirty-six that were selected. And out of the hundreds who sought admission into Bauchi Teachers College, I was lucky to be among the ninety that were admitted. In the whole of the (Boarding) School, I was the only person to have two options of either going to Bauchi Secondary School or Bauchi Teachers College. I was also among the only three candidates who passed the examination to Barewa College but I was rejected in the interview because of my size. If not because of the mistake in gazetting my results, I would have gone to the A.T.C. straight away. In my set at the A.T.C., only three of us were lucky to get direct admission into this University.

2. THE SOCIAL ROOTS: FAMILY AND TRADITION

The data on family background in the preceding chapter demonstrated how typical the above life histories are of the great majority of students. As the student progresses upward through levels of formal education, he is likely to move further away from his home community in the physical sense, and deeper and deeper into an initially alien culture distinct from that of his parental home and his home community. All post-primary education in most Nigerian communities is (among other things) training and equipment for life "abroad" as Nigerians say, i.e., outside the home community.[12] The bulk of university graduates (after completing the long struggle described in the preceding section) will embark on careers within complex bureaucratic organizations which will keep them physically separate from home communities during their entire working lives. Viewed historically, the graduate is the functional equivalent of the young British 'cadet' of colonial days, joining a ministry at a junior level of the higher ranks, or the field administration as a D.O. or A.D.O.[13] In post-colonial society it is largely correct to say that the *achievement* to which the university degree testifies carries with it what becomes almost an *ascriptive right* to certain roles, which in turn have implications for the material accoutrements of the post-graduate life. Viewed in these terms it is not so surprising that the content of higher education, particularly at the university level, largely retains its assimilationist character. Quite evidently there is an element of cultural transformation involved in formal education up through university level in Nigeria. To find out how much of a personal transformation is involved, we asked the students whether they would agree or disagree that 'university education makes one a different person'. In five different administrations two-thirds or more of student respondents agreed that university education does make one a 'different person' (Table 18).

Table 18. Personal Transformation

'If someone said that "University education makes one a different person", would you agree or disagree?'

	ABU, 1970	Ibadan, 1972	Lagos, 1972
	%	%	%
Agree:	65.3	61.7	68.9
Disagree:	34.7	38.3	31.1
	100.0	100.0	100.0

This educational 'Odyssey' has implications for the individual's sense of social identity. It was common during the colonial period in British Africa to assume that the highly educated African had lost touch with his community of origin. In Rattray's words:

> The educated African . . . has been cut off from and is out of sympathy with the life of his own people.[14]

Traces of Rattray's attitude are evident in far more recent writings which consider whether the highly educated new elites of Africa are 'deracinated', 'detribalized' or 'detraditionalized'. We should therefore consider the extent to which a conscious sense of cultural alienation accompanies the acquisition through formal education of a 'second culture'; whether many students, like the student quoted above, feel they are fluent in neither English nor their first language; the extent to which a sense of social alienation results from the undeniable fact of physical separation from family and home community; whether a sense of belonging to primary levels of social organization is replaced by a sense of membership in wider levels of community and organization (in particular, that represented by Nigeria); and finally, whether such an examination of the situation of the university students can provide any useful information about the processes of change which are generally, if somewhat misleading, referred to in terms of 'tradition' and 'modernity'?

The question presented in Table 19 is based on a hypothesis evolved from the knowledge we had already gained on the general pattern of

Table 19. Education and family relationships
'Does your education tend to reduce the understanding between you and your parents and other members of your immediate family?'

	ABU, 1973	Ibadan, 1972	Nsukka, 1973
	%	%	%
Yes:	17.0	11.1	11.1
No:	83.0	88.9	88.9
	100.0	100.0	100.0

students' family background in terms of parental education, occupation and income, rather than from the generally accepted concept of a deracinated African elite. Less than one fifth felt that their education—in a different language from that spoken in the home and far above that of the parents and most other members of the family—reduced understanding.[15] The wording of the question should be noted; the phrase 'reduce understanding' does not suggest a traumatic and absolute divide. These findings immediately call into question the basic idea of deracination.

The results produced by two other questions point in the same direction. Students were asked to whom they would generally turn when faced with serious personal problems; the kinship categories of mother and father were placed above the non-kin categories of friend and wife by most of the students.[16] In another question we asked the students 'what are the best uses of money, when people make more than enough to satisfy their immediate personal needs?' Of the five alternative answers

'Help members of the family' received the most support, while the individualist and hedonist 'Live a full and exciting life' was ranked lowest. The same family ties manifested themselves in a more negative guise when students were asked what they thought were 'the most important sources of worry or strain in the lives of most university students.' 'Family problems' ranked highest after worry about failure, low marks and fees.

Finally, we explored the depth and intensity of family loyalty by putting it in conflict with what, for Nigerian university students, has to be a crucial value: the university degree itself, for which in most cases such effort has already been expended. The questions asked and responses obtained are shown in Table 20. The results suggest deep ambivalence. A

Table 20. Sacrifice for Family

A. *'Do you think that a university student should feel duty bound to leave the university and sacrifice his degree if his family badly needed him at home?'*

	ABU, 1973	Ibadan, 1972	Nsukka, 1973
	%	%	%
Yes:	36.1	29.5	37.1
No:	40.7	51.9	39.1
Not sure:	23.2	18.6	23.8
	100.0	100.0	100.0

B. *'Do you think most students would do so?'*

	ABU, 1973	Ibadan, 1972	Nsukka, 1973
	%	%	%
Yes:	5.7	5.4	12.6
No:	64.1	67.1	56.3
Not sure:	30.2	27.5	31.1
	100.0	100.0	100.0

sizeable minority made use of the 'not sure' alternative. The rest, when the question was posed in terms of the abstract moral dilemma, split between those who felt that a student is duty bound to make this kind of supreme sacrifice, and those who did not. When the question was made 'behavioural' only a small minority thought that most students *would* make the sacrifice. Almost two-thirds thought that students in general do not have this level of family loyalty. It should be noted, in partial explanation of the answers, that some students may see the dilemma posed as an impossible one; families expect to benefit in many ways from the educational achievements of members, and thus *familial duty* as well as personal interest would in almost any conceivable circumstance call for completion of the university degree.

Apparently, then, we find a situation here quite different from that of the scholarship boy in relation to English working class society as described by Richard Hoggart.

> He cannot go back; with one part of himself he does not want to go back to a homeliness which was often narrow; with another part he longs for the membership he has lost, 'he pines for some Nameless Eden where he never was'. The nostalgia is the stronger and the more ambiguous because he is really 'in quest of his own absconded self yet scared to find it'. He both wants to go back and yet thinks he has gone beyond his class, feels himself weighted with knowledge of his own and their situation, which hereafter forbids him the simpler pleasures of his father and mother'.[17]

Nigerian students have moved much further away in knowledge from their parents than have most such English scholarship boys. They will shortly overtake them in terms of salary and influence. But the bonds are there. Personal knowledge of the Nigerian students indicates that, although in other dimensions they tend to be educational elitists, the majority retain strong feelings of respect for their parents. One final year student writes:

> Both my parents are very intelligent and hardworking people, probably more intelligent than myself.

We have not infrequently heard such comments from students about parents who may not be literate in any language. Bonds of respect and strong bonds of affection, especially for the mother, are reinforced by pragmatic considerations of help and support. Probably the real secret of the continuing strength of family structures in modern Nigeria is that in general they remain relevant to the new needs and problems of their individual members.[18] Factors of personal security, advancement and material change supplement the bonds of affection. There are relatively few students who are not deeply enmeshed in a complex web of rights to assistance and obligations to assist, above all with school fees, by which (hopefully) the whole family is elevated. A woman student writes:

> I am the eldest of nine children but we lost two, so there are seven of us now... Because I am the first, my parents... had to pay my school fees when I was doing my teacher training... After my five years training in Kaduna, I had to pay my immediate junior (half) sister's school fees and this I did until she finished her five years' training in the same school as I went last June and she is now a Grade II teacher. As the eldest in the family I had to give my mother some money every month when I was teaching and this she used as pocket money

... Also being the eldest in the family I was supposed to buy clothes once in a while for all my junior ones at ceremonial periods ... Now that my junior sister is out of school, she too will be expected to help the family. My step-father and my mother now pay the younger children's school fees.

This sort of pattern is utterly typical. Graduating university students often feel that there is such a built-up accumulation of expectations of a reversed flow of goods and services once their education is complete that they almost dread the achievement of post-degree status. Such uneasiness, where it exists, reflects the strength, not weakness, of family bonds.

Moving beyond the family, we can also consider the students' relations to their home communities and to what might be called 'first culture', i.e., the language, mores and traditions of the home community and the 'tribe'. We already have some notion of the distance (in every sense) travelled by the students by the time they enter the university. If, as we shall see, they tend to be a conservative elite socially and politically, they experience social change in their personal lives. Their early formative years are spent in an indigenous cultural medium. Their formal education has an undeniably 'Western' content. If a typical Westerner surveys their situation 'objectively' by comparison with his own, he finds the students richer in that they are adepts in at least two languages and cultural traditions (and often more), but poorer in not being absolutely part of either. We were interested in the extent to which a sense of cultural alienation and confusion is characteristic of students. Is the Nigerian poet Mabel Imokhuede's sense of unbearable ambiguity characteristic?

> Here we stand
> Infants overblown
> Poised between two civilizations,
> Finding the balance irksome,
> Itching for something to happen
> To tip us one way or the other,
> Groping in the dark for a helping hand—
> And finding none.
> I'm tired, O my God, I'm tired.
> I'm tired of hanging in the middle way.[19]

Or is the robust eclecticism of the Gambian poet Lenrie Peters more characteristic?

> Open the gate
> To East and West
> Bring in all
> That's good and best.[20]

Quite obviously, there are strong elements of both among the students as a whole. We asked the question reproduced in Table 21 to find out the number of students who considered themselves to be in the same position as their fellow student cited above who was fluent in neither Ishan nor English.

Table 21. Knowledge of Language
'If someone said to you that you neither spoke English perfectly nor your own language perfectly would you agree or disagree?'

	ABU, 1970	Ibadan, 1972	Nsukka, 1973
	%	%	%
Agree:	50.0	40.9	46.0
Disagree:	50.0	59.1	54.0
	100.0	100.0	100.0

There is something deeply poignant in the fact that so many students agree that they speak no language perfectly.[21] It is probably true as well that the responses do not indicate two distinct and different groups within the student body, but rather that the great majority of individuals are divided in themselves on this point.[22] This question was supplemented by the ones presented in Table 22, which attack more directly the central questions.

Table 22. Knowledge of Language and Traditions
A. *'How well do you consider that you speak your own language?'*

	ABU, 1970	Ibadan, 1972	Nsukka, 1973
	%	%	%
Very well:	31.9	38.3	30.8
Well:	54.9	49.4	55.4
Not very well:	13.2	12.3	13.8
	100.0	100.0	100.0

B. *'How well do you consider you know the traditions of your own people?'*

	ABU, 1970	Ibadan, 1972	Nsukka, 1973
	%	%	%
Very well:	18.9	22.3	12.5
Well:	48.6	47.1	43.1
Not very well:	32.5	30.6	44.4
	100.0	100.0	100.0

The results confirm those of Table 21 and also offer a corrective perspective on the earlier responses. In terms of language, when presented with the three-fold scale, only about one-third of the students felt that they knew their first language 'very well.' It is easy to see how half could agree that they had a perfect knowledge of neither the first language nor English. Well over 80 per cent, however, felt that they knew their first language 'well' or 'very well'. Not surprisingly fewer felt that they knew the traditions of their people well. Here the years of boarding school undoubtedly have a greater influence, yet only about one third felt completely cut off from an indigenous cultural tradition; the rest rated their knowledge of their traditions either 'good' or 'very good'.

The results of the above questions show that overall, the formal education these students experience *does* have a cost in terms of relation to 'first culture'. The feelings of the student who remarked that he was not completely at home in either English or his first language were shared by at least half of the students. About a third of the students felt that they did not know the traditions of their own people very well. However, it would seem quite unjustified to talk of general and pronounced cultural alienation. The students must bridge cultures, but the same is true of educated persons around the world outside the major developed countries. Nigerian students may not speak any language 'very well', but almost universally speak two (and often three, four or more) languages 'well'. Many of those students who in our survey reported that they did not speak their own language well were probably brought up outside their own communities, and may speak another Nigerian language fluently. Taken as a whole these results confirm the continuing strength of links between students and their 'first cultures' rather than the reverse.

3. *HOME COMMUNITY*

Traditionally, with the exception of some aristocratic groups among the Hausa, Fulani and Kanuri, there was little overall sense of ethnic identity among Nigerian peoples. Hierarchical groups such as the Yoruba did not identify beyond particular kingdoms, e.g., Oyo, Ijebu-Oe, Abeokuta. Acephalous groups usually found their identity in and gave their loyalty to a village or group of villages. The imposition of colonial rule, the spread of communications, the growth of an awareness of cultural similarities and the exigencies of political organization widened social horizons. Everywhere, local communities lost their semi-exclusive status as units of social, political and economic organization. District or division (or other intermediate level of organization), region, ethnicity (district almost always from home community), and the Nigerian State as a whole acquired new significance. The 12 States created in 1967 have taken on much of the importance of the former Regions (while, inevitably, a residue of regionalism remains as well).

Despite this development, however, the local communities retain great strength as a source and focus of social identity. Between 1950 and 1960 the communities were by and large the real building blocks of electoral politics—which had to be combined to forge an appearance of ethnic or regional unity.[23] The local community is generally the only level of social organization beyond the family at which co-operation and trust provide a lasting foundation for collective effort. The majority of university students, however, have been physically separated from their home communities since they commenced secondary education (and many before that). Our experience as teachers over the years suggests to us that while students visit their home communities at least once a year (and often during all major university holidays) few spend a long time actually at home. The students' occupational future is in the modern organizations and urban sectors that transcend the local community. These thoughts lead one to wonder whether students' sense of belonging to home communities remains as strong as their sense of family membership.

We explored the problem in our questionnaires. The most direct question is presented in Table 23. To avoid forcing responses to a question that might not seem relevant to the students, we offered the 'cannot say' option, which was utilized by about 15 percent of the students. Of the total students only one-third felt they were less members

Table 23. Home Community Membership

'Do you feel that you are as much a member of your home community as men and women your age who have not had education and who reside there permanently?'

	ABU, 1973	Ibadan, 1973	Nsukka, 1973
	%	%	%
Yes:	50.2	51.8	62.1
No:	33.2	34.0	20.3
Cannot say:	16.6	14.1	17.6
	100.0	99.9	100.0

of their community than those who will spend all their lives there and participate fully and constantly in its affairs. Well over half of the students who answered either 'yes' or 'no' felt that they were just as much members of their home community as the permanent residents. The wording of the question was designed to establish a level of *maximal* membership. That half of the total felt that they met this *maximal* definition of home community membership illustrates in a striking fashion the continuing strength of local communities.[24]

We also asked students about the influence of students as a group within their home community (Table 24). Influence of 'secondary and

Table 24. Influence in Home Community

'List in order of importance the groups which most influence opinion in your home community: (Number in order of importance).'

	Modal ranking	ABU, 1973 Percentage of first rankings	Percentage of last rankings
Traditional leaders:	1	61.0%	15.4%
Secondary and university graduates:	2	21.3%	35.0%
Middle level groups (clerks, traders, small contractors, etc.):	3	17.7%	49.6%
		100.0%	100.0%

university graduates' was compared by the students with that of 'traditional leaders' and 'middle level groups (clerks, traders, small contractors, etc.)'. The responses give an impression of communities which, while far from closed to the influence of the well-educated, have their own independent momentum to which the students, to the extent that they participate, must accommodate themselves. Almost two-thirds of those who answered ranked 'traditional leaders' first in influence.[25] An approximately equal number of students assigned graduates or the new 'big men' (the 'middle level groups') of the towns and villages second or third place. About one-quarter of the students, it should be mentioned, ranked the secondary or university students in first place in influence. These students may come from highly modernized areas or from some of the communities where for a variety of reasons strong 'traditional' leadership does not exist. Table 25 indicates another way of approaching the question of students' relations to communities of origin. The great majority of university students will be 'migrant workers' in the urban centres throughout their post-graduation working lives, analogous in this

Table 25. Residence

'Do you expect ever again to live (as opposed to visit) in your home community?'

	ABU, 1973	Ibadan, 1972	Nsukka, 1973
	%	%	%
Yes:	44.9	66.5	51.0
No:	22.5	11.6	17.5
Not sure:	32.6	21.9	31.5
	100.0	100.0	100.0

respect to migrant labour at other economic levels. It is interesting to consider to what extent the highly educated graduates regard *their* urban residence, which will be highly remunerated and characterized by access to all of Nigeria's amenities, as a temporary stage of life, and look forward to an eventual return to the home community. Only time can answer this question, but we tried to find out what the students *thought* they would do. We were surprised to find that less than one-quarter were willing to reject the possibility of living in (as opposed to visiting) the home community. It should be borne in mind that at present the majority of home communities do not have electricity, may have no health facilities, are poorly served by roads and have few, if any, retail shops.

To put these results in perspective we can ask what proportion of British or American university students from small towns and villages would expect to return to them eventually to live.

These data confirm the strength of home community identification, but they may also be taken as an indication of the incompleteness as a *social environment* of the new, urban Nigeria. The urban centres, with their pattern of elite amenities, were originally designed for a clientele of 'sojourners'—colonial expatriates residing there temporarily during a period of employment. At this stage of development, as indicated in the responses discussed above, the urban centres tend to remain for the new elites also a sort of no-man's-land which one makes the best of, but never regards as completely 'home'.[26] The culture of the urban elite world will probably develop and lose this temporary and incomplete character, just as many elite members, and certainly their children, will gradually lose contact with home areas and with the members of the family who remained behind. Already it is noticeable that some of the children of the present generation of highly educated elites do not speak the language of the 'tribe' to which they categorically belong.

4. THE ELEMENTS OF SOCIAL IDENTITY

We have examined the students' sense of personal relationship to families, 'first cultures', and home communities, and referred to some of the multiple social levels and categories that form part of, or condition personal identity. In the Nigerian social (and political) context home community, home State and ethnic group generally have the most significance among levels of social identity. To this list we added the inclusive levels of 'Nigeria' and 'Africa'. In our second questionnaire, we asked students to rank these levels in order as an experiment. We had reservations about this format; loyalties are notoriously situational and sequential and the relative importance of each may shift with circumstances. Questioning students on the relative importance of identities in the abstract and simultaneously might be illuminating in some respects but artificial and misleading in others. The results obtained were in fact more diverse and inconclusive than those resulting from most other ranking questions, suggesting uncertainty (see Table 26). In our final stage, therefore, we employed the format shown in Table 27.

Table 26. Sense of Social Identity

'If you were asked to reckon your own sense of social identity in what order would you place the following? (Number in order of importance).'

	Modal Ranking	ABU, 1971* Percentage of first rankings	Percentage of last rankings
Identification with Nigeria:	1	37.9%	0.9%
Identification with home State:	3	6.5%	4.4%
Identification wih home community:	4	17.2%	15.0%
Identification with Africa:	5†	26.4%	40.5%
Identification with ethnic group:	5	12.0%	39.3%
		100.0%	100.0%

* The same question was administered at Ife (1973); broadly similar results were obtained.
† Responses for 'Identification with Africa' were sharply bimodal with first and last ranking together accounting for the considerable majority of responses.

This ranges the levels of membership in two-way contests and permits cross tabulation.

A high degree of complexity if not fragmentation of social identity is apparent in Table 27. It is evident that not only did the students divide

Table 27. Elements of Social Identity

'How would you compare the following as elements in your own social identity (sense of belonging to social categories)?'

		ABU, 1973	Ibadan, 1973	Nsukka, 1973
African identity is stronger than Nigerian identity:	Yes: No:	% 37.2 62.8	% 30.5 69.5	% 32.3 67.7
		100.0	100.0	100.0
Home community identity is stronger than ethnic identity:	Yes: No:	62.0 38.0	71.0 29.0	67.0 33.0
		100.0	100.0	100.0
Nigerian identity is stronger than home State identity:	Yes: No:	48.0 52.0	58.6 41.4	35.6 64.4
		100.0	100.0	100.0
Nigerian identity is stronger than ethnic identity:	Yes: No:	48.0 52.0	54.7 45.3	39.3 60.7
		100.0	100.0	100.0
Home community identity is stronger than Nigerian identity:	Yes: No:	57.1 42.9	54.0 46.0	64.8 35.2
		100.0	100.0	100.0

into substantial segments on every question but that the sample group taken as a whole were divided in their approach to a hierarchy of choice of social identity. The artificiality of our earlier format which asked the students to resolve complexity by imposing a hierarchical order becomes obvious, but it is valid as an indication that identities have to be combined in practice, whereas the later format reveals deeper attachments and suggests what would happen in the event of conflicts of identity.

Referring to the second format (Table 27), the distribution of responses may be mentioned. For the majority of students at ABU and

Nsukka Nigerian identity was not as strong as membership of a home community, an ethnic group, or a home State.[27] At Ibadan, Nigerian identity was stronger than home State and ethnic identity (but not as strong as home community identity). For about one-third of each of the three groups being an 'African'—that rather nebulous but basically racial and geographical category—was a more important part of 'self' than being a Nigerian. The relative strength of home community and ethnic (when put in competition with Nigerian) identity in the Nsukka results should be noted as probably related not only to strong traditions of local community but also the experience of the civil war and its aftermath.

There are some apparent inconsistencies. For instance, whereas Nigerian identity and ethnic identity were chosen almost equally in a direct choice between them, in the choice between home community identity and Nigerian and ethnic identity, identity with the home community was felt more strongly in comparison with ethnic identity than with Nigerian identity. Cross tabulation of the pairs, however, shows that the responses are generally consistent. Thus, to take an example, those who placed ethnic identity before Nigerian identity were also likely to place home community identity ahead of Nigerian identity (Table 28).

Table 28. Cross Tabulation: Nigerian identity vs. ethnic identity and Home Community identity vs. Nigerian identity

A. *Percentages of column totals:* ABU, 1973

Which is more important:	Which is more important Nigerian identity	Ethnic identity
Nigerian identity:	77.5%	11.7%
Home community identity:	22.5%	88.3%
Total	100.0% (N=129)	100.0% (N=145)

B. *Percentages of grand total:* ABU, 1973

Which is more important:	Which is more important: Nigerian identity	Ethnic identity	Total:
Nigerian identity:	36.5%	6.2%	42.7%
Home community identity:	10.6%	46.7%	57.3%
	47.1%	52.9%	100.0% (N=274)

The cross tabulation of ABU results shown in Table 28B focuses attention on the 37 percent who might be called 'Nigerians' (placing Nigerian identity above both ethnic and home community identity) in contrast to the 47 percent who might be called 'communalists' in terms of placing both ethnic and home community identity above Nigerian identity. Only 17 percent of the total group (274) mixed their responses, placing either ethnic or home community identity, but not both, before Nigerian identity.

The present 12 States of the Nigerian Federation were created only in 1967. Our data conform what already seem aparent from unsystematic observation: that the States, intermediate between home community and the Federation, have in the seven years of their existence grown remarkably as foci of social identity and allegiance.[28]

Research in certain Western countries has shown that the deepest and most significant of the individual's political orientations is his sense of belonging to the political community coinciding with the national state. It is evident that for Nigerian university student membership at the 'national' level does not dominate social-political identity as it has been found to do in other countries. It could be argued that 'nation' in the sense of ethnic group (and so much of Nigerian and African politics have been interpreted in ethnic or tribal terms)[29] might offer a foundation identity. But the data do not bear out this hypothesis: rather, they suggest that for about two-thirds of the students sampled home community identity is stronger than ethnic identity. Moreover, for a little over half the students, Nigerian identity is more significant than ethnic identity; the Ibo students are the only exception to this. In the most integrated Western countries, the various identities of individuals tend to be cumulative and mutually reinforcing, with the national identity dominating the rest. A Nigerian who is ethnically a Yoruba may be Ekiti or Ijebu or Oyo, etc., he may be from the Western State, Lagos State or Kwara State, so he may be a northerner or a southerner; and he has a home community within these other categories which, according to our data and many other indications, remains the most likely capital of his social self.[30] These identities are not necessarily mutually reinforcing. Frequently the opposite is the case, nor does any one identity act as the hub for the rest. No level can be discounted absolutely. Each level means *something* to the individual, even if not *everything*.

The following data, on specifically national issues, reinforce the impression of weakness of a Nigerian identity for most students. They indicate how groups reject the use of a local language as a national language and reveal how late students arrive at national awareness.

The language issue illustrates some of the problems of nation building

72   SOCIAL ORIGINS AND IDENTITY

and unity in a post-colonial situation. The deeper bases of disunity in Nigeria are historical and cultural, and they have been sharpened by elite competition and uneven social modernization. If political and cultural disunity is to diminish, differences must to some considerable extent be overcome in a superseding political, and even social, culture. Yet the legacy of colonialism is singularly weak in terms of the instruments by which this might be accomplished. In the post-colonial Nigerian situation so much of what is not particularistic (mainly ethnic) is alien. Thus, the pan-Nigerian language, and official language of the country, is English. A considerable proportion of those in Nigeria who use English best feel that this non-African language can never be fully 'Nigerianized'. In recent years there have been many serious proposals for the adoption of a local language as a national language (to replace English as a pan-Nigerian medium of communication).[31] In several of our university administrations we asked the question 'Do you favour using one Nigerian language as a national language of the country?' The strong and very unusual variation in the results at the four universities was striking. Cross tabulation showed that the respondent's association with ethnic group was even sharper than association with university, and that the ethnic composition of the various university student bodies thus seemed to explain the variation by university. Table 29 gives breakdowns by ethnicity of the ABU and Nsukka results.

Table 29.   National Language

'Do you favour using one Nigerian language as a national language of the country?'

| | Ethnic affiliation of respondents | | | | |
| | ABU, 1973 | | | Nsukka, 1973 | |
	Hausa	Yoruba	Northern Minorities	Ibo	Southern Minorities
Yes:	71.8%	24.6%	46.3%	19.4%	34.2%
No:	28.2%	75.4%	53.7%	80.6%	65.8%
	100.0%	100.0%	100.0%	100.0%	100.0%

The factor behind these ethnic and regional diversities is the prominence of Hausa as a candidate for the national language. In other words, the Hausa (and those Hausa-influenced groups that themselves use Hausa as a *lingua franca*) gave considerable support to using a Nigerian language as a national language.[32] All the other groups were more or less strongly opposed because they know that Hausa is the only realistic candidate. The breakdown of opinion reflected here suggests that there would be great danger in any attempt to impose a single

Nigerian language on the whole country for official communication purposes.

The students also acknowledged that, while they themselves were nationally minded, they came late in their schooling to thinking in national (Nigerian) terms (See Table 30).

Table 30. Recognition of National Identity

'At what level of education do you think you begin to think in National (Nigerian) terms?'

Level of Education	ABU, 1971	Ibadan, 1973	Ife, 1973
	%	%	%
Primary:	6.6	8.2	11.9
Secondary:	64.6	62.2	57.7
University:	16.0	21.4	21.1
Cannot say:	12.9	8.2	9.3
	100.0	100.0	100.0

Three-quarters or more said that they began to think in national terms only during their secondary education or even later. The 'cannot say' alternative, offered to guard against forcing answers to a question that was not understood or seemed artificial to respondents, drew only modest support which suggests to us that most of the students found the question meaningful. Cross tabulation of these results by language groups shows that there are no significant variations in responses among the various ethnic groups. In Western nations it is generally agreed that basic national orientations are consolidated before the end of primary schooling, but the student responses shown in Table 30 suggest that only a little more or less than 10 percent of students in Nigeria leave primary school with sharp consciousness of the national-level social and political entity. Our data on social identity suggests, in addition, that the sense of the national whole must thereafter coexist, often on unequal terms, with the students' sensitivity to other levels of social interaction.

Social identity then—the bedrock of political self—is by no means a simple matter for these Nigerian university students. We shall see in a succeeding chapter that one of the students' central political values is a very deep and sincere longing for unity, focused at the national level. These findings will be relevant, namely that the longing for unity must and does coexist with a clear realization of the existence of disunity, even fragmentation—the latter existing not only in the society at large, but *within the individual personality.* The highly educated Nigerian must be cosmopolitan in order to survive socially and psychologically—a man or woman of many identities, used to being one thing in one place and something else in another.

In contrast with the Western integrated nation-states social identity is fragmented by a complexity of levels, not resting on one another and not truly hierarchical. The situation of multiple levels of identity can be described in terms customarily applied to international relations: they are coexisting and polycentric. Depending on circumstances, contradictory imperatives are likely to be produced for the individual, but these are often successfully managed as sequential rather than as simultaneous and competitive. The result, both on the level of the individual and the society is a considerable element of unpredictability, especially since circumstances may make the manipulation of identities and allegiances as separate and sequential impossible, and force individuals and potential groups at least temporarily to choose one and renounce another.[33]

5. *THE AMBIVALENCE OF ETHNICITY*

Among the categories of social identity discussed above ethnicity must receive special attention. Nigerians sometimes resent outsiders stressing the importance of ethnicity in Nigerian society. Nearly every foreigner interested in Nigeria has encountered abroad the student who when asked about his ethnic origin replies curtly that he is a 'Nigerian.' Yet in meeting one another for the first time two Nigerians are as discreetly anxious to establish one another's ethnicity as two men from Northern Ireland are to establish one another's religion—and for the same reasons. Ethnicity structures relationships; it also draws on deep and readily activated sentiments. We will see (in Chapter VI) that our student samples consider ethnicity to have been the single most important factor in Nigerian electoral competition (between 1950 and 1966) and Nigeria's greatest political problem. In Chapter V we will see that national unity—the positive converse of ethnic division—is held by most students to be the supreme value and aspiration of the Nigerian polity. The university students are almost agonizingly conscious of the evils that have befallen the country through ethnic differences and rivalries, and they do not want these evils to recur. At the same time the students acknowledge the reality of ethnic differences and competition and realize that they have to be taken into account.

It is clear from the above discussion of social identity that ethnicity is only one of a number of levels of identity and loyalty which are important for most students. Ethnicity itself is complex. Whereas it is sometimes thought of, by Nigerians as well as others, as a 'traditional' allegiance, ethnicity today is for the most part not traditional in the historical sense; ethnicity tends to rest on modern interpretations and reorientations of the primordial factors of language, shared tradition and sense of social belonging. One of the basic if somewhat ironical truths about Nigeria is that the modern integrating forces at work in the society frequently have the effect of making ethnic and communal ties more rather than less important to the new urban populations.[34] Ethnic identity was most often forged in the towns and schools. In the new towns to which the former students moved, members of traditionally rival or hostile village clusters discovered how much more they had in common with one another than with members of other social and linguistic groups. A common language underpinned a 'complementarity of communication' (Deutsch) and traditionally understood forms of cooperation were re-interpreted in the new conditions of the towns. In other words, ethnic affinity offered a *useful* device for social organization, just as it later offered a *useful* basis for political organization. Since formal and informal organization was so often ethnic, it was along ethnic lines that social boundaries were drawn and it became difficult to maintain communication across the boundaries. The result in a highly competitive situation, aggravated by the introduction of politics, was that ethnic groups tended to regard one another as stereotypes, often as dangerous and a little less than human. The casualty of modernizing and competitive ethnic aggressiveness is trust, which is already a scarce commodity in rapidly changing societies where social predictability is rare. The temptation in a society where 'no condition is permanent' is to 'love all, trust few'. And ethnicity often comes next after kinship and local community as a criterion for determining who can be trusted.

A number of factors underlie instances of ethnic conflict, ranging from the most specific and immediate competitions (especially for jobs) to the deeper 'primordial' factors of culture and history. We were interested to see the importance students would attach to various bases of ethnic conflict (see Table 31). The first two pairs of alternatives pose the general problem of the relative weight of the more immediate and material factors versus the cultural and historical factors. The third pair offers a 'devil', asking whether 'foreign influences' are more important than the weakness of national loyalties. To take the last pair first, it is interesting that only a minority (about one-third) saw foreign influences as more important than the indigenous factors that add up to 'weakness of overall sense of national identity'. Even in the case of the Nsukka students, most of whom were affected by the Biafran crisis in which foreign factors *were* important, only slightly more than one-third placed foreign influences

Table 31. Bases of Ethnic Conflict

A. 'In relations between ethnic groups what causes more harm? (Mark one alternative in each pair)'

	ABU, 1973	Ibadan, 1973	Nsukka, 1973
	%	%	%
Distrust of one another based on mutual ignorance of traditions:	64.0	69.7	69.9
Competition between elite members for jobs:	36.0	30.3	30.1
	100.0	100.0	100.0
Uneven development of different groups:	68.8	66.3	53.4
Different historical, social and religious traditions:	31.2	33.7	46.6
	100.0	100.0	100.0
Divisions between groups created by foreign influences:	31.7	30.3	38.6
Weakness of overall sense of national identity and solidarity:	68.3	69.7	61.4
	100.0	100.0	100.0

B. 'Do politicians primarily create tribalism or primarily make use of existing sentiments?'

	ABU, 1971	Ife, 1973
	%	%
Create it:	35.9	32.7
Use existing sentiments:	64.1	67.3
	100.0	100.0

above the generalised 'weakness of . . . national identity. . . .'

Responses to the first pair are consistent with the last pair in that a majority of about two-thirds opted for the "deeper" cultural explanation rather than the more immediate and material one. Only about one-third thought that competition for elite jobs came ahead of distrust based on ignorance of traditions. Consistent as well is the fact that about two-thirds thought that politicians could not be blamed for the existence of 'tribalism' and only for using already existing sentiments. The pattern is reversed, however, in the case of the second pair shown in Table 31A, where the majority thought that uneven development of different groups caused more harm than differing traditions. This apparent shift can be explained by the fact that 'uneven development' concerns whole peoples (and areas) and not just the elite members, and that it is itself a 'deeper' and historical explanation of ethnic conflicts. It is interesting that the majority who chose 'uneven development' over different traditions at Nsukka was considerably smaller than the two-thirds majorities recorded at ABU and Ibadan.[35] Cross tabulation shows that the Ibo students at Nsukka rather than the students from other ethnic groups varied sharply from the ABU and Ibadan results, yet the bitter conflicts between Ibo and northern groups were founded on the factor of uneven development. Possibly Ibo reject this explanation of ethnic conflict as tending in some way to *justify* bitterness against groups more favoured by economic history. Ibo students may also be more sensitive to historical and social differences and stress the latter as a factor in ethnic relations.

The question in Table 32 throws some further light on the students' understanding of ethnic loyalties and conflicts. This poses a problem which for several years has had an intense reality for a number of ethnic groups; at the time of writing, appeals for or against regrouping of ethnic groups in a new structure of States appear frequently as paid announcements in the newspapers. A great majority of the students agreed that

Table 32. Ethnicity and State Reorganisation

'If they had the choice, which one of the following situations do you think most members of most 'ethnic' groups would choose?'

	ABU, 1970	Ibadan, 1972	Lagos, 1973
	%	%	%
Form minority in rich State:	20.1	14.0	21.8
Have own State, even if economic advantages are less:	79.9	86.0	78.2
	100.0	100.0	100.0

most ethnic groups would prefer to have the security against 'domination' represented by political autonomy within the group's own State, even when there is an economic cost attached. The 'possession' of a State represents a safeguard in relations with other groups and States analogous to that provided by the sovereign stage in international relations.

In their views on relations between ethnic groups the students indicated their understanding of the depth of the phenomenon. This will help to explain the data presented below on attitudes towards government policy on ethnicity and expectations as to how long ethnic attitudes will persist in the future.

To the students, as was indicated in the previous section on social identity, ethnicity is not only a social phenomenon, but also, in various guises, a part of personal life. We will see (in Chapter 6) that university students consider themselves to be the most nationally-minded (i.e. most free from ethnic and other sectionalist loyalties) group in the country. Yet in the questions on social identity, the majority of students acknowledged the pull of loyalties at levels below the national one, and about half placed ethnic identity above national identity. Ethnicity (and regionalism) impinges on the lives even of students on the campus; four-fifths of the students acknowledged that campus friendships tended to follow home area and thus ethnic lines.

As we saw in the discussion of social identity, for most students an ability to think in 'national terms' is a recently acquired one, dating from the secondary school level of education for the majority.

These various findings are supported by our own informal observations and, we believe, would come as no surprise to other observers of the Nigerian scene. Everyone who knows Nigeria well knows how very pervasive ethnicity *tends* to be, both on the social and the personal level. It is necessary to emphasize 'tends', for while the general pattern holds true, there are many important exceptions. If student friendships tend to follow the lines of home area and ethnicity, one is constantly aware of close and enduring friendships that cut across these lines. If national consciousness is new and weak, nevertheless large proportions of the students evince a willingness to respond to national leadership and to make personal sacrifices for national goals. University graduates consider membership of the same ethnic group a relatively unimportant factor in the selection of their husbands or wives. Above all, we are aware, both through our formal research and our longer-term observation, of the revulsion that the great majority of students feel for the competitive ethnicity that Nigerians call tribalism. The students themselves retain strong ethnic affiliations in terms of culture and social ties, but we have evidence that they do not want to be personally ethnic. Their strictures on ethnic politics, and the desire, referred to below, to emphasize the non-ethnic principles of political organization such as ideology, testify to their desire for the country to break out of ethnic politics. At the same time, the events of the past have shown how political crises may force the majority of even the most highly educated strata of the country to retreat, at least temporarily, behind ethnic lines. But if under certain circumstances most of the students are potential 'tribalists', we think it is important to emphasize that they are never more than 'reluctant tribalists.'

If we are right in thinking that the students strongly deplore the existence of ethnic loyalties, yet at the same time acknowledge their reality both in the society and in themselves, it is important to know whether they see any speedy solution to this problem. We asked three questions (Table 33).

Table 33. Changes over time in ethnic and national loyalties

A. *'Do you think that the generation of university graduates which is emerging from the universities now has a more national outlook than those of ten years ago or more?'**

	ABU, 1970	Ibadan, 1972	Lagos, 1972
	%	%	%
More national in outlook:	50.1	57.9	57.1
Less national in outlook:	22.9	24.3	21.8
About the same:	27.0	17.8	21.1
	100.0	100.0	100.0

B. *'Do you think that ethnic loyalties as a divisive factor in Nigerian life will be less important 20 years from now?'*

	ABU, 1970	Ibadan, 1972	Lagos, 1972
	%	%	%
Much less important:	12.5	14.7	16.8
Less important, but still a factor to be reckoned with:	70.3	64.7	62.6
About the same:	17.2	20.5	20.6
	100.0	100.0	100.0

C. *'Do you think that 10 or 15 years from now your closest friendships and social life will have any tendency to follow 'ethnic' lines?'*

	ABU, 1970	Ibadan, 1972	Lagos, 1972
Yes:	7.8	5.1	9.0
No:	48.4	54.4	50.4
Cannot say:	43.8	40.5	40.6
	100.0	100.0	100.0

* A similar question (used only in the spring, 1973 ABU administration) which asked 'Do you think that national unity in Nigeria is less or greater now than at the time of independence' produced almost identical results to the pattern found here.

The students as a whole expressed only limited optimism. Comparing the present with the past (Table 33A) small majorities felt that there had been progress in building national unity. It seems remarkable to us that comparing the early 1970's with the early 1960's, when the country was already involved in the bitter regional and ethnic conflict that was to lead to the ruin of the system, nearly half of the students thought that there had been no progress over the last decade, and between one-fifth and one-quarter actually thought the country had regressed in terms of the development of unity. Looking toward the future the great majority (some four-fifths) thought that in 20 years ethnicity would be a less divisive force in Nigerian society (Table 33B). But here again, the optimism was guarded. Less than one-fifth thought that the problem would be 'much less important' in 20 years, and about one-fifth thought that there would be no progress at all in the next 20 years. The final question (Table 33C) shifted the problem to a personal level, asking about the respondent's own social life '10 or 15 years from now'. Only a tiny minority (less than ten percent) said that their social life would follow ethnic lines. About one-half said 'no', supporting the suggestion made above that the students wish to diminish and if possible eliminate ethnicity from their personal lives. Yet nearly half, forty percent, utilized the 'cannot say' option, which was provided as a safeguard against forced answers. The strong emotive dislike of ethnicity felt by the students must come to terms with the reality of its existence. Thus nearly half found themselves unable either to answer 'yes' or 'no' to the questions asked.

Recognition of the reality of the existence and persistence of ethnic feelings in the country is clearly illustrated by a question which posed a possible solution to the problem of ethnic division. We asked whether government power should be turned directly against ethnicity, whether government should pretend that ethnic loyalties do not exist, or whether government should accept their reality and reconcile them (Table 34).

Table 34. Government Policy

'How should a government act about ethnic loyalties?'

	ABU, 1973	Ibadan, 1972	Nsukka, 1973
	%	%	%
Ignore them:	7.5	5.7	10.6
Abolish them:	14.6	22.8	17.0
Reconcile them:	77.9	71.5	72.4
	100.0	100.0	100.0

The great majority of the students preferred the latter alternative; consistent with the recognition of the reality of ethnic feelings noted above, the majority thought that government would be successful neither in ignoring nor 'abolishing' ethnic sentiments.[36] When we remember the students considered ethnicity the country's greatest political and social problem (and unity its greatest aspiration) their realism is impressive. As a test of idealist versus realist predispositions on questions of political action to achieve social goals, this problem is probably more significant (because more important to the students) than others, such as 'socialism' versus 'capitalism', or attitudes toward imperialism. According to this test, the majority of our respondents would be characterized in terms of their 'realism' and pragmatism.

CONCLUSIONS

Earlier in this chapter we noted the long tradition of misconception which has reduced the ability of Western observers to understand Africa's highly educated elites. This tradition of misconception, which has its historical roots in the period of British colonial rule (and many of its theoretical roots in Lugardian theories of Indirect Rule) has involved the use of word-concepts such as 'detribalization' and 'deracination', and 'traditional' and 'modern'. Persons and elite groups are assumed to be 'tribal' or 'detribalized'; 'traditional' or 'modern'. If a person, through pursuit of higher education, puts down a personal tap root deep into the Western cultural tradition, it is assumed that he must previously have been uprooted from his native soil. In thinking about elites in Africa one encounters the analogy to the fault noted by Gulliver:

> Anthropologists have too often sought to describe *the* traditional system of a tribe, or to eliminate 20th century innovations from their analyses; and they have therefore tended in effect to give support to facile lay views which conceive of immutable patterns of culture and of tribal alignments that 'have not changed for generations'.[37]

There has recently been a growing recognition, in all social fields, of the wrong that has been done by the old dichotomous imposition of the 'traditional'/'modern' labels. In some social areas there must be war between the old and the new, the indigenous and the imported: the god of smallpox of the old creeds is being killed by vaccination and the spirits of the creeks are likely to be frightened away by motorboats. Yet people do not change their structures and values more than is necessary. Historical tradition in the sense of previously existent social values tends also to go on existing where it is to some degree contrary to modernizing structures because social relations are not constructed according to inexorable consistency. It may in certain cases be easier to modernize where continuing tradition softens the pangs of change. Finally, traditional structures, family and community links as well as links of trust among aristocrats from ruling groups, offer crucial organizational devices for achieving modern goals.

The data presented in this chapter encourages the rejection of the old stereotyped views. It is clear that at this stage in Nigeria's development, 'deracination'/'detribalization' are not central problems for most university students. The students retain ties with their home communities; the majority has some sense of cultural loss, but only a limited one. Relations with families seem, in the students' own view, surprisingly unaffected by the cultural gap between most students and their relatives. The analytical gap between 'traditional' communities and 'modern' elites is in reality reduced on both sides: highly educated elites remain participating members of their local communities on the one hand; on the other other, the communities themselves are anything but 'traditional' in the sense of unchanging, and are only partially 'traditional' in a historical or anthropological sense.

The important factors which emerge in the above analysis are the strength of the links with social origins and the polycentricity of social identity. As we remarked above, nothing else contributes so much to form the character of Nigerian social and political interaction. There are value implications. On the one hand, there is here a social basis of the ethnicity and political tribalism that is Nigeria's curse. On the other hand, the continuing ties between the elites of the central apparatus and their rural origins constitute one of the major forces for the rapid social development of the country.

FOOTNOTES

1. Compulsory service for a year in a National Youth Service Corps was introduced first for those who graduated from Nigerian universities in 1973. One of the main features of this service period is that graduates are usually directed to different parts of the country by the Federal government to work in States other than their own. They are well paid: in 1973 they were allocated N120 a month; in 1975 it has been raised to N150. The National Union of Nigerian Students (NUNS) has been carrying on vigorous negotiations with the Federal government in an effort to raise the stipend to N180 a month.
2. From an excellent study of towns in Nigeria, see Mabogunje, *Urbanization in Nigeria* (London: University of London Press, 1968).
3. Hausa proverb: *Allah ya ce ' ka tashi, zan taimakeka.'*
4. All the subsequent quotations in the text from students are taken from these short autobiographies. We cannot claim that these statements prepared by ABU students wholly

correspond with the experience of students at the other Nigerian universities but the consistency between students at different universities in answering our questions suggest that similar accounts could be elicited from students outside ABU. The autobiographical accounts in the text may be interestingly compared with the 'I am' statements drawn up by East African students for K. Prewitt. *Education and Political Values* (Nairobi: East African Publishing House, 1971), pp. 228-242.

5. *Comparative Statistics of Educational Development in the Six Northern States of Nigeria: 1962-68.* (Zaria: Institute of Education, ABU), p.9. 72.8 percent of these pupils were male and 27.2 percent were female.
6. R. P. Clignet and P. Foster give their book on secondary schools in Ghana and the Ivory Coast the title, *The Fortunate Few*. The Public Service Review Commission, 1974, *Main Report*, p.136, reckons that only 4 percent of those who complete secondary education enter the tertiary level of education.
7. A Hausa student from a Sokoto district, writing an essay on social modernization in his area during the past ten years, says: 'Not so long ago the people of the district held some sinister ideas about Western education. I could remember that when I started my primary school in that area, my mates and I were called by those not in school "Yan bokon karshe daga gareku sai tashin duniya", meaning that we were "the last of the students, after us it would be Doomsday". As if that was not insulting enough, they said that we could not read the Koran and say our prayers—despite the fact that we were taught religion in school. These verbal blasts were part of efforts to discourage parents from sending their children to school. They did succeed to some extent. Some parents even went to the extent of paying money so that their children were not taken to school.' This student goes on to say: 'However the situation has improved considerably over the years. Seeing men who went to school in earlier periods with cars and "big" salaries... and realizing that one can improve one's life through Western education, it is no longer looked at with disdain. A few regard it as a necessary evil, but most people have no doubt whatsoever as to its importance.'
8. In his autobiographical statement one student remarks: "I tried to be an obedient boy to minimise strokes of cane on my body.' A Nigerian novelist, C. Agunwa, in *More Than Once* (London: Longman's, 1967), p.209, sums up a view of teachers: 'There was a time school teachers were known for two things, namely for cruelty and miserliness. They whipped like masquerades....'
9. It is interesting that since independence there has been little or no trend away from boarding schools at the secondary level. In some States a few rare day schools at that level have been reconstituted as boarding schools.
10. In the earlier years of the University College, Ibadan, when each undergraduate had a room to himself, many students reported that it was the first time in their lives that they had slept alone in a room—and a few preferred to share a room with a friend during the first few nights.
11. One educationalist, reflecting on Nigeria's need for more primary teachers, asks how teachers can be induced to remain in teaching after training. Because of 'the unenviable social and economic status of teachers in the country... most people take to teaching as a last resort while they continue to search for more lucrative jobs.' L. Adesina, "How to avoid shortage of teachers for UPE", *Daily Times* (Lagos), 3/10/1974. See the remarks of a Western Region Commission, *Report of the Commission Appointed to Review the Educational System of Western Nigeria* (Ibadan: Government Printer, 1961), pp.14-18.
12. Agunwa, describing the 'sons of Ndigwe' who are meeting at Onitsha which he describes as a mere thirty miles from their home town, calls them 'abroad members'. C. Agunwa, *op. cit.,* p.1.
13. For a thoughtful and informative account of the experience of a young English recruit in the administrative cadre during the 1950's, see J. Smith, *Colonial Cadet in Nigeria* (Durham, N.C.: Duke University Press, 1968).
14. R. S. Rattray, cited in D. E. Apter, *Ghana in Transition* (New York: Atheneum, 1963), p.146.

15. Certain correlations can be mentioned: the Hausa much less than other ethnic groups think that education has reduced understanding with their families; Muslims are less inclined to think so than Christians; and women students less than men. Age and university major seem to make no difference. Children of farmers indicate marginally more than others a reduced understanding.
16. In this question which is not reported in the text we listed a number of persons—wife, mother, father, uncle, brother, sister, friend—and asked in which of them they would place trust in the event of being confronted with a situation of extreme personal difficulty. 'Mother' ran well ahead of other categories—which is all the more interesting in view of the fact that two-thirds of the mothers in the sample (ABU, 1970) are illiterate.
17. R. Hoggart, *The Uses of Literacy* (London: Penguin, 1968), p.250. See also E. Ashby, *African Universities and Western Tradition* (London: Oxford University Press, 1964), pp.41-42.
18. In this connexion there is an impressionistic but convincing account of life in African urban centres in M. Kelly, "The Secret Heart of the Urban Monster: An African Hypothesis", *The Month* (October, 1974), pp.676-677.
19. The poem is entitled "Conflict" and appears in F. Ademola (editor), *Reflections: Nigerian Prose and Verse* (Lagos: African Universities Press, 1962), p.57.
20. Quoted by P. Theroux, "A Study of Six African Poets" in U. Beier (editor), *Introduction to African Literature* (London: Longmans, 1967), p.115.
21. The Udoji Commission discusses the issue of language and among other things says: 'An overriding problem, which affects the public service as it does all aspects of society, is language . . . it is perfectly clear to the careful observer that below the topmost levels in the various sectors of society, most people are conducting their business in a language, which, in varying degrees, they have not in fact mastered.' Public Service Review Commission 1974 *Main Report,* p.4.
22. The question used the word 'perfectly', thereby setting a very high standard. We think from subsequent discussions with students that they took it to mean 'very well', i.e., with ease and accuracy, as was the intention of our phrasing.
23. On the communal patterns of voting, see K. W. J. Post, *The Nigerian Federal Election of 1959* (London: Oxford University Press, 1963), pp. 376-476; also J. O'Connell "Political Parties in Nigeria" in L. F. Blitz (editor), *The Politics and Administration of Nigerian Government* (London: Sweet and Maxwell, 1965), pp. 165-166 where it is argued that Nigerian political parties were 'parties of communal integration'.
24. Employing Hobbesian introspection as an aid to hypothesis, both the authors would not hesitate to affirm that *they* are much less members of their communities of origin than school peers who have remained there.
25. There were considerable ethnic differences in the answers to this question. Thus 84.6 percent of the Hausa placed 'traditional leaders' first in influence; 63.5 percent of the Ibo and 59.6 percent of the Yoruba students did. Inversely only 12.9 percent of the Hausa students placed 'graduates' first, while 31.5 percent of the Ibo and 29.6 percent of the Yoruba did. The contrast between the Hausa and the other two large ethnic groups is striking.
26. For an excellent short overview of urban problems in Nigeria and the attachment of Nigerian workers to their communities of origin, see A. Mabogunje, "Urbanization in Nigeria—a Constraint on Economic Development", *Economic Development and Cultural Change,* Vol. 13, No. 4, Part 1 (July, 1965), pp. 413-438.
Onigue Otite in discussing Nigerian political integration remarks: 'There is . . . an imperceptible feedback of ideas and practices from the rural systems. This communication between urban and rural actors and systems is found everywhere in Nigeria . . . From a sample of 50 urban dwellers in Benin City, Sapele and Warri in the Mid-Western State in 1967, I found that 70 percent visited their rural homes at least once monthly, eight percent did not, while the rest visited home when necessary but generally once or twice a year. On the whole, 94 percent of my respondents were in unbroken communication with

their rural kinsmen and indigenous social systems . . . although only 50 percent were members (generally nominal) of their Town Union or ethnic organization.' O. Otite "On the Concept of a Nigerian Society", *Nigerian Journal of Economic and Social Research*, Vol. 14, No. 1 (March, 1972), pp. 307-308.
27. The Hausa at ABU tended more than other groups to support Nigerian identity against the other identities. The Ibo at Nsukka supported Nigerian identity much less than other ethnic groups: they chose as follows:

                Nigerian identity 32.1%   Home State identity 67.9%
                Nigerian identity 36.5%   Ethnic identity 63.5%
                Nigerian identity 33.8%   Home community identity 66.2%
28. The federal military government from the first creation of States out of the old Regions (1968) accepted the principle of establishing more States. After the ousting of General Gowon in July 1975 one of the first acts of the new government was to set up a committee to advise on the issue of States. Shortly after receiving the committee's report the government set up seven new States that came into formal existence on 1st April 1976. There are now 19 States. Six of the previous states—Lagos, North Central, Kano, Mid West, South East and Rivers—remained unchanged except for minor boundary adjustments. Three existing States received new names— the Mid West became Bendel, North Central became Kaduna and South East became Cross River. Since our data were collected under the previous system of States we have left names and references unchanged.
29. For a defence of the use of the term 'tribe' to describe African peoples, see P. H. Gulliver in *Tradition and Transition in East Africa* (London: Routledge and Kegan Paul, 1969), pp. 5-35; for an argument in favour of using the term 'nation' (and 'multi national state'), see J. O'Connell, "Senghor, Nkrumah and Azikiwe: Unity and Diversity in the West African State", *Nigerian Journal of Economic and Social Studies*, Vol. 5. No. 1 (March, 1963), pp. 77-93.
30. A Yoruba, for example, may be a Dahomeyan rather than a Nigerian. A Fulani may be—among other things—a Nigerian or a Camerounian or a Guinean (etc.). Many African groups spread across national boundaries.
31. This issue constantly recurs in the press: see, for example, *New Nigerian* (Kaduna) 3/2/1975. The Udoji Commission calls for 'vastly expanded research in all aspects of linguistic science with a view to developing a national lingua franca.' Public Service Review Commission, 1974, *Main Report,* p.4.
32. Over 95 percent of those respondents who actually named a language put forward Hausa.
33. L. Plotnicov, writing about workers in a Nigerian mining town, Jos, says: 'A man must choose the proper social identity as frequently as the social context changes.' L. Plotnicov, *Strangers to the City: Urban man in Jos* (Pittsburgh: Pittsburgh University Press, 1967), p.8. Politically problems arise when a social context forces a choice between two or more identities. Robert Melson deals with the conflict of ethnicity and economic interest among Nigerian workers, "Ideology and Inconsistency: The "Cross-Pressured" Nigerian Worker" in R. Melson and H. Wolpe (editors) *Nigeria: Modernization and the Politics of Communalism* (Michigan State University Press, 1971), pp. 581-605.
34. R. Melson and H. Wolpe have an excellent discussion of these issues in their introductory chapter "Modernization and the Politics of Communalism: A Theoretical Perspective", *ibid.,* pp. 1-43.
35. At Nsukka 51.2 percent of the Ibo students chose 'uneven development' while 48.8 percent chose 'different traditions'.
36. The Yoruba and the Ibo students who elsewhere stress their ethnic and home community loyalties are marginally stronger than other groups in their desire to ignore or abolish ethnic loyalties. Possibly these two large and relatively developed groups prefer more than others to see ethnicity de-emphasized in relation to government jobs and other such matters. Both these groups are also more likely than others to say they will look for jobs in large private enterprise which itself is a commentary on how they see their prospects.
37. P. H. Gulliver, *op. cit.,* p.11.

4 Career and Happiness: Perspective on the Future

The largest group of university students studied here are in transition between rural farming backgrounds and high-level bureaucratic occupations. Almost all, upon graduation, will take their places in the lower echelons of the Nigerian elite, and many, before too many years have passed, will themselves wield power and amass wealth within the society. For most the 'elite' status of which university education is the guarantee (and, more specifically, the occupations to which the *achievement* of university education gives a nearly *ascriptive* right) is the reward of years of relative sacrifice. In some cases it is the result of two decades or more of effort.

We were interested in students' perceptions and evaluations of various aspects of their future. We asked specific questions about the values affecting the choices the graduates would make when they entered the job market. We also elicited more general attitudes toward the opportunities awaiting graduates within the society. Finally, we were interested in evaluations of the elite life toward which the students were proceeding.

This chapter first presents data related to jobs and career opportunities, then material on students' general outlook and the question of happiness, and concludes with an examination of the university graduates' relation to the West.

1. CAREER: HARD WORK OR 'LONG LEG'?[1]

Viewed in functional terms, Nigerian university students are being trained to fill the roles in society that were pioneered by the white colonial elite. The public sector still dominates the market for university-educated labour to a far greater extent than in the Western developed countries. The administrative state and the culture and status system that grew up around it, in which the administrator was supreme, is a colonial heritage.

Aspects of this heritage can be seen in the career plans of university students.[2] In one sample (ABU, 1971) some 52 per cent of those stating career plans expected to go into either the Federal or State governments. Another 13 per cent expected to go into teaching, which is also almost entirely public sector employment, (in fact most graduates who go into teaching will be administrators within a few years).[3] Almost 20 per cent more planned to go into large-scale commercial concerns, mainly either foreign-owned, owned by State or Federal governments or with mixed government and private ownership, where organization, duties and conditions of service resemble those in the government agencies.[4] Large-scale 'modern' bureaucratic organizations, mainly under auspices of government, thus account for the great majority of the graduates, and most of the remainder goes into teaching, almost exclusively in the public sector. The number of graduates left to disperse to smaller private enterprises or to self-employment is small indeed.

We were interested in the extent to which general preferences (as opposed to expectations) in terms of the kind of employer would reflect the values of the administrative state heritage. We present the results (ABU only) in Table 35. The pattern of preferences clearly reflects government dominance. Two-thirds of the students ranked government

Table 35. Employer Preference

'When you start working, for whom would you prefer to work? (Number in order of preference)'.

	ABU, 1973				
	1st	2nd	3rd	4th	Total
Government administration:	69.8%	15.7%	7.4%	7.1%	100.0%
Large private enterprise:	27.9%	50.0%	14.6%	7.5%	100.0%
Small private enterprise:	4.7%	8.5%	46.9%	39.8%	99.9%
Have own enterprise:	15.2%	17.5%	26.3%	41.0%	100.0%

highest; only about 15 percent placed government administration in the two lowest ranks. Large private enterprise was preferred as a first choice by a little more than one quarter, but was the clear modal second choice. Most of the students were divided as to whether 'small private enterprise' or 'have own enterprise' should occupy last place. But it is noteworthy that while 'small private enterprise' owned by another person drew few votes in either first or second place, there was a significant minority of would-be entrepreneurs who ranked 'have own enterprise' in either first or second place: 15 percent of those ranking the alternative would actually prefer to have their own business rather than government employment.

One would expect to find certain regional differences in preferences as to employer, reflecting differential economic developments in the country, but in fact the same basic pattern is found in data from Ibadan (1973), Nsukka (1973), and Ife (1973). In the data from these universities, where a slightly higher proportion of students come from commercial families, the proportion of students preferring 'large private enterprise' to government employment is also higher; about 35 percent of those answering ranked 'large private enterprise' first. However, government employment was still ranked first by the majority. The minority preferring 'own enterprise' was not significantly higher at the three southern universities. The majority preference for government employment is the more interesting in that salaries for graduates are well-known to be *lower* in government than in the larger private enterprises.[5]

Two other preference factors help to shape patterns of graduate employment in Nigeria, and we elicited student attitudes on each. First, it is a commonly held view in Nigeria that university graduates are as loath as any of the other educated strata to work in rural areas; i.e., 'in the bush'. This is widely considered as a constraint on rural development and on rational use of high level manpower resources. Our question (Table 36) assumes a basic preference for urban employment and thus posits a

Table 36. Location of Employment Preference

'would you consider taking a higher paid job in a rural area before a lower paid one in a city or town?'

	ABU 1970	Ibadan 1972	Lagos 1972
Yes:	44.1%	47.4%	53.8%
Yes, but for a limited period only:	39.1%	37.8%	32.6%
No:	16.8%	14.8%	13.6%
	100.0%	100.0%	100.0%

measure of financial inducement—a technique in practice in some of the states. The results generally bear out the stereotype view as slightly more than 50 percent either would refuse to work in a rural area or would do so only temporarily. Yet more significantly, approximately 50 percent of the students indicated that they could be induced to work in rural areas for a higher salary; another 36 per cent indicated a more temporary willingness. Taking into account that it is fashionable to express concern for rural areas and that many would ultimately refuse, these results suggest that the State and Federal governments may have wider scope for the use of graduates in rural and less developed areas than is generally realized, provided that the governments are willing to deploy them, and willing to pay inducements.[6]

The other factor which limits and shapes the flow of graduates to jobs is preference on the basis of Region and State, both by potential employees and by employers. Only the most naive observer (and none of the students are that) would assume that Nigeria is one large, internally undivided free labour market. The States now tend to form the same 'units of indigenisation' as the Regions did formerly, giving preference in State employment to their 'indigenes'. In extreme cases, some far northern States, short of highly educated men, hire skilled persons from the southern States on a limited-duration contract which is usually reserved for foreign staff in Nigeria. In numerous circumstances restrictions or quotas are tacitly or covertly applied in hiring employees. Within the states as well recruitment to the central institutions is balanced according to areal and ethnic considerations.

We asked students whether they themselves would prefer a job in their own home State (Table 37). About 50 percent said they would. It is fair to say that when real factors of security and community were included, and allowing for a natural reluctance to acknowledge 'home-statism' in this context, the 'yes' vote would be even higher. However, this is preference only, which in many cases would certainly be overridden by a variety of other factors. We might have expected a variation in the responses from

Table 37. Employment and State Origin

A. *'Would you prefer a job in your home state to one in a different part of the country?'*

	ABU, 1973	Ibadan, 1972	Nsukka, 1973
Yes:	51.1%	59.4%	47.2%
No:	48.9%	40.6%	52.8%
	100.0%	100.0%	100.0%

B. *'Do you think that in filling jobs requiring university degrees there tends to be too much emphasis placed on the place of origin of applicants?'*

	ABU, 1973	Ibadan, 1972	Nsukka, 1973
Yes:	75.8%	71.5%	73.6%
No:	24.2%	28.5%	26.4%
	100.0%	100.0%	100.0%

the various universities, but no significant differences were found. Seven samples at four universities answered 'yes' in proportions a little above or below 50 percent.

We turned the question around and asked the students whether they thought 'that in filling jobs requiring university degrees there tends to be too much emphasis placed on the place of origin of applicants?' (Table 37B). 75 percent of the students said yes. Once again the proportions returned from administrations at the different universities were remarkably similar.

Thus, we find that slight majorities exhibited the expected preferences (urban and home State), but in both cases a very sizeable minority would appear to be open to employment anywhere, and while 50 percent acknowledged they would give preference to a home State job, 75 percent disapproved of discrimination on the basis of State of origin by the major employers of university graduates.

More specifically, we were interested in the particular qualities that students valued in a job. We had hypothesized, based on our own observation and on received theory (see section 2 below) that students might be interested in security above all other factors, including salary. We put the question shown in Table 38.

Table 38. Job Security

'Which of the following would you be likely to choose?'

	ABU, 1970	Ibadan, 1972	Lagos, 1972
An exciting and well-paid job which would last only for two or three years:	26.0%	19.6%	26.0%
A job which was somewhat dull and gave only an average salary but which offered an assured career:	74.0%	80.4%	74.0%
	100.0%	10.0%	100.0%

75 percent of the students gave the expected answer. Once again the responses from the various universities were consistent. While the Ibadan, 1972, results seem to diverge slightly from the ABU and Lagos ones, the Ibadan, 1971 sample gave results of 24.6 percent to 75.4 percent, almost identical to those at ABU and Lagos. Our expectations regarding the security factor seemed to be confirmed, but fortunately we also put a more subtle question which provides both a more balanced and a more complex view of job preference (Table 39). In this test five job

qualities including security were put in competition. Interestingly, security was ranked lower

Table 39. Job Qualities

'In what order would you list the qualities you look for in a job?'

	ABU 1973		
Alternative:[1]	Modal ranking	Percentage of first rankings	Percentage of last rankings
Personal fulfilment:	1	33.4%	9.8%
Usefulness to the community:	2	24.6%	10.7%
Security:	1 and 3	29.2%	8.6%
High salary:	4	7.5%	18.4%
High status in the community:	5	5.3%	52.5%
		100.0%	100.0%

[1] Order of alternatives has been rearranged to reflect responses. See Appendix 2.

than the two most 'idealistic' alternatives: 'personal fulfilment and maximum use of talents' and 'usefulness to the community'. 'Status' was ranked last by the majority. It is clear that most of the students believe they are motivated by a far more complex set of variables than security and salary. These answers may also be considered together with the ones given in Table 36 and 37 as evidence that a sizeable proportion of the students would be open to appeals to contribute to social purposes were they convinced of the value of government programmes and their own ability to make a contribution.

Next, we explored attitudes about factors important in careers. In casual conversation and perusal of the newspapers, it is easy to gain the impression that elite careers are determined solely by 'long legs' as Nigerians say, favouritism based on various kinds of influence. We were interested to see the extent to which such a view was prevalent among the students as they looked forward to their own post-graduation careers (See Table 40). The responses are remarkable both for the relative absence of cynicism and for the emphasis on what in a Western group would be considered a middle class ethic. Academic qualifications, hard work and competence were considered the most important factors in getting promotion by most students. It is impossible in Nigeria at the present time to discount completely the factors of home State and ethnicity, for it is obvious to all that a university graduate from one of the

Table 40. Promotion

'What factors help a graduate to get ahead quickly in his career? (Mark the three most important)'.

Alternative:*	ABU, 1971 Percentage Marking alternative†
Academic qualifications:	75.3%
Hard work:	63.2%
Competence:	52.4%
State of origin:	27.4%
Ethnicity:	23.1%
Paying exaggerated respect to superiors:	14.8%
Family connections:	13.7%
Luck:	12.9%
Friends:	6.2%
Seniority:	3.8%

* The order of the alternatives has been rearranged to reflect the responses received. See Appendix 2.
† Each student could mark up to three alternatives: percentages add to more than 100%.

major ethnic groups from an educationally backward State has much brighter career prospects than a graduate from an educationally developed State who is one among hundreds or even thousands of graduates. In fact 'State of origin' and 'ethnicity' were each chosen by about a quarter of the students. 'Family connections' was considered important by relatively few students. Gross deference to superiors was at least not considered a *sufficient* condition of rapid success by most of the students. It is interesting that almost none felt that advancement was possible only through the inexorable working of seniority. This may in part be a reflection of the rapid expansion which most organizations into which the graduates will go are currently experiencing.

With reference to this expansion, we were interested in the students' general outlook on the market for their skills. This is a post-independence generation. The period of general rapid indigenisation was in the 1940s, the 1950s and early 1960s when university graduates were scarce. Particularly in the Northern Region the highest government posts were filled by men without university education. In some sub-Saharan African countries, quite apart from North African countries, the production of graduates in relation to available jobs has already proceeded far enough to require some redefinition of what jobs are regarded as suitable and attractive for new graduates. Such a situation is of social and economic interest, and also political significance. The university-educated elites' political outlook is inevitably coloured heavily by the extent of satisfaction with the roles and status afforded it by the social, and above all the political system. In Nigeria certain factors have postponed any possible glut of graduates. In particular, in 1967 the creation of States meant that 12 State capitals replaced four Regional ones, thus vastly increasing the number of government jobs, particularly in the north where there were six capitals instead of one. The phenomenal growth of oil revenues since the civil war has also made possible the continued expansion of public sector employment.

However, the most rapid growth in the number of jobs was probably completed by about 1970. More university graduates are now produced annually than in the whole pre-independence period. It seems probable, therefore, that Nigeria will fairly soon be overproducing graduates in relation to the available jobs traditionally defined as requiring degrees and as providing an income and status appropriate for graduates.[7] In some States already only a proportion of 'indigene' graduates can be recruited into the public sector except for teaching at the secondary school level which is an occupation desired by few of the graduates.

Against this background, we wondered how the present generation of students regarded the opportunities they saw open to them, and whether

Table 41. Opportunities for graduates

A. *'How would you rate the opportunities for getting ahead which are open to people getting their degrees now, in comparison with those who graduated ten years ago?'*

	ABU. 1973	Ibadan. 1972	Nsukka. 1973
Better:	35.9%	19.5%	30.6%
About the same:	13.4%	15.6%	12.1%
Worse:	42.3%	57.8%	46.2%
Much worse:	8.5%	7.1%	11.1%
	100.1%	100.0%	100.0%

B. *'How satisfied are you with what your own career prospects are likely to be after graduation?'*

	ABU 1973*
Very satisfied:	32.7%
Satisfied:	55.3%
Somewhat dissatisfied:	10.6%
Very dissatisfied:	1.4%
	100.0%

* This question was employed only in the ABU 1973 survey.

they felt bitter or disadvantaged in comparison with earlier generations of students. We posed two types of questions, both shown in Table 41. The first question compared the present with an earlier student generation; the second simply asked for an evaluation of personal prospects. In response to the first, between 50 and 65 percent of the students thought prospects were worse than those open to the graduates of ten years ago, but an appreciable minority, up to 35 percent, said they were better! Only a very small minority (ranging from 7 to 11 percent) said that prospects were 'much worse'.[8] The greater than usual variation in the results by university which is apparent in Table 41 disappears when the results of the seven administrations available are compared; the ABU 1970 sample varied in the direction of the Ibadan 1972 results shown, while the Ibadan 1971 results varied in the direction of the ABU 1973 results shown in the table.

We were somewhat surprised by the rather positive outlook, since it seems evident to us that the prospects of graduates from a number of the States are in fact not as good as those of graduates ten years ago. We think the relatively high proportion of positive responses reflects the enormous expansion of public organizations over the past years; this generation probably regard this extraordinary expansion as normal. It should also not be forgotten that the States of the far north are many years behind the southern States in the production of graduates.

That extreme dissatisfaction is confined to a small minority is confirmed by the more direct evidence of Table 41B. Only a tiny minority of the ABU students pronounced themselves 'very dissatisfied'. Only about 10 percent saw themselves as dissatisfied in any degree. 33 percent were highly satisfied and another 50 percent were satisfied.

To summarise, these results show a considerable degree of apparent satisfaction with what the system provides. There is even, surprising in the outwardly cynical climate of Nigeria, an apparent faith in the institutions: a faith that the middle class virtues of preparation, hard work and competence are sufficiently untrammeled to be the key to success in careers. There is no evidence of general bitterness; if some of the students will be trapped in a graduate glut based on accelerated production of graduates and a stabilizing demand for their skills, few seem aware of this.

2. *PROMISED LAND, OR EDUCATED MAN'S BURDEN?*

Most of these students have spent most of their lives struggling to enter the realm of graduate status and careers. We now consider whether they look forward to a land of milk and honey (bungalows and mercedes) or whether they seem painfully conscious of the strain, discontinuity and personal insecurity of their lives, both past and future. In his influential *Politics, Personality, and Nation Building,* Lucian Pye argues

> First, there is the problem of certainty or predictability: people in transitional societies can take almost nothing for granted; they are plagued on all sides by uncertainty and every kind of unpredictable behaviour. In their erratically changing world, every relationship rests upon uncertain foundations and may seem to contain unlimited potential for good or evil. Above all else, the individual cannot be sure about himself... There is the ultimate problem of a lack of trust in human relationships... The feeling of basic distrust leaves people unsure of their control over their world and hence fearful that the world is either against them or indifferent to them. Distrusting others, they must distrust their own capacity to influence others, and hence they have a feeling of impotence.[9]

Is the outlook of *these* individuals marked by similar insecurity and impotence?

West African 'mammy wagons'[10] have a rich tradition of mottoes expressing philosophical positions and bits of folk wisdom. In one of our questionnaires we offered students two lists of mottoes, inviting students to indicate the ones that most appealed to them. In the first list NO CONDITION IS PERMANENT was chosen most frequently. In the second series the students ranked first: ONE PLUS GOD IS MAJORITY. Choice of the first would seem indeed to indicate an image of life not dissimilar to Pye's 'erratically changing world'. Yet while one may regard no condition as permanent, it does not necessarily follow that all situations change erratically. As to the second motto, it would seem that to have only God on your side is to be very lonely. At the same time the message does not suggest a sense of impotence.

On the basis of our evidence Pye's hypothesis is not proved correct in this instance. While the students are persons in a transitional society, they have enduring social links. They are not generally conscious of alienation from their home communities and cultures or from their families. They seem generally to have more than enough stability within themselves and in their social relations to cope with the continuing changes.

The material presented earlier in this chapter on careers is particularly relevant. In terms of qualities preferred in jobs, 'security' was an important factor for most students, but far from the most important one for the majority. Moreover, the students saw the structures they would professionally inhabit not as erratic, personalized and unpredictable, but, on the contrary, as an orderly world in which competence and diligence would finally prevail.

We asked a general question of the students which tested for a general sense of personal competence and efficacy within the society as a whole (Table 42). While we have no comparative data we would hypothesize that

Table 42. Future Role

'Do you feel that you personally will be able to make a significant contribution to Nigeria's future?'[11]

	ABU, 1973	Ibadan, 1972	Nsukka, 1973
Yes:	60.9%	83.6%	70.6%
No:	2.1%	1.3%	0.4%
Cannot say:	24.7%	9.9%	20.4%
Some contribution, but not a very significant one:	12.3%	5.3%	8.6%
	100.0%	100.1%	100.0%

far smaller proportions of university students in the U.S.A. or Britain would have a sense of being able to have a significant impact in the context of the nation as a whole. In each of ten different administrations at four universities the percentage answering 'no' to this question was under three percent. Between 60 and 80 percent answered 'yes', displaying a resolute confidence in their own social significance. If there is the sense of individualism suggested by ONE PLUS GOD IS MAJORITY, it is a rugged individualism.

If we reject the Pye model, as applied to *these* citizens of a transitional society, we must still consider whether the students see themselves as approaching a social promised land, or as the new bearers of what used to be called the 'white man's burden'. Early in our survey project we asked the question reproduced in Table 43. We were somewhat surprised at the results. More than half of the students considered that the 'African peasant living in a traditional culture' was likely to have the happiest life, yet those students have worked for so many years to escape this role. We offered the alternative of 'high African civil servant' as representing the pinnacle of possible personal achievement for a majority of the students, and the pinnacle role in the value structure of the heritage of the colonial administrative state. We were surprised to find that the majority ranked it so clearly behind the peasant alternative. The happiness of the 'high African civil servant' was ranked only marginally above that of the

Table 43. Happiness

'Which do you think is likely to have a happier life? (Number in order)'.

Alternative*	Modal ranking	ABU 1972† Percentage of Rankings			
		1st	2nd	3rd	4th
African peasant living in a traditional culture:	1	57.1%	14.5%	9.5%	13.6%
High African civil servant	2	27.2%	42.4%	31.1%	2.1%
Western industrial worker:	3	8.5%	35.7%	44.8%	13.4%
High African political leader:	4	7.2%	7.4%	14.7%	70.9%
		100.0%	100.0%	100.0%	100.0%

* Order of alternatives has been rearranged to reflect results. See Appendix 2.
† Similar results were obtained in administrations at Ibadan and Lagos universities.

'Western industrial worker', whose 'happiness' could scarcely be considered more than mediocre, even by non-Marxists. And none of the alternatives challenged the 'high African politician' for lowest ranking—that person so supremely positioned to enjoy (while it lasts) the fruits of society.

We know from other formal evidence (and from our informal experience) that students are well aware that the 'happiness' of their home communities is flawed by poverty, disease, ignorance and exploitation by the more well-to-do and the politically powerful. Yet, it is evident that for large numbers the simpler life of the home communities has a quality of idyll. These results, overall, introduced a note of doubt to

Table 44. Stress

'Would you say that the lives of university graduates are generally characterized by worry and emotional tension by comparison with people living in their traditional societies?'

	ABU, 1973	Ibadan, 1972	Lagos, 1972
Much more stress and tension:	21.6%	17.3%	30.1%
More stress and tension:	36.0%	37.2%	24.1%
About the same, though the tensions are different:	31.8%	32.7%	30.1%
Less strain and tension:	10.6%	12.8%	15.8%
	100.0%	100.0%	100.1%

our image of the highly educated elite, forging ahead self-confidently, with no doubts about the value of the goal. A related question asked for comparison between the situation of the graduate elite and the members of the rural communities (Table 44). Consistently some 55 to 60 percent considered the life of the graduate to be more stressful, but 30 percent or less thought there was 'much more' stress and tension. Between 42 and 46 percent thought that there was about the same, or even less, stress in the graduates' lives.

3. 'MODERN' OR 'WESTERN'?

The university graduates are knowledgeable in Western culture. While we think the point is easily exaggerated, Fanon and others have drawn unflattering portraits of the highly educated bureaucratic elite functioning as mediators between 'Europe' (i.e. the developed world) and the African people. It is certainly true that the education the university students receive is still largely based on the British structural model. It is interesting that the students themselves agreed overwhelmingly that their education is too Western and should be more Nigerian (see Table 45).

Table 45. Assessment of University Syllabus

'Do you think that the syllabuses of Nigerian universities should undergo major revision to make them less 'Western' and more 'Nigerian'?

	ABU, 1970	Ibadan, 1972	Lagos, 1972
Yes:	89.5%	87.9%	82.3%
No:	10.5%	12.1%	17.7%
	100.0%	100.0%	100.0%

Partly as a consequence of these findings, we wondered how students would see university-educated Nigerians as a group in their relation to the West. We also wanted to see how they saw the uneducated — the unprepared and uninitiated — in relation to Western culture.[12] We asked the questions shown in Table 46. The results would seem to indicate basic acceptance of the commonly held view of the university-educated elite as an imitative and at least superficially 'Westernized' one. 'Imitation' was chosen almost twice as often as any other alternative. The other responses were diverse, expressing both positive and negative reactions to Western culture. Besides 'imitation' the student group as a whole, if not the individuals, seemed ambivalent which is scarcely surprising in the

Table 46. Attitudes toward Western Culture

A. *'What attitudes do you think most university-educated Nigerians have towards Westerners and Western culture? (Check as many answers as seem to you appropriate)'*

Alternatives*	ABU, 1970 Percentage marking alternative
Imitation:	76.7%
Contempt:	41.7%
Respect:	36.5%
Ambivalence:	32.4%
Envy:	29.7%
Hostility:	27.2%
Avoidance:	20.6%
Other (write in:)†	—

B. *'What attitudes do you think most non-educated Nigerians have towards Europeans‡ and European culture? (Check as many answers as seem to you appropriate)'*

Alternatives*	ABU, 1970 Percentage marking alternative
Inability to understand:	67.3%
Respect:	64.4%
Fear:	52.9%
Suspicion:	49.5%
Imitation:	37.1%
Envy:	22.0%
Contempt:	20.5%
Ambivalence:	12.9%
Other (write in:)†	—

* The order of the alternatives has been rearranged to reflect results.
† Write-ins, in case we failed to anticipate wide-spread feelings in our alternatives, were too few and too scattered to code.
‡ 'Westerner' was changed to 'European' in the non-educated version because some students might have been bothered by the fact that the idea of 'Western' would not be understood by many uneducated persons. 'European' on the other hand is the common translation for most of the various words used in Nigerian vernaculars to apply to whites.

confusing and culturally unsatisfactory situation of post-colonialism.

The answers to the second part are interesting. 'Inability to understand,' 'respect', 'fear', and 'suspicion' all drew response from half of the students answering. It is to be noted that the latter three are all related to 'inability to understand'. The alternatives which imply *empathy* with Europeans or European culture (imitation, envy) received lower numbers of choices.

A further insight into what seems to be a general area of ambivalence is provided by the responses to the questions reproduced in Table 47, which

Table 47. Evaluation of Colonialism

A. *Do you agree or disagree with the following statement: "On balance, colonization in Africa brought more advantages than disadvantages"?*

	ABU, 1973	Ibadan, 1973	Nsukka, 1973
Agree:	56.6%	44.3%	66.3%
Disagree:	43.4%	55.7%	33.7%
	100.0%	100.0%	100.0%

B. *'Which one of the following statements do you most agree with?'*

	ABU, 1973	Ibadan, 1973	Nsukka, 1973
'The Third World Countries are poor because they have been and are exploited by the developed countries:'	47.5%	50.8%	36.3%
'The Third World countries are poor because they are underdeveloped (i.e., lack structures, skills and resources);'	52.5%	49.2%	63.8%
	100.0%	100.0%	100.0%

attempt to explore what would seem to be the most basic problem of African/Western relations: the evaluation of colonialism and the contemporary post-colonial (or neo-colonial) situation. On both questions some differences between the university results are apparent, with a slightly greater proportion of the Ibadan (1973) group inclining toward an anti-colonial view of the past and the Fanonesque interpretation of present poverty. However, the differences should not be overemphasized. On the first question, nearly half the students, even at Ibadan, were willing to say that colonization brought more good than harm, and half or more of the students at each of the universities rejected the fashionable exploitation theory of Third World poverty in favour of a more pedestrian one focusing on the internal factors of development. Poverty was seen by this group as deriving more from intrinsic than from extrinsic causes. It can be suggested (if not proved) that these results reflect not so much the existence of sharply divided groups within the student body as a tendency toward ambivalence within individuals when such questions are raised.

4. CONCLUSION

We do not ask that a great deal be made of the responses on colonialism and neo-colonialism. Taken together with other questions such as the felt need to revise university syllabi to make them more Nigerian, we have some indication that large numbers of the students are troubled by their relationship to the West. We mention this in part because our unstructured interchange with the students has convinced us that this is an area of unresolved intellectual concern for large numbers of the most thoughtful students. As observers we can suggest that this represents at least a partial consciousness of an underlying structural and cultural situation which is inherent in the post-colonial situation, and which will be fully resolved only as various presently inchoate forces within the society work themselves out.

We think that generally the university students have a high level of understanding of their situation. They accept the responsibility for that multitude of important things in modern Nigeria which transcend the world of the village. What data we have on the point suggests that the students accept 'the educated man's burden'. They look back on the village as a place of happiness. But we would say that on balance most students regard their own future positively; only a tiny minority seems embittered. They are satisfied with their opportunities; they seem to have basic faith in the roles and institutions to which they go; and most important of all, they feel that they personally are important within the country's future.

FOOTNOTES

1. 'Long leg' is common Nigerian slang for improper influence in procuring jobs, etc.
2. In a survey of 1972 graduates from Ibadan, Ife and Lagos it was reported that by 1973, 42.9 percent worked in the Federal or State civil service; 32.1 percent under state school boards; 11.8 percent in Federal State corporations; and a mere 13.2 percent in the private sector. Interestingly, though graduates in education were the most likely to work in schools 22.7 percent of them were already working in the civil service. A check on 1973 graduates showed that only a little over 10 percent of them were working in the private sector, *University Graduate Employment: A Sample Survey of Employment Experience amongst Nigerian Men and Women Graduating in 1972* (Lagos: National Manpower Board, 1973), pp.25-31.
3. Teachers are more likely than others to change jobs within a year of graduating, *Ibid.*, p.43.
4. There is a regional and ethnic pattern in this choice. Of the Yoruba students at ABU 33.3 percent put large private enterprise in first place which is consistent with the students at the southern universities.
5. The survey by the Manpower Board reports '. . . graduates who do go into the private sector are likely to do proportionately considerably better as regards annual emolument than their counterparts who take up careers in government service. No (1972) graduate taking an appointment in the private sector reported earning less

than N1,600 and less than N2,000 (compared with 75 percent in the public sector and 90 percent in the teaching sector), whilst just under 40 percent gave salaries in the range of N2,000 to N2,400 and another 30 percent or more were earning N2,400 or more.' *University Graduate Employment,* p.35. The effect of the Udoji Commission's recommendations on these differentials is not yet clear.
6. The financial inducements suggested are all the stronger in that living expenses in the rural areas are mostly lower than elsewhere.
7. The Federal Public Service Commission in a letter to the University of Ibadan during the 1974-75 session informed the university that it was not going to interview final year students in mechanical, electrical, civil and petroleum engineering, agriculture, veterinary science, zoology, food technology and science subjects. *Daily Times.* 17/2/1975.
8. At least up to 1972 the optimism of the graduates seems well founded. In that year some 86 percent of male graduates found employment in less than two months after graduation. Female graduates took a little longer but nearly 75 percent of them had found jobs within two months, *University Graduate Employment,* pp.23-24.
9. L. Pye, *Politics, Personality, and Nation Building: Burma's Search for Identity* (New Haven: Yale University Press, 1962), p.55.
10. This term is more frequent in Ghana than in Nigeria. It refers to lorries that are often converted in most ingenious ways into buses that carry passengers and their baggage between towns. Mottoes and slogans are painted on the back, front and sides.
11. We consider that this question—couched at the highly general level of 'significant' contribution to the future of the national whole—does not produce results which are comparable with Almond and Verba's civic competence data (see G. A. Almond and S. Verba, *The Civic Culture: Political Attitudes and Democracy in Five Nations,* (Boston and Toronto: Little Brown and Company 1965), Chapters VI and VII. We experimented with a question based on their highly specific and political 'unjust law' formulation, but we found that the Almond-Verba problem did not translate well into Nigerian conditions, particularly under military rule, and could well produce misleading results. For an attempt to use the Almond-Verba formulation in a survey of African elites, see V. T. Levine, *Political Leadership in Africa* (Hoover Institute, Stanford University, 1967).
12. We are far from satisfied with the format of these questions, particularly Table 46B, because the choices offered are unduly restricted and overly negative.

5 General Political Values: Order and Unity

The next two chapters deal with the focal point of our survey project, namely, the political dimensions of attitudes. The present chapter attempts to describe general political orientations; the succeeding chapter deals with the more immediate level of political interaction. Political orientations, however, can only be understood in relation to the objects and interactions of specific political environments. We begin this chapter, then, with a section designed to be introductory both to this chapter and the next. It will serve not only to sketch the main lines of recent Nigerian political history but also indirectly to make clear the authors' own perspectives on Nigerian political history which inevitably helped to shape our inquiry.

1. POLITICS NIGERIAN STYLE: 'IN OUT OF THE RAIN'[1]

Political activity informed by a clear consciousness of the colonial quasi-state may be dated from 1923 when Herbert Macaulay founded the Nigerian National Democratic Party.[2] Macaulay, while speaking in terms of Nigeria and its people, was, along with his allies and rivals, mainly concerned with those Lagos issues that touched the creole and coastal intelligentsia.[3] With the founding of the Lagos Youth Movement (soon afterwards renamed the Nigerian Youth Movement) in 1934, new men from the southern hinterland made their presence felt in Lagos and linked its politics more closely with the preoccupations of a greatly increasing group of educated Nigerians in the other 'modern' towns. These developments were the reflection of a myriad of micro-events (especially schools, missions and cash crops) in the rural areas of southern Nigeria. This generation of 'new men' (there have been several in Nigerian politics) took the Lagos seats in the Legislative Council away from Macaulay's NNDP in 1938. The NYM then split in 1941 (reflecting the increasing complexity of the Lagos political environment). However, its members kept nationalist politics alive during the Second World War. In the post-war world they were ready to demand power from the colonial government and its officials, and also to compete for it among themselves.

Some of these new men were university graduates and professional men; others were small businessmen, produce buyers, petty traders, clerks and teachers. They made their appeal to an audience that consisted of the middle and lower ranks of government employees and large-scale foreign private enterprise, all people who had received some formal schooling. But they also appealed to petty traders and others who had grievances against both government and foreign enterprise and to groups ranging from mission catechists to cocoa farmers. These participants in politics had roots in the traditional communities of the southern countryside (a small number, however, came from the north), and they maintained connexions with their communities of origin.

The British government made plans during the Second World War for constitutional evolution towards independence in its West African colonies. The British however envisaged this development on a time scale much longer than the nationalists were prepared to accept. Moreover, the colonial officials on the spot tended to be more grudging than the metropolitan government and fought a rearguard action against nationalist demands. The first constitutional step in Nigeria was taken with the Richards constitution that came into force in January, 1947. It was designed to give a very limited political autonomy that did not amount in practice to much more than an elaborate form of consultation. It expanded the Legislative Council, but not its directly elected component. It drew political representation from among the ranks of the local authorities rather than from among the nationalists. The latter had not only been by-passed in the drawing up of the constitution but they were mostly to be left out of its working. Inevitably they intensified their opposition to the colonial government and to the shape and pace of its decolonisation programme. The Richards constitution made an unexpected and important contribution to developing nationalism, as opposition to it provided an unprecedented unifying and energizing impulse which was particularly important in bringing educated young men in the north into contact with the nationalist currents in the south.

In addition, the Richards constitution brought two crucial factors to bear on the Nigerian political scene. First, it consolidated the existing groupings of provinces (Eastern, Western and Northern) for both political and administrative purposes. Future politics would develop within this three-way framework and the administrative cleavages would become social and political. Second, northern representatives were to sit for the first time in an all-Nigerian political assembly.[4] Thus it became clear that the future of the north lay with the rest of the country, at the same time that the country's regional pattern was confirmed.

The Richards constitution was speedily acknowledged to be outmoded, and consultation on the terms of its replacement began soon after its promulgation. A new constitution (called the Macpherson constitution) established true legislative assemblies in the Regions and at the centre, again confirming the pattern of political development within a three-way regional framework. The most important immediate result of the new constitution was that country-wide (but indirect) elections were held, which stimulated political organisation with far reaching results. The Lagos-centred NYM had decayed after Azikiwe[5] had withdrawn from it in 1941. Azikiwe in collaboration with Macaulay founded the National Council of Nigeria and the Cameroons (NCNC), a congress-type party (originally it had only group membership) that gathered together a wide range of associations and politically conscious individuals. The 1951 elections stimulated the formation of new parties in the west (the Action Group, formed a few months before the 1951 elections) and north (the Northern People's Party, formed in the crucible of the elections in 1951). From the beginning the emergent party system adopted a regional pattern derived from colonial administrative history.

The 1950s in Nigeria were filled with constitution-making as a constantly accelerating process of formal decolonization developed. Constitutional conferences took place throughout the 1950s. The regionalist pattern was consolidated in the 1954 constitution which was avowedly Federal, and provided the structural basis for regional political machinery. The 1959 constitution provided a uniform electoral system throughout the Federation (except that only males could vote in the north) and led to the first country-wide direct general elections (to the Federal House of Representatives) in 1959.

As the structures of political input were thus elaborated (all, it is important to note, in only slightly more than a decade) the personnel of Nigerian politics developed apace. An understanding of the developing 'political class' is, in fact, considerably more important than the structural details of the new system. Southern politicians from the Eastern and Western Regions came mainly from among those who had joined the nationalist ranks early. They included well-educated leaders such as Dr. Nnamdi Azikiwe and Mr. Obafemi Awolowo, professional men who had early on joined them such as Dr. Michael Okpara and Mr. S. L. A. Akintola and business men such as Mr. Festus Okotie-Eboh and Mr. S. A. Sonibare. To them should be added the northern leaders who stepped into the power vacuum created when the imminence of British withdrawal was understood. Ahmadu Bello and Abubakar Tafawa Balewa were foremost among these. These leading politicians were quickly joined by hosts of others from all over the country who had some education, organizing ability and traditional connexions or patronage, and who made their way into politics as champions of local communities that had become aware of the need to be represented where laws were made, taxes decided and amenities allocated.

By the time of the 1951 elections the southern nationalists had split largely along ethnic lines, although the splits owed much as well to personal dislikes and even to business competition among the leading activists. At about the same time the civil service was opening up to Nigerians. The resultant scramble for jobs also caused deep cleavages along ethnic lines among the more highly educated Nigerians. It was a difficult period as elite groups competed with one another: social communication took on ethnic patterns, and members of different groups started more than ever to see one another through tribalist eyes. Ethnic organisation in politics worked all the more easily through the regional structures. By 1959 the largely Yoruba-led Action Group controlled the Western Region but had some following or allies among minority peoples in the other Regions. The largely Ibo-led NCNC controlled the Eastern Region and had strong support among dissident Yoruba groups and among the mid-western Edo and Ibo. It is important to emphasize here that ethnicity itself was a relatively new organizing principle in Nigeria, and that rural communities where the bulk of the population was to be found saw politics as communal before they saw it as ethnic. The British creation called Nigeria brought together several hundred language groups, each composed of many thousands of town and village communities. Right up to the end of the Second World War communications between most communities remained rudimentary and trade was limited. Not until the 1950s did community leaders all over the country begin to realize the full implications of the idea of British withdrawal, and the extent to which the lot of all the communities was linked. Socialization, for all but a few, was communal and ethnic rather than 'national' or even regional.

In the simultaneous rush toward political power and decolonization, it was natural that political organization should rest heavily on the social cleavages which were most obvious (and which had their inevitable impact on social communication): those of language group or 'tribe' in Nigerian parlance. In the effort to construct (in a hurry, be it remembered) new solidarities transcending accustomed patterns of interaction ethnicity was simply (in many cases) the most pragmatic basis of organization. But influential as ethnicity became in Nigerian politics it seldom operated as a monolithic factor. To refer only to the largest groups, the Yoruba have divided in party politics along lines that recall the 19th century wars; Ibo groups who stayed mostly within one party nevertheless split acrimoniously over constituency nominations; and the Hausa emirates saw age-old tensions resurface. Indeed, while ethnicity has been the most prominent organizing pattern in politics, the basic organizational unit within the pattern has been the home community. Ethnic affinities offered a basis on which traditional communities and their opinion leaders could collaborate with one another and take up positions vis-a-vis other groups in a developing struggle for shares of what came to be called the 'national cake'. Analysis and summary at the macro level have tended to obscure the primacy of social identity with the home community and political organization.

As well as the factors of home community and ethnic group, the regional level must also be kept in mind—particularly with reference to the developing politics in the north. The growth of politics there had less to do initially with resistance to colonial government. It was rather caused by northern fears that the southern lead in education would permit southerners to take over power and posts in the north, undermining its social structures, and harming its traditions. Though power in the far northern emirates was traditionalist and quasi-feudal, it was also highly structured through the native authorities which included the vast majority of the able, educated and traditionally prestigious persons in their areas. The traditional ruling classes had reacted slowly to the constitutional concessions being wrested by the nationalists from the British. On the one hand they were prompted to organise themselves politically by the British officials who were more aware of the direction of their own government. On the other hand they were shaken by the initial successes of the challenge from their own young Muslim Hausa radicals,[6] particularly in the first stage of the 1951 indirect elections. The Northern People's Congress which took over in the Northern Region once the 1951 election was over was sponsored by the traditional ruling classes.[7] It was less a party organization as such than collaboration between the ruling classes in the native authorities and their own new men with modern education. The British colonial authorities helped discreetly. It is most important to note how defensive these Northern developments were. Though NPC leaders made remarks such as Abubakar's on continuing the jihad (the holy war which the Fulani had waged during the 19th century) to the sea, their real concern may have been to prevent a southern march to Kaduna, while at the same time forestalling premature attempts by their own young radicals to reform the native authorities out of recognition. They were also engaged in defeating challenges by the ethnic and communal leaders of the traditionally pagan peoples of the Region who did not form a natural part of a Hausa-Fulani/Kanuri coalition. Many of the leaders of these groups argued for a Middle Belt (largely a riverain and southern sector of the north) State of their own.

Nigerian constitutional change after 1951 was worked out with the British by the leaders who had emerged in the 1951 elections and the period immediately before them. These leaders used their newly acquired control of the regional government apparatus to win over community and business leaders by a judicious award of posts and patronage, and they defeated opposition groups by withholding patronage from them and by discriminating against them in taxation and law enforcement. The leaders of the main parties worked out and accepted a constitutional settlement that envisaged a weak centre and strong Regions, and they refused to countenance the setting up of new Regions.

The top elites that were recruited through the 1951 elections, and the party organizations which they constructed around themselves, were in fact able to dominate and largely control events during the period of dyarchy in the twilight of colonial rule.[8] It can be clearly seen with hindsight—and was more dimly perceived by many at the time—that the logic of the developing system was a live-and-let-live coexistence between the regional machines which would then ally and oppose within the framework of the Federal parliamentary institutions. Only control of a regional government provided sufficient security for the major political elites to interact at the Federal level. The Action Group's acceptance of the role of official opposition at the Federal level—so much appreciated by liberal observers abroad—was made possible by the fact that until 1962 the Action Group was also a party in power in the Western Region.

This interesting structural 'solution' might have endured longer (though it was unsatisfactory and unfair to many minority groups within the regions) but the Action Group and to a lesser extent the NCNC continued to try to invade the NPC's base in the north. The Action Group endeavoured also to build up support among dissident groups in the Eastern Region and the NCNC strove to maintain its strong position in the Western Region (where it had actually won a majority of seats in the 1954 Federal elections). In 1962 the northern and eastern leaders did not resist the temptation to activate Federal powers to collude in ousting the main group of Action Group leaders from control of the government of the Western Region (in favour of a government and party which became largely satellite to the NPC), and they also set up a fourth Region (the Mid-West). Moreover, the Federal centre had come to be seen to have more financial and legal control over the regions than had originally seemed to be the case. It was still true however to say some five years after independence that the centre was politically only 'a collection of regions'.[9]

GENERAL POLITICAL VALUES: ORDER AND UNITY   109

Beyond the competition for power, and in many ways more fundamental, was the general closing of ranks by the leading political activists in each Region. Those who had arrived first on the scene, the founder members, brought in some new recruits as deaths or ministerial expansion created vacancies or new posts, but they themselves remained solidly entrenched in the Regions and at the centre. Even when the Action Group was destroyed, most of its leaders simply changed sides and regained their posts. If the political leaders had conveyed an image of integrity and competence, they might not have provoked the resentment and dislike that they did; but they tended not only to flaunt wealth acquired through politics, they also did not bother to conceal its unscrupulous acquisition. Nor did certain irresponsible statements and childish public squabbling convey an image of competence to a political audience that was growing both more sophisticated in its interpretation of politics and more alienated from the political class. What particularly exasperated educated Nigerians was that they felt they could do nothing about the low calibre politicians they had inherited from the era of the independence movement. The Nigerian novelist Chinua Achebe gave expression to the frustrated and ambivalent reactions of many educated Nigerians in *A Man of the People* as a central figure thinks:

> A man who has just come in from the rain and dried his body and put on dry clothes is more reluctant to go out again than another who has been indoors all the time. The trouble with our new nation—as I saw it then lying on that bed—was that none of us had been indoors long enough to be able to say, 'To hell with it'. We had all been in the rain together until yesterday. Then a handful of us—the smart and the lucky and hardly ever the best—had scrambled for the one shelter our former rulers left, and had taken it over and barricaded themselves in. And from within they sought to persuade the rest through numerous loudspeakers, that the first phase of the struggle had been won and that the next phase—the extension of our house—was even more important and called for new and original tactics; it required that all argument should cease and the whole people speak with one voice and that any more dissent and argument outside the door of the shelter would subvert and bring down the whole house.[10]

There were two main reasons for this sense of impotence and frustration. First, the existing leaders not only controlled the rudimentary political organisations that existed, but they also controlled, and were willing to use ruthlessly, the apparatus of government to maintain themselves in power. Second, the politically aware groups were ethnically and regionally divided among themselves. In consequence, they feared to injure the interests of their own groups in opposing their leaders without at the same time a move being made against all the other leaders. The educated intelligentsia was expanding rapidly, however, as increasing numbers of university graduates returned from abroad or graduated from the University College, Ibadan. The new graduates tended to be embittered by their own impotence as they watched men, whom they despised as both incompetent and corrupt, represent and guide the interests of the country. It was the 'intelligentsia-in-uniform'[11] (who shared the views of the rest of the intelligentsia) that finally moved against the political regime in January, 1966, but they did so only after the country had undergone a long series of constitutional crises over rigged elections and falsified censuses, had witnessed the exacerbation of ethnic bitternesses, and had recoiled from unconcealed corruption. During all this time the politicians had been treating the country as a personal patrimony from which they could not be dislodged. For all their faults, however, they had been performing a brokerage function. Once that was removed the country quickly lurched into governmental instability with a second coup (July, 1966) and came up against ethnic and regional cleavages that culminated in massive repatriation to Regions of origin and then in a war of secession.

It is against this background that the perceptions and attitudes of our university students towards politics must be seen and gauged. Several points emerge as having probable relevance to the attitudes of the present generation of university students (or any other educated and politically conscious group in the society). First, while British colonial rule lasted for a little over half a century, electoral politics on a countrywide basis existed for less than a decade before independence. Second, during the whole period of electoral politics (1951-1966) electoral success or failure never led to a peaceful changeover of government at either the Federal of the regional level. The regional political elites manipulated both democratic and governmental structures and processes to maintain themselves in power. In this sense, Nigeria's experience with electoral democracy was both brief *and* incomplete. Third, the politicians discredited themselves in the eyes of the politically aware populace. Knowledge of the personal corruption and incompetence of many of the political leaders was widespread, and the reactions to the January 15 coup indicated very general disgust with the politicians and the many crises which marked their rule. Fourth, at the same time as the 'input' institutions were being hurriedly constructed and set in motion, the accelerating curve of Nigeria's developing educational system was changing both quantitatively and qualitatively the character of the Nigerian intelligentsia. The politicians who mobilized sufficient support to gain power at the beginning of the 1950's included many who were poorly educated. By the end of the political era in the mid-1960's many of the politicians were being judged by younger men with much higher education. The result was that, among the most highly educated at least, the common view was that politicians were not only corrupt and tribalist, but ignorant and under-educated as well.

A hiatus of over nine years has now occurred since the 'end of politics'. The country has been divided and put together again. The educational institutions have taken vast numbers of boys and girls from the rural villages and turned them into 'elites', as the term is used in Nigeria. Oil has made Nigeria a rich-poor country and the evidence of spreading wealth is everywhere. Following the cataclysms of 1966, and the subsequent civil war the military government stabilized at both Federal and State level as a coalition of high ranking military and police officers with civil servants and some civilian representatives (including a number of former politicians chosen from among those less associated with the excesses of the First Republic). After recovering from the efforts of the civil war the government embarked upon a number of major reforms (the most important of which involved economic indigenisation) and programmes of public expenditure (especially roads and education). The Gowon government however, which had come into power in the second coup of 1966 and which had led the country through the civil war and the first stages of reconstruction became progressively seen as incompetent and corrupt, and was replaced by the Muhammed government after a bloodless military coup in July, 1975. However, little has changed fundamentally in the pattern of government which remains a combination of military officers, bureaucrats and civilian commissioners. The situation in which an authoritarian government rules 'for the people' as it sees their interests, consulting and coopting representatives as it sees fit, bears a striking resemblance to the colonial situation itself. As a transition to popular democratic rule is eventually engineered and presided over by the authoritarian government, the resemblance will become more striking. Viewed from this perspective it scarcely seems surprising that the colonial administrative state with its deeper roots in history should show more persistence than the democratic system which saw the light of day so late.

Yet there is impatience with the military regime—for its particular faults, errors and omissions, but also, seemingly, *because it is authoritarian*. It was naive to believe—as the British colonial decision makers and many others seemed to—that a system of electoral democracy would immediately find sufficient support within the relevant portions of a new State's population to become self-sustaining. Yet the history of the last few years, here briefly surveyed, suggests that the converse assumption—that the predominant value patterns of significant elite groups in Nigeria make democratic structures permanently dispensable—would be at least equally false. Rather, the major facts—consensual acceptance of failure of the first regime, the unbalanced experience of the colonial period, and, above all, the contemporary pressure for a return to a system of electoral democracy—suggest that the question of democracy in Nigeria remains unsettled, and as such is the most significant element of unfinished business in the process of becoming an independent State and political community. It is significant that the government that succeeded General Gowon's acknowledged that some of its predecessor's unpopularity derived from its going back on its pledge to restore civilian rule in 1976 and laid down a new programme to prepare for civilian rule in 1979.

A number of points thus arise. We can consider the nature and implications of the general acceptance of the failure of democracy, and examine whether the structures of the First Nigerian Republic were inappropriate, or whether they were not permitted to operate within even the broadest outlines of their normative definitions. In terms of the present situation, we can question whether the visible support for a return to democracy is genuine or whether it is simply a desire for change from the present regime (which can most easily and thoroughly be disposed of through return to democracy). Where there is support for the idea of democracy we can examine which elements are seen as essential to democracy, and whether there is support for a vaguer, more inchoate *idea* of democracy which is poorly connected to the specific structures and processes (elections, parties, competition, etc.) which the Western tradition defines as appropriate to its realization. Finally, looking to the future, we can consider whether Nigeria is doomed to pendulum swings between civilian and military rule and democracy and dictatorship (civilian or military), and what factors might lead one to expect different patterns in a future political regime; we can examine, in particular, the possible effect of the substitution of States for the Regions, and the immense expansion of the highly educated intelligentsia.

This survey of recent Nigerian history and the points listed above indicate in a cursive way the set of hypothesis-producing concerns and ideas with which we began our study, attempting to cast light on questions of broad importance through a study of one limited, but sharply definable and highly accessible portion of Nigeria's highly educated elite.

2. A TOLERANCE OF SOCIAL CHANGE: 'NO CONDITION IS PERMANENT'

Underlying the political change described above has been an enormous degree of social change. The motivational pull of change—social influence through formal education, security of salaried employment, money from cash crops, new positions and wealth, freedom from traditional controls in new towns and new circumstances, surer defences against hunger and disease, comfort in cement buildings, and speed and ease in motor and rail transport—has been extraordinarily powerful wherever the demonstration effect of modernity (in the sense of more powerful rationality, technology, and organizational forms) has been grasped. In the process many old ways have been altered, social structures have been modified, and confidence in the ability to deal with the physical environment has grown. These changes have not taken place without cost: social influence changes hands or is modified with some difficulty, new forms of social predictability and trust are only slowly established and new skills are often painfully and slowly acquired. But it is clear that most communities and their most energetic members have valued the benefits more than they have deprecated the costs of change.

Important and obvious as change is, it is important not to exaggerate its impact on the country. There are two main reasons why the effects of change remain limited. First, a great many communities still remain only marginally affected by modernizing factors. Many communities are poorly served by the communications network and only a minority of the country's population has gone to school. Modern medicine is not fully available to most groups, and for many it is not available at all. Second, social structures have in good measure withstood the pressures of change. For example, in spite of the considerable take-over of power by politicians and bureaucrats many traditional ruling authorities, be they title-holders or elders, still wield great power within their communities. Family and lineage structures have adapted and used new technological possibilities and organizational opportunities rather than been broken by them and many social and personal values, even in the new towns, show basic continuity with the old. In short, social change is a package deal of benefits and costs, and persons and groups try consciously and unconsciously to maximize the benefits as they see them and to minimize the costs.

This changing social situation is complex. We generalize about it only hesitantly. If it is true, as we have argued, that there is much more continuity than first appears and that people want only selective change, how do highly educated persons like university students who seem to have benefited most from social change formulate their attitudes to it? Some observers think that the intelligentsia is doctrinally commited to change. Van den Berghe's view is typical:

> The emerging classes of the newly independent states ... have eagerly adopted a pervasive ideology of change. Everybody is in favour of change, especially economic development.... The ruling elites of the Third World favour development largely because it is fashionable, prestigious, and frequently lucrative to themselves.[12]

We were uneasy about accepting this view and could think of several reasons why an intelligentsia might be less than whole-hearted in its readiness to embrace a 'pervasive ideology of change'. First, since nearly all of them have made great adjustments in the course of their lives, they may well have come close to the limits of tolerable change, at least for themselves. Second, they do not any longer suffer from the wants of the population generally, and so may be less sensitive to these wants and to the changes required to cope with them. Third, further social change of certain kinds (a revision of salary structures, for example) could challenge their hard-earned status and privileges, and they might well resist this kind of challenge. In short, it cannot be taken for granted that elite groups are unreservedly in favour of promoting social change, so there is good reason for trying to explore their views on the subject.

We posed a question in the widest terms, asking whether social changes that are bound to come sooner or later should be put through rapidly, even at the cost of some disruption, or whether they should be managed in a slower, evolutionary way. The question expresses a real dilemma for third world countries. A strong majority of the students at all the universities surveyed favoured evolutionary change. The Ibo students at Nsukka, who come from a society that has been vocally proud of its

Table 48. Rapid or Evolutionary Change

'Which is the better way to bring about major social changes which are bound to come about sooner or later?'

	ABU, 1973	Ibadan, 1972	Nsukka, 1973
Rapid change*	20.7%	31.0%	14.5%
Evolutionary change†	79.3%	69.0%	85.5%
	100.0%	100.0%	100.0%

* Full text was: 'Rapid change which "gets it over with", but at the cost of some disruption of the lives of individuals and groups'
† Full text was: 'Evolutionary change which is less disruptive but moves slower'

progressiveness (but which suffered the disaster of the civil war), opposed disruptive change even more strongly than other groups.

This general reaction to the problem of change is revealing because the question focused mainly on the tolerance of an educated group for change in the abstract and avoided connecting it to other issues—especially those linked with their own status or privileges. When law and order and the order-related values of national unity and stability were placed in competition with economic development the importance of order became very clear (Table 49). However, these questions alone

Table 49. Order and Economic Growth Contrasted

'*Which is more important in a developing country? (Mark one out of each pair of alternatives)*'

	ABU, 1973	Ibadan, 1973	Nsukka, 1973
Economic development:	11.9%	14.0%	12.3%
National unity:	88.1%	85.9%	87.7%
	100.0%	100.0%	100.0%
Economic development:	17.2%	16.5%	19.4%
Political stability:	82.8%	83.5%	80.6%
	100.0%	100.0%	100.0%
Economic development:	14.9%	13.0%	9.3%
Law and order in society:	85.1%	87.0%	90.7%
	100.0%	100.0%	100.0%

provide no sure grounds for concluding that the student majorities are highly conservative. We shall see that economic development is not a primary preoccupation for most of the students. It should also be noted that order, defined in terms of the unity of the community and the stability of government, has only to be threatened to become immediately a main concern of any society. A great majority of educated Nigerians have no wish to hasten change in such fashion as to impose disruptive strains on their society. Perhaps more than most groups they know how fragile order is. They have learned about disorder from folk memories of pre-colonial wars, and the students have in their own lifetime witnessed the breakdown of political and social order in their country culminating in communal massacres and civil war.

The students' views on order cannot be taken to indicate uncompromising support for the present *status quo*. It is striking that a majority of the students thought that a Chinese-style transformation of Nigerian society was desirable (Table 50), but a majority also doubted that it would be

Table 50. Transformation of Society

'Do you think it is possible to transform Nigerian society as thoroughly as the Chinese Communists seem to have transformed their society?'

	ABU, 1973	Ibadan, 1973	Nsukka, 1973
It is possible	38.6%	41.8%	37.5%
It is not possible	61.4%	58.2%	62.5%
	100.0%	100.0%	100.0%

'Whether or not you think it is possible, do you think it is desirable?'

	ABU, 1973	Ibadan, 1973	Nsukka, 1973
It is desirable:	60.4%	59.3%	56.9%
It is not desirable:	39.6%	40.7%	43.1%
	100.0%	100.0%	100.0%

possible to transform Nigerian society in this way. The only value gaining considerable, if still minority, support in a contest with law and order was 'restructuring society to bring social justice' (Table 51).

Table 51. Stability

'Mark the one that you consider more important:'

	ABU, 1973	Ibadan, 1973	Nsukka, 1973
'Law and order and political stability':	65.1%	57.9%	56.6%
'Restructuring society to bring social justice'	34.9%	42.1%	41.4%
	100.0%	100.0%	100.0%

We introduced a practical—and painful—question about the problem of privilege in the post-colonial era. We asked whether elite incomes should be 'slashed (i.e., reduced by one-third or more)' in order to reduce the elite-mass gap that is so prominent a feature of the post-colonial situation (Table 52). It should be noted that the question was asked of young men and women who are on the point of joining the 'elite'

Table 52. Income Gap

'Should the incomes of Nigeria's elites be slashed (i.e., reduced by one third or more) in order to narrow the gap between them and the common people?'

	ABU, 1973	Ibadan, 1973	Nsukka, 1973
Yes:	46.6%	37.3%	38.7%
No:	53.4%	62.7%	61.3%
	100.0%	100.0%	100.0%

themselves (often after years of relative sacrifice). Somewhat to our surprise between one-third and one-half thought that elite incomes should be 'slashed'.[13] The southern students tended to oppose reduction of elite salaries with slightly stronger majorities than the northern students. Our data does not permit extensive exploration of the question, but we think it probable that those groups who feel most secure about their own future (based on a presently unsatisfied demand for their skills) are more likely to feel generous toward the masses.

Two qualifications need to be made. First, this question may have forced respondents to take a position on a problem which they would not themselves have seen as relevant. In informal conversations with students we repeatedly found that the formulation they preferred was not that elite incomes should be lowered, but that mass incomes should be raised! Second, apparent support by one-third or more for 'slashing' salaries almost certainly exaggerates the effective support this kind of radical policy would in fact find among the intelligentsia. The intelligentsia, as Nigerian experience in the civil service and the army shows, are unlikely to play down their own benefits. Initiatives toward social sacrifice will always tend to founder in practice on the problem of ensuring that all groups see themselves as making an equal sacrifice.[14]

These opinions suggest a general feeling of caution towards advancing social change rather than resistance to particular forms of change, even to forms of change that challenge vested elite interests. The opinions expressed above indicate that a sizeable proportion feel Nigerian society is not justly ordered. This was confirmed when we asked about the extent of satisfaction among various groups with the results of independence (see Table 53).

The students considered top civil servants and big businessmen were the two groups that had gained most out of independence. It is interesting that only some 20 percent thought that the common people were not disappointed with what independence had brought. The data suggests

Table 53. Perceptions on the Results of Independence

'Do you think that there is disappointment with the results of independence among the following groups?'

	ABU, 1970*			
	Much	Some	None	Total
Common people:	59.9%	18.4%	21.7%	100.0%
Lower civil servants:	32.9%	50.3%	16.8%	100.0%
Small businessmen and traders:	22.3%	50.2%	27.5%	100.0%
University students:	32.0%	34.7%	33.3%	100.0%
Big businessmen:	11.5%	34.7%	53.8%	100.0%
High civil servants:	12.6%	30.6%	56.8%	100.0%

* Similar results were obtained at Ibadan and Lagos universities.

that should an upright and competent reforming leadership emerge, it would not encounter an educated elite entirely opposed to reform. Such a leadership would, however, do well to stress the justice of individual reforms and to avoid the resistance and uneasiness that would arise from impressions of over-fast and disruptive change.

3. *THE AUTHORITY OF THE STATE: THE FRAGILITY OF STABILITY*

In discussing social change and reform the question of the State as a sphere of activity is inevitably introduced. Political power centres mainly around the State and its authority groups. The State has varied in its activities in different cultures and at different epochs. The early 19th century Western State, like the early colonial State in West Africa, was primarily geared to maintaining law and order. In the West during the 19th and early 20th centuries, technology and social organization became more complex and the socialist movement increased in influence. The interventionist activities of the State in the economy grew and emphasis in government shifted to include social welfare. Similar developments took place in the colonial States. By the time of independence Nigerian political leaders were deeply committed in public promises to promoting economic growth, spreading education still further and improving health facilities. Law and order received less emphasis in public statements, but some people were disturbed by the use of thugs by the political parties and even more disturbed by the misuse of governmental powers to suppress the regional oppositions.[15]

The appearance of a lack of concern with order was deceptive. Nigerians generally did not take law and order for granted and they were sensitive to the fragility of their new political institutions. For most of Nigeria the second half of the 19th century had been a turbulent period. Folk memories of danger lived on in small communities that had often been threatened with devastation by raiding. The colonial officers had also employed no small measure of force in various areas. Implicit in colonial rule itself was the threat of force. For a long time also (and still to some groups within the Nigerian State) the apparatus of the modern State seemed foreign, new and strange. Finally, one of the most uncomfortable aspects of the new order was that communities were grouped together that had in the past either lived apart or been hostile to one another. Independence removed the colonial arbiter and threw the communities into a direct power relationship with one another that was only barely moderated by constitutional safeguards. If the two military coups showed how fragile political *authority* was, the outbreak of civil war in the

Table 54. Political and Economic Values

A. '*Which are most important for a developing country? (Choose* three).'

Alternative*	Percentages†		
	ABU, 1973	Ibadan, 1972	Nsukka, 1973
National unity and patriotism	78.0%	90.7%	75.1%
Modernizing and technical skills	66.8%	74.7%	59.2%
Abundant economic resources	61.9%	69.1%	58.3%
Efficient civil service	40.2%	30.9%	30.7%
Integrity in all ranks of society	17.8%	22.0%	14.8%
Respect for authority	4.2%	7.4%	8.8%

* Order of alternatives rearranged to reflect results.
† Each student could mark three alternatives: percentages add to more than 100%.

B. '*Number the following in order of importance for a developing country.*'

		ABU, 1970*	
	Modal rank	Percentage of first rankings	Percentage of last rankings
Stable government	1	58.2%	2.2%
National unity	1	29.8%	1.6%
Honest leadership	3	18.8%	3.6%
Rapid economic development	3	8.9%	8.7%
Democratic freedom	5	3.5%	26.7%
Independent foreign policy	6	0.8%	57.2%
		100.0%	100.0%

* Other administrations (Ibadan, 1971 and 1972; and Lagos, 1971 and 1972) produced similar results.

C. *'Rate the following as problems of most African countries.* (Number in order of importance)'

Alternatives*	Modal rankings	ABU, 1973† Percentage of first rankings	Percentage of last rankings
Ethnic and regional loyalties, as opposed to national ones	1	36.2%	7.4%
Corruption among politicians	2	18.8%	4.4%
Corruption among civil servants	3	10.5%	8.5%
Interference and exploitation by developed countries	6	18.8%	25.8%
Lack of educated administrators and technicians	6	10.9%	24.7%
Lack of tolerance and fair play among political activists	6	4.7%	29.2%
		99.9%	100.0%

* Order of alternatives rearranged to reflect responses. See Appendix 2.
† This question was also administered at ABU (1970), Ibadan (1971, 1972), Lagos (1971, 1972), and Nsukka (1973). Ethnicity and corruption were always ranked highest as problems.

country which was the culmination of various ethnic and communal strains showed how fragile the national *community* was.

Nigeria's political background and the students' views on social change led us to expect that student views on politics would lean towards the values of political order. This proved to be the case: national unity and governmental stability were consistently ranked first. The majority of students saw 'ethnic and regional loyalties, as opposed to national ones' as the leading problem facing African countries (Table 54C). Paradoxically, the only student group who did not rank this latter first among problems (they rated ethnic loyalties as a strong second behind 'corruption among politicians') were the Ibo students at Nsukka University who had themselves experienced an ethnically organized secession. The sheer size of the general support for national unity and governmental stability suggests that these values mean a great deal to the great majority of the students. In the contrasting either/or questions presented above in Table 49, unity, stability and order were placed ahead of economic development by all but small minorities. When compared with 'democracy' as a value, as we shall see in Chapter VI, the order-related values again prevailed (see Table 76).

Unity seems to be the crucial expression of the central political value of order. Not only did unity receive considerable direct support in our questionnaires but it also lays behind other answers. Chapter VI contains some evidence of the students preference for a pluralistic unity rather than an absolute and monolithic one. They undoubtedly support unity because they know that it is both a fragile acquisition and a necessary good for peoples who have no alternative to living with one another within one country. In other words, unity is the concrete embodiment of political order in a vast multi-ethnic country.[16] The students almost certainly value it all the more because they come from traditional backgrounds where the unity of the community, particularly the unity of the village, was a value constantly kept before people and a value that was in many cases crucial to the political and ecological survival of the village community.

The emphasis on unity and stability logically entail an appreciation for the role of government. In this respect Nigerians contrast strongly with the distrust of government inherent in, for instance, Western traditions, where modern systems took their shape from long struggles against oppressive and inefficient autocracy. We found little abstract fear of government power on the part of the majority (see Table 55). Over one third of the students were willing to let government have more powers to 'secure greater political unity and faster economic growth' than the (very considerable) powers it already possessed. Only a tiny proportion thought government should be able to exercise only 'weak controls' (Table 55A). Interestingly the considerable majority of ABU students (the only group to whom this question was put) thought that weak government was more dangerous than strong government (Table 55B). They were also more afraid that government would favour a particular group or groups than that it would oppress citizens generally (Table 55C). These findings, it should be emphasized, come after some eight years of military rule and during a period in which many of the students (judging by their conversations) consider that human rights, especially free speech, have been unduly restricted, and in which there is evidence of growing malaise over the lack of freedom in choosing rulers.

The positive attitude towards government is all the more surprising when one thinks of the alien origin, operation and personnel of modern government during the colonial period, and the grievances widely held against the post-independence regimes. Resentment seems to focus on the actual possessors of power or on their incompetent or corrupt use of power rather than on the measure of power vested in their offices. It seems to us that it is the aspiration towards unity and the value placed on stability that underlie the acceptance of government. In recent Nigerian experience weak government has been associated with military coups and communal violence. It is also generally true that in tradition misfortunes are associated with weak rulers in the kingdoms (Bini, Hausa,

GENERAL POLITICAL VALUES: ORDER AND UNITY

Table 55. The Powers of Government

A. *'To secure greater political unity and faster economic growth what kind of powers would you be willing to let government have over its citizens?'*

	ABU, 1971	Ibadan, 1973	Ife, 1973
Absolute control:	9.5%	10.3%	11.4%
Very strong controls:	36.8%	24.7%	24.4%
Medium control (as in Nigeria at present):	48.4%	61.9%	57.0%
Weak controls and let citizens get on with the job themselves:	5.3%	3.1%	7.3%
	100.0%	100.0%	100.0%

B. *'Which do you think is generally worse for a country?'*

	ABU, 1973(A)*
Very strong government:	15.7%
Very weak government:	84.3%
	100.0%

C. *'Of which possibility do people tend to be more afraid?'*

	ABU, 1973 (A)*
The government will amass too much power:	27.1%
The government will be dominated by groups other than those they identify with:	72.9%
	100.0%

* Non-probability sample. See Appendix 1.

Yoruba, for example) and with divided community among the lineage segmentation groups (Ibo, Idoma, Tiv, for example). It is worth remembering that oral traditions among the Hausa testify that one of the reasons why the British with minuscule military forces were able not only to conquer but to maintain control over the huge area of northern Nigeria was that they were quickly able to demonstrate a superior ability to maintain order and peace: 'they would', foretold the malams (surely with some hindsight), 'stop wars [slave raiding], they would repair the world, they would stop oppression and lawlessness'.[17]

We do not want to emphasize order alone. Welfare is also a factor as people look to government for modernizing initiatives, especially in terms of the provision of infra-structure (roads, water supplies, electricity), location of industrial and agricultural projects, and the distribution of social welfare amenities (schools and clinics).

The students' views on the relation between the Federal centre and the States are consistent with their support for strong government. We said in Chapter 3 that the States represent an important level of social identity; the preference for strong government (and for unity) helps to explain the general centralist position on Federal problems. The majority were willing to have Federal power expand at the expense of state power (Table 56A), and most of them would prefer to participate in politics at Federal rather than State level (Table 56B).[18] The support for Federal power is historically interesting.[19] Events during the post-independence period, especially from 1964 to 1970, showed the dangers of participation at the Federal centre, and large numbers of people demonstrated by migration that they

Table 56. Federal and State Power

A. *'In most Federal systems elsewhere in the world, either the Federal government gets more powerful at the expense of the States, or the States get more powerful at the expense of the Federal government. Assuming that one or the other has to happen, which would you prefer in the Nigerian case?'*

	ABU, 1973	Ife, 1973
States to have more power:	17.4%	21.3%
Federal government to have more power:	82.6%	78.7%
	100.0%	100.0%

B. *'If you were to become a politician, at which level would you most like to participate?'*

	ABU, 1971	Ife, 1973
Federal:	72.1%	62.1%
State:	27.9%	37.9%
	100.0%	100.0%

C. *'Should the new (12) States have the same or less powers than the former Regions?'*

	ABU, 1971	Ibadan, 1973	Ife, 1973
More:	18.7%	20.6%	21.9%
About the same:	25.9%	40.2%	46.9%
Less:	55.4%	39.2%	31.2%
	100.0%	100.0%	100.0%

felt they needed to return to their home areas to be safe. Yet once educated groups, such as the students, accept the need for Nigerians to live together within one State, the majority seems to realize that there is no alternative to a national, even if understood in a Federal sense, constitutional logic. They may fear that centrifugal tendencies in the country would be fostered by increasing State powers. Under the present constitutional arrangements, the States have, in fact, inherited the powers of the former Regions, but their multiplicity and their administrative and economic failings have weakened them in relation to the Federal government. The relative strength of the centre and the States is going to be a crucial issue in future constitutional discussions in Nigeria. A willingness on the part of the intelligentsia to accept a stronger centre and a move towards Federal politics (the latter is in stark contrast with decisions in the past by leading politicians) could consolidate the unity of the country and allow time to find a balance between its components as well as a central sense of direction.

4. POLITICAL VALUES AND ECONOMIC DEVELOPMENT

Earlier in this chapter we cited van den Berghe's expression of a widely-held view: that Third World elites 'have eagerly adopted a pervasive ideology of change, . . . especially economic development . . .' We adopted this widely-held assumption as a hypothesis, expecting that for young, highly educated Nigerians the achievement of rapid economic development would function as a prime value. We have indicated already that we were forced by our results to modify this expectation considerably. The tests reported above (Table 49), where economic development was placed in competition with political order values, indicated that the students' concern for economic development was not an overriding one. Few students were willing to sacrifice stability and unity to achieve more rapid economic development.

A more complete perspective on the relation of economic development to other valued objects of government policy is provided by the two-way competitions reported in Table 57. All of the problems posed in Table 57 are relevant to Nigeria. The first four pairs represent major problems of contemporary public policy. The economic growth alternatives performed better when ranged against such objects of public policy as indigenisation of ownership and management of the economy, jobs for (university) graduates, and expanding the educational system, than when they were placed in competition with the primary political values of stability and unity. However, the groups of students still tended to divide about equally as to relative importance in these contests. An important

GENERAL POLITICAL VALUES: ORDER AND UNITY 125

Table 57. The Importance of Economic Development

'In each pair mark the one that you consider more valuable or important'.

	ABU, 1973	Ibadan, 1973	Nsukka, 1973
Rapid economic indigenisation:	43.5%	52.2%	36.3%
Rapid economic growth:	56.5%	47.8%	63.7%
	100.0%	100.0%	100.0%
Keeping up with the demand for jobs for qualified graduates:	53.3%	55.7%	73.7%
Rapid economic growth:	46.7%	44.3%	26.3%
	100.0%	100.0%	100.0%
Rapid expansion of education:	59.8%	49.7%	44.5%
Expansion of industrial capacity:	40.2%	50.3%	55.5%
	100.0%	100.0%	100.0%
Agricultural development:	73.5%	52.2%	57.7%
Industrialization:	26.5%	47.8%	42.3%
	100.0%	100.0%	100.0%
Overcoming poverty:	34.9%	32.4%	37.7%
Overcoming ignorance:	65.1%	67.6%	62.3%
	100.0%	100.0%	100.0%
Creating a strong national culture:	25.1%	27.0%	26.4%
Creating a strong national economy:	74.9%	73.0%	73.6%
	100.0%	100.0%	100.0%

priority emerged when the problem of 'poverty' was posed against 'ignorance': for about two-thirds of the students, overcoming ignorance was the more important of the two problems. For most the two are probably inseparably linked, but ignorance was seen as the most urgent in terms of solution.

Variations between the university samples reflect regional economic disparities. Both the ABU and the Nsukka students showed less enthusiasm for indigenisation against economic growth than the Ibadan students who tend to come from ethnic groups, and often from families, more likely to profit from indigenisation in the immediate future. A considerably larger proportion of students at Nsukka, mainly from the Ibo ethnic group and the East Central State where, since the war opportunities for graduates have been inadequate, opted for graduate jobs over rapid overall growth. We can consider whether this should be taken as a suggestion that as university students in other parts of the country begin to face a diminishing demand for their skills they are likely to put their group interests ahead of wider ones. A clear majority of ABU students, mostly from the northern States where underdeveloped educational systems are a major obstacle to all forms of development, favoured expansion of education over industrial expansion. The majority of Nsukka students, from areas where the educational systems are already relatively well-developed, opted for industrial expansion. Nearly three-quarters of the ABU students voted for agricultural development over industrialization. At the two southern universities smaller majorities were in favour of agricultural development.

These variations between the university samples seemed to be provoked by questions on relatively specific and concrete problems which were readily translatable into government policies. It will be recalled (see Table 49) that when economic development was tested against the relatively abstract values of unity and law and order, little inter-university variation was apparent. It is interesting that when the education problem was posed in more abstract terms ('poverty' versus 'ignorance') systematic variation between the university samples disappeared.

The same lack of variation is apparent in the equally abstract contest between 'strong national culture' and 'strong national economy'. Some readers may be surprised by the very strong majority (almost three-quarters) against the cultural alternative. On the basis of unstructured observation, we suggest that this result is a true reflection of an area of unease and ambivalence among the members of Nigeria's highly educated elite. When Nigeria was preparing during 1974-75 to act as host in a grand manner to the Black Arts Festival,[20] all around the country large competitive festivals were held to develop Nigeria's own entries. There was, in consequence, a great emphasis on Nigeria's indigenous culture, especially dancing, with widely reported festivals occurring in the capital cities of the States. At the same time letters to the newspapers, statements at academic symposia, etc., indicated that many educated persons felt uneasy about the emphasis on purely indigenous cultural expressions.[21] Some felt that movements towards 'authenticity' as in Chad and Zaire could develop; others reacted against the association of cultural traditions with tribal ones; and others again reacted against elements of the indigenous traditions such as semi-nudity. Above all, many complained that money in a poor country was being badly spent; and that Nigeria in any case would be judged by the rest of the world in the immediate future much less by cultural than by economic achievement. Understandably under these circumstances the Muhammed government decided both to postpone and to scale down the festival. At the same time we have noted in Chapter 4 the ambivalence toward the 'Western' (properly, world) culture of modernity in which the educated elites are participants. Ambivalent attitudes towards cultural affairs reflect both the collective historical experience of colonialism and the personal experience of an educational system still only partially reoriented from its colonial origins.

The results presented in Table 57 together with other questions reproduced above provide us with a considerable range of information, though rather inexact information, about the place of economic development in the students' value structure. The most significant finding is that economic development seems to lack for most students the imperative value quality which the hypothesis mentioned at the beginning of the section would have suggested. If hypothetically extended to wider circles of educated elites, in particular those already occupying high positions of political power, then the often lackadaisical approach to comprehensive development policy in post-independence Nigeria becomes easier to understand. However, economic development has a solid place in a middle range of values where the students as a whole divide fairly evenly in deciding between various objects of government policy.

The general lack of visible concern in Nigeria with the idea of Stalinesque forced development through the sacrifice of a generation, or even the more gentle prescriptions of liberal development economists regarding public savings and productive investment, become more

Table 58. Economic Development and Sacrifice

A. *'Do you agree or disagree with the following statement: "The sacrifice of present generations for future generations is a choice which must be made if rapid economic development is to be achieved"?'*

	ABU, 1970	Ibadan, 1972	Lagos, 1972
Agree:	85.8%	96.1%	91.0%
Disagree:	14.2%	3.9%	9.0%
	100.0%	100.0%	100.0%

B. *'Should present generations be made to sacrifice for future generations so as to achieve rapid economic development?'*

	ABU, 1973	Ibadan, 1973	Nsukka, 1973
Yes:	80.0%	83.1%	74.6%
No:	20.0%	16.9%	25.4%
	100.0%	100.0%	100.0%

understandable when we see that economic development is ranked in a middle range of public priorities rather than in the highest rank. Yet our surveys persistently showed that strong majorities accepted sacrifice as necessary to achieve rapid economic development (see Table 58A). When we subsequently put the question in value terms strong majorities were in favour of the proposition (Table 58B).

The willingness to accept present sacrifice seems surprising when juxtaposed with what has already been shown in terms of the overall priority given to economic development. It should be related to the willingness expressed by between one third and one half of the students to have the incomes of their own social stratum 'slashed' in order to narrow the gaps in income differentials (Table 52). It can also be related to the willingness discussed below (Table 62B) to put rural development ahead of jobs for university graduates. There seems to be in the student culture a certain generalized predisposition toward sacrifice for social goals, not only in terms of the society as a whole but also in terms specific to the interests of the highly educated elite. In our opinion this predisposition toward the abstract idea of sacrifice shared by considerable numbers of the students is not generally recognized in Nigeria, and until the establishment of the 'National Youth Service Corps' for university graduates in 1973 was not drawn on by government. The experience of the National Youth Service Corps, on the other hand, has illustrated the inevitability of difficulties in translating an abstract willingness to sacrifice into concrete effort.

The phrase 'economic development' tends to bring to mind central government planning and action. It is in this light that the findings so far reported (including the willingness to sacrifice for development) have been interpreted. But it should be recognized that 'economic development' may have a different meaning for many of the students. This is suggested by the results of the question reported in Table 59. The question was phrased in terms of groups rather than institutions, policies, or technical and material inputs. It is striking that the two groups, civil servants and 'able politicians', connected with a national government role in economic development were considered the least important 'force' by the majority of students, whereas a strong modal first place was accorded to innovative rural communities ('farming communities that accept innovation'). The modal second choice was the other 'communalist' alternative, the role played by the educated persons (the 'elites') in their communities of origin: bringing and remitting money, stimulating innovation and helping to secure 'amenities' for the community. Together, these two alternatives accounted for nearly two-thirds of first and second choices. Similar results were obtained in administrations at two southern

GENERAL POLITICAL VALUES: ORDER AND UNITY

Table 59. Factors in Economic Development

'*What are the most important forces in economic development? (Number in order of importance)*'

Alternative*	Modal ranking	ABU, 1971† Percentage of first rankings	Percentage of last rankings
Farming communities that accept innovation:	1	42.8%	6.0%
Educated persons who help their own communities:	2	17.7%	19.5%
Businessmen with initiative:	2-3	14.6%	13.5%
Civil servants committed to the public good:	3-4	12.6%	12.6%
Able politicians:	5	6.9%	48.3%
		100.0%	99.0%

* Order of the alternatives rearranged to reflect results: see Appendix 2.
† Administrations at Ife (1973) and Ibadan (1973) produced similar results.

universities (Ife, 1973 and Ibadan, 1973). In all cases, 'farming communities' was consistently ranked in first place, and civil servants and politicians were fourth and fifth, respectively.

These findings suggest that for the students economic development consists of the development of the communities: improved income through innovative farming and local commerce, communications, and creation of educational, health and other facilities. This is an interesting reminder that all over the country much of the transformation that has occurred over the last half century is in fact largely due to the responsiveness and initiative of communities, much of which can be traced to the action of 'educated persons who help their own communities'.

With reference to the role of government in economic development, interesting results were produced by the question shown in Table 60. Students were asked to choose between faster economic growth and even distribution. Modern governments in every country must balance the two functions of growth and distribution. The problem is particularly clear and acute in Nigeria, with its history of bitter regional conflict and the heritage of differential development which has provided much of the basis for that conflict. Nigeria's planning documents have attempted to balance the objective of growth with distribution, allocating major new projects to the various parts of the country even at some cost to growth. When faced with a stark choice, two-thirds or more of the students

Table 60. Distribution of Wealth

'If you had to choose, which do you think is preferable?'

	ABU, 1973	Ibadan, 1973	Nsukka, 1973
'Faster economic growth which creates inequalities between areas now, but which promises to make every area richer some time in the future'	19.6%	30.9%	28.3%
'Slower overall economic growth in which benefits are more evenly spread among different areas'	80.4%	69.1%	71.7%
	100.0%	100.0%	100.0%

considered distribution more important than rapid growth.[22] These answers again confirm that rapid growth is seen as secondary in value to political stability and unity, for it is stability and unity that is at stake when the question of equality and inequality is raised. Finally, the results suggest that the predominantly northern ABU students were still more willing than the students of the southern universities to place even distribution ahead of rapid growth. It is the north which historically has suffered from the disparities in educational and industrial development, and in fact the call for more balanced development has been something of a rallying cry for northern leaders. The fact that the southern students were nevertheless willing in almost as high proportions to put distribution before growth is another confirmation that the stability of the whole is valued ahead of strictly economic interests.

The question shown in Table 60 focused on *areal* inequalities in the distribution of economic benefits. Historically, inequalities within, but especially between, the major Regions have been a most important source of political conflict and have posed the greatest problems for political stability. There is now evidence of a growing awareness on the part of Nigeria's privileged highly educated elite of the significance of the extreme inequalities in the post-independence society. Sensitivity to inequality is indicated in the students' responses to the question shown in Table 61. The students were asked to rank the three forms of inequality most important in contemporary Nigeria: between the rich and the poor; between the cities and towns and the rural villages; and between the different areas and regions. Among each group of students the largest proportion felt that closing the rich-poor gap was the most important objective. It is interesting that a larger proportion of the ABU students, predominantly from the

Table 61. Inequalities

'Which of the following political objectives do you consider the most desirable in Nigeria?'

	ABU, 1973	Ibadan, 1973	Nsukka, 1973
Reducing the gap between the rich people and the poor people	43.1%	53.1%	45.2%
Reducing the disparity between the towns and the countryside	19.8%	27.1%	25.9%
Closing the gap in development between different areas	37.1%	19.8%	28.9%
	100.0%	100.0%	100.0%

poorer northern States, inclined to the areal distribution alternative, while the Ibadan students, predominantly from what are presently the best developed areas, were least concerned about that alternative. More of the Nsukka and Ibadan students than the ABU students showed concern with the discrepancy between city and village.

We were interested in knowing more about the directions of the students' sympathy for the underprivileged groups of Nigeria. We asked the questions shown in Table 62. The striking feature of the results is the strong sympathy for the farmers. The foreign observer of the Nigerian scene would be likely to say that it is the urban unfortunates (the unemployed above all, and the clerks and workers secondarily) who are most miserable in present day Nigeria. Unlike the farmers, they must rely on the market for food, pay for their housing (often at exorbitant rates) and they are intensely exposed to the demonstration effect of minority affluence. They suffer in a most exposed way from the impact of inflation. Yet the sympathy of the majority of the students was overwhelmingly with the farmers, and the primary teachers edged out the urban unemployed for second place. A larger majority of ABU students ranked farmers in first place on this question than students from Ibadan and Nsukka. At Nsukka in fact primary teachers were given almost as much sympathy as farmers.[23] It is noteworthy that a significantly smaller proportion of the Nsukka students come themselves from farming families (see Chapter 2). The sympathy for the teachers can best be explained by occupational similarity with the students and the latter's regard for men who have helped them to advance. Many of the students have been teachers themselves, at least briefly. Often primary teachers are established elders in the communities; the students have all been in a position to judge at first hand their material

Table 62. Dimensions of Sympathy

A. *'A number of groups in Nigerian society are sometimes described as exploited and/or suffering. For which do you have the most sympathy? (Number in order of most sympathy)'.*

Alternatives*	Modal ranking	ABU, 1973† Percentage of first rankings	Percentage of last rankings
Farmers:	1	62.7%	4.5%
Teachers (primary level):	2	16.5%	12.2%
Urban unemployed:	2	14.8%	15.9%
Low-level clerical, messengers, etc.:	4	2.8%	18.4%
Urban industrial workers:	5	3.2%	49.0%
		100.0%	100.0%

B. *'In each pair, mark the one you consider more important'.*

	ABU, 1973	Ibadan, 1973	Nsukka, 1973
Keeping up with the demand for jobs for qualified graduates:	19.1%	23.5%	28.2%
Raising the standard of living of the farmers:	80.9%	76.5%	71.8%
	100.0%	100.0%	100.0%
Urban amenities:	15.1%	10.9%	16.6%
Rural amenities:	84.9%	89.1%	83.4%
	100.0%	100.0%	100.0%

* Order of alternatives rearranged to reflect results; see Appendix 2.
† Ibadan (1973) and Nsukka (1973) produced the same overall pattern but farmers were lower and teachers higher than in either the ABU, 1973 sample shown or the ABU, 1971 sample.

circumstances. Primary teachers are in fact badly paid by the standards of other elite groups; they are often badly housed, they do not have the prestige of the more highly educated elites and the majority have to serve in the smaller towns and the villages. In Nigeria the teachers are the wretched of the educated classes. Yet for all this the teachers are better paid, better fed and better housed than the majority of urban workers.

Nothing demonstrates more clearly the rural origins of the vast majority of university students than their lack of sympathy for urban workers in comparison with farmers and teachers. The students know little of the industrial workers; only a tiny proportion at any of the universities come from urban working class families. It is probable that they tend to see the worker as a new and interstitial rather than an enduring and structural element on the Nigerian urban scene. One suspects that the students attitudes cast light on general attitudes of the administrative and other educated groups towards lower paid workers. The authors of the 1970-74 Nigerian development plan, for instance, advanced the argument (based on estimates of cash income) that the town workers were doing disproportionately well in comparison with the farmers.

The pattern of rural sympathies is confirmed by the two competitive pairs shown in part B of Table 62. A very strong majority of the students ranked raising the standard of living of farmers ahead of keeping up with the demand for jobs for university graduates. It will be recalled that only a minority were willing to put the more general objective of 'economic development' ahead of jobs for graduates (Table 57). An even stronger majority thought that 'amenities' (i.e. services and infrastructure) should be directed to the underdeveloped rural areas rather than the already better served urban areas (in which latter, it should be remembered, most of the graduates will spend most of their working lives). It is noteworthy, however, that in the south, where the question of graduate employment is closer to being a real problem, the majorities in favour of raising farmers incomes were slightly lower, just as earlier we saw that Nsukka students, who will tend to have the most trouble finding jobs, were considerably less willing to rank economic development above jobs for graduates. The suggestion is that, ironically, as sacrifice becomes more likely to be called for, it may be less forthcoming.

As a final perspective to the question of economic development we can consider the present ebullience of the oil-fed Nigerian economy, which may account for some of the mixed and partially contradictory attitudes reviewed above. A general question on students' expectations with regard

Table 63. Rate of Economic Development

'How fast do you expect that Nigeria's economic development will progress in the next twenty years?'

	ABU, 1973	Ibadan, 1973	Nsukka, 1973
Very rapidly:	6.4%	15.6%	8.0%
Rapidly:	54.6%	38.3%	36.7%
Moderate speed:	34.8%	42.2%	45.6%
Slowly:	4.2%	3.9%	9.7%
	100.0%	100.0%	100.0%

to economic development indicated optimism among the majority. Seven separate administrations of this question at four universities are available; in only one (Nsukka, 1973) was the proportion marking either 'very rapidly' or 'rapidly' less than 50 percent. The proportion opting for 'slowly' was less than 5 percent in all administrations except for Nsukka, and even there it was less than 10 percent. This general optimism undoubtedly conditions attitudes toward economic development; undoubtedly, also, it helps to condition personal expectations and to explain the general satisfaction with personal career prospects or expectations.

5. CONCLUSION

This chapter has revolved around issues of social change, economic development and political order. University students (and graduates) are simultaneously subjects, agents and beneficiaries of the rapid change taking place in developing countries like Nigeria. Western observers have in general been quick to assume their commitment to rapid change in the direction of 'modernization' and 'development', but our findings emphasize that most students are cautious with regard to social change in the abstract, and that the political values of order, stability and unity are placed above all other values. Few students were willing to accept social disruption in order to achieve more rapidly goals involving major social change and thus to 'get it over with'. Emphasis on order, however, does not necessarily imply an uncompromising or even a general support for the status quo. The majority of the students indicated at least an abstract support for a Chinese-style transformation, and a surprisingly strong minority indicated support for 'slashing' the incomes of Nigeria's elites. 'Restructuring society to bring social justice' won strong minority support even against the alternative of 'law and order and political stability'. Our examination has made it clear that one can assume neither automatic support for social change nor automatic opposition to social change. Students are undoubtedly sensitive to issues that touch on their own interests, and their reactions will probably be determined by how closely specific issues of change are associated with positive values such as social justice, on the one hand, and with the negative values of disorder, disunity, and instability on the other. It seems fair to say that for the majority strong impulses toward justice and improvement co-exist with an even stronger appreciation of order and resistance to disruptively rapid change.

In the political realm, our surveys demonstrate repeatedly the primacy within the student value structure of an order-related triad: law and order, political stability and unity. We have argued that the emphasis on political stability and national unity can be understood both in the more recent historical context of Nigerian electoral politics and in relation to the older traditions of smaller-scale societies. As is made clear by the results described in Chapter 4, the value placed on unity does not imply the existence of overriding nationalist impulses among the students. The students also accepted the reality of social diversity, reflecting an understanding of the post-independence multi-ethnic structure. Unity is for the students what might be called an 'aspirational value'. The value exists, and is given much of its force, by the understanding of the fact of disunity in the country. It is the very fragility of stability which helps to explain its prime value for the great majority of the students. Taken together, we consider that the order triad of values can be expected to act as a powerful mediator when students react to other value problems, whether posed in the abstract or raised by topical issues.

The emphasis placed by students on unity and stability was associated above with a general appreciation of the role of government. Few expressed abstract fear of strong government; weak government was feared more than strong government. Similarly, a strong majority supported Federal power against State power when forced to choose between the two. Given that most of the students acknowledged strong positive orientations toward their own States, we believe that the greater strength of the positive orientation toward strong central government, associated with the stability and unity of the whole, explains why so many adopted a Federalist position when the question of Federal-State power relations was posed. This is one reason for the weak defence since 1966 of the States' rights dimension of Federalism in the face of the steady erosion of States' powers.

We were interested, in particular, in student attitudes towards economic development. Our major finding was that for the majority of the students economic development was subsidiary in priority to the fundamental political values (the order triad). Economic development, contrary to expectations deriving from some descriptive literature about third world elites, was ranked instead in a middle value range, and was considered less important than the more particular interests of certain groups, such as farmers and university graduates. The lack of concern with rapid overall national economic growth may be connected with the weakness of social identification with the State. The majority of students demonstrated their overriding concern with the maintenance of Nigeria's fragile unity and political stability by attaching greater importance to the government's role in the *distribution* of resources than its role in *growth*. Two other factors also condition the lack of concern with the government's role in economic development. First, for the majority of students, 'economic development' denoted the development of the communities at least as much as change in the macro indicators. At the community level, the initiative of the people themselves was considered most important in bringing development. Second, only a tiny minority was pessimistic about Nigeria's economic progress in the coming years; the majority was optimistic, reflecting the reality of Nigeria's current oil boom in the context of which 'development' seems to look after itself.

Finally, in connection with economic development, we explored the directions of sympathy for less privileged groups which might condition attitudes toward patterns of future economic change. We found that the mainly rural origins of this generation of university students were apparent in the strong patterns of sympathy toward the farmers and the rural underdeveloped areas. At the same time we found strikingly less sympathy among the majority for the underprivileged groups of the urban sector, especially the industrial workers. We think that this pattern of rural/urban sympathy/non-sympathy both helps to explain certain past and present patterns of public policy, and also would seem to be fraught with important consequences for Nigeria's future.

A conception of the State is implied in the answers we have been discussing. The students saw the State as a framework rather than a motor; they expected political authority to arbitrate rather than to lead and saw the political system as distributing rather than creating economic wealth. Both traditional and colonial conceptions of the State probably buttress such attitudes. The colonial State, in its origins and over much of its life-span, was geared to the maintenance of order, presiding over a mass of individual communities. In traditional systems power was used to arbitrate and regulate, above all to maintain the order of the community against internal and external threats. Traditional authority's economic role often included functions of conservation (against emergencies) and distribution, but rarely creation of new wealth.

The last decades of colonial rule (and the first years of independence) reinforced the image of the political authority providing and dispensing the things valued by communities. It is not surprising that this image should be stronger than that of the State as the macro-level organizer of overall growth. Sklar rightly emphasizes the theme of distribution (using the concept of welfare) when he describes the political party appeals to the electorate in Nigeria and summarises:

> In a sense the welfare state is a cultural imperative of communal society: industrialization at the expense of welfare would require the repudiation or disregard of communitarian principles which have been affirmed by Nigerian leaders.[24]

But if distribution is more important than growth, the relation—in a complex multi-ethnic society— of distribution to order must be kept in mind. The fragile unity of the Nigerian whole must be maintained through an adequately fair distribution to areas, ethnic groups and social classes. In this fashion the primary value position of the order-related goals of unity, stability and law and order can be expected to mediate positions on issues which involve other political values.

FOOTNOTES

1. The phrase is found in C. Achebe, *A Man of the People* (London: Heinemann, 1966), p.42; See quotation above, p.105.
2. The most comprehensive study of the nationalist period is J. S. Coleman, *Nigeria: Background to Nationalism* (Berkeley and Los Angeles: University of California Press, 1958). There is supplementary material in R. S. Sklar, *Nigerian Political Parties* (Princeton: Princeton University Press, 1963); K. W. J. Post, *op. cit.*, (London: Sweet and Maxwell, 1963); K. Ezra, *Constitutional Development in NIgeria* (London: Cambridge University Press, 1960); L. Blitz (editor), *The Politics and Administration of Nigerian Government* (London: Sweet and Maxwell, 1965); B. J. Dudley, *Parties and Politics in Northern Nigeria* (London: Frank Cass, 1968); J. P. Mackintosh, *Nigerian Government and Politics* (London: Allen and Unwin, 1966); C. S. Whitaker, Jr., *The Politics of Tradition: Continuity and Change in Northern Nigeria 1946-1966* (Princeton: Princeton University Press, 1970); R. Melson and H. Wolpe, *op. cit.* For the period of Legislative Council politics, see T. N. Tamuno, *Nigeria and Elective Representation 1923-1947* (London and Ibadan: Heinemann, 1966) and J. Wheare, *The Nigerian Legislative Council* (London: Faber, 1950).
3. An early manifestation of the problem of indigenization was the resentment that developed on the part of the native-born Nigerians against the 'Sierra Leonean' elite dominance of the elected legislative council seats as well as of civil service posts open to Africans.
4. The northern Provinces, where Lugard's policy of indirect rule had been given freest rein, were not represented in the Legaslative Council arrangements from 1923 to 1947.
5. Benjamin Nnamdi Azikiwe (he later dropped the 'Benjamin') was born at Zungeru, Northern Nigeria in 1904. He came of an Onitsha Ibo family. In 1925 he made his way to the United States where he received a university education. He returned to Nigeria in 1937 (after a spell in the Gold Coast). He founded *The West African Pilot* and other newspaper and gave a skilled and flamboyant twist to nationalist journalism. He was the effective founder of the NCNC and eventually became the first President of the Federal Republic (1963).
6. In addition to the parties whose formation has already been noted the Northern Elements Progressive Union (NEPU) was founded in 1950, which grouped the more radical of politically conscious young men in the North many of whom were not only strongly critical of British rule but also of the emirate native authority system.
7. See C. S. Whitaker, *op. cit.*, pp.363-375 for NPC organisation, and pp.375-384 for NEPU.
8. On the 'political class' see J. O'Connell, "Political Integration: The Nigerian Case" in Hazlewood (editor), *African Integration and Disintegration* (London: Oxford University Press, 1967), especially pp.159-160.
9. O. Aboyade, "Relations Between Central and Local Institutions in the Development Process" in A. Rivkin (editor) *Nations By Design* (Garden City, N.Y.: Doubleday, 1968), p.101.
10. C. Achebe, *op. cit.;* p.181.
11. H. Seton-Watson, *Neither War Nor Peace* (London: Methuen, 1960), p.176.

12. P. van den Berghe, "Major Themes in Social Change" in J. S. Paden and E. W. Soja (editors), *The African Experience* (Evanston: Northwestern University Press, 1970), Vol. I, p.255.
13. An earlier and less abrasive version of this question had asked 'Should the standard of living of Nigeria's civil servants be revised downward to be closer to that of the "masses"?: the answers were much the same as those to the question discussed in the text.
14. On incomes in Nigeria, see O. Teriba and O. A. Philips, "Income Distribution and National Integration", *Nigerian Journal of Economic and Social Studies,* Vol. 13, No. 1 (March, 1971), pp.77-122. The Udoji Commission remarked: 'The overall range of salaries from the bottom to the top of the salary schedule is too great for a public service which intends to move in the direction of an egalitarian society, a differential of which employees at the lower ranks of the salary scale are very conscious'. *Public Service Review Commission Main Report,* p.159. The Commission claimed to make recommendations that reduced salary differentials from 30:1 to 10:1. Yet the upshot of both the Commission's report and the Federal government's white paper on the report is to create much greater absolute differences than before between upper and lower salary earners. It looks as if the road towards closing salary gaps in Nigeria is paved with good intentions.
15. The Nigerian novelists in particular have depicted how people disliked, feared and reacted against violence in politics. This theme recurs constantly in Achebe, *op. cit.,* Ekwensi, *Iska* (London: Hutchinson, 1966), and T. M. Aluko, *Chief the Honourable Minister* (Heinemann, 1967).
16. Perhaps what Aristide Zolberg has written in a related context is worth citing in relation to our findings: 'What is striking is that the regimes (one party systems in West Africa) ... do not find it desirable to maintain even the public facade of debate. Since it can be assumed that this could easily be arranged, we must conclude that the desire to maintain unanimity is greater than the concern to demonstrate the persistence of democracy.' A. Zolberg, *Creating Political Order* (Chicago: Rand McNally, 1966), p.112.
17. M. F. Smith, *Baba of Karo: A Woman of the Muslim Hausa* (London: Faber, 1959), p.66.
18. Throughout the independence period the leader of the NPC, Alhaji Sir Ahmadu Bello, and the leader of the NCNC, Dr. Michael Okpara, remained as Regional Premiers in their base Regions, North and East respectively.
19. It should be noted that Ibadan and Ife opt much more than ABU to leave the States with similar powers to those of the former Regions. But overall the results in Table 56 seem to indicate that once more States are created there is likely to be a greater acceptance of reduced powers for them.
20. Second World Black and African Festival of Arts and Culture.
21. See, for example, contrasting views in the *New Nigerian* 20/2/1975 and 26/2/1975. Of the spate of polemical articles and letters that the festival has generated the considerable majority has been hostile. One of the first decisions of the re-constituted Federal Military Government in July, 1975 was to postpone the Festival.
22. Perhaps the attitudes of the students bear more than a passing resemblance to the outlook on the planning of development under the civilian governments that Ojetunji Aboyade writes about bitterly: 'For purposes of planned development, there was not so much a government as a collection of regions at the centre ... (The Federal government) was caught in the continuous struggle for regional economic advantage, especially as the resource picture became less promising as the years rolled by ... This struggle for regional economic advantage—known in Nigerian journalistic parlance as 'sharing the national cake'—provides the key to understanding the planning strategy and plan implementation'. O. Aboyade in A. Rivkin (editor), *op. cit.,* p.101.
23. The Ibo students at Nsukka put 'teachers' slightly ahead of 'farmers' for sympathy in their first place choices: 47.4 percent against 44.2 percent.
24. R. S. Sklar, *op. cit.,* p.504.

6 Participation and Democracy: The Dynamics of Politics in Nigeria

1 INTRODUCTION

'If'—Almond and Verba have argued:

> ... there is a political revolution going on throughout the world, it is what might be called the participation explosion. In all the new nations of the world the belief that the ordinary man is politically relevant—that he ought to be an involved participant in the political system—is widespread. Large groups of people who have been outside of politics are demanding entrance into the political system. And the political elites are rare who do not profess commitment to this goal.[1]

These generalizations are obviously relevant to the period of terminal colonialism when in fact colonized majorities were "exploding" into participation within colonial systems of power previously closed to them, and political elites were claiming authority deriving from the (liberal) rights of the common man. A decade later, however, we must acknowledge that there is a naive ring to this statement.

There are two reasons for including the above statement by Almond and Verba. The first, which is disciplinary and methodological, is our conviction that a fairly simple ideological/normative adherence to the basic tenets of the Western liberal democratic heritage is deeply imbedded within the major theoretical work so far done in the study of political culture, and one might as well be conscious of it. The second, more substantive, reason for the initial reference is that it points us toward what seems at present to be the major structural and normative problem facing the Nigerian policy: *the institutionalization of participation (input) within a heritage of authoritarian administration (output).* Students (like most other politically conscious groups in the society) consider Nigeria's first experience (up to January 15 1966) with democratic institutions to have been a failure. As elsewhere in Africa, many of the students argue against the simple equation of "democracy" with the competitive party forms which derive mainly from Western European and North American experience. Yet it is likewise clear that for a sizeable majority of politically conscious Nigerians the present situation of military government, which can be seen as a return, in its broad outlines, to the heritage of the benevolent colonial administrative state, cannot be considered a permanently satisfactory institutional solution.[2] It is striking that in Nigeria, as in most other African situations of military rule, the military itself has not asserted the legitimacy of permanent military rule, but rather continues to acknowledge the ideological principle that government can only be finally legitimated by some kind of formalized participation by "the people" in the selection of power-holders and the determination of policies. It is likewise striking that despite criticism of Western competitive democracy's exclusive right to the title "democracy", and a certain envy for the apparent simplicity and unity of the presently stable African single party systems, most Nigerian political thinking continues to assume that political parties will again compete for legislative and executive roles within a universal suffrage system.

We are not imposing our Western traditions, therefore, when we say that democracy remains perhaps the largest structural problem of the Nigerian polity, meaning by democracy some form of elections, parties, legislature and executive in which rules are made by elected representatives, and the whole (including the top executive figures) are normatively responsible to "the people". Democracy is at the moment Nigeria's major unfinished business. The question is likely to retain its significance for a long time. The abstract alternatives, after all, are not many. At the two extremes are stable one-party rule, able more or less permanently to contain the dynamics of Nigerian society, and permanent military dictatorship. In between, there is the possibility, already pioneered by other African politics, of pendulum systems, alternating between elected civilian regimes and military rule.[3] It is for these reasons that we have chosen to order this discussion of student attitudes regarding political dynamics in Nigeria around the overall theme of democracy.

2. PERCEPTIONS OF POLITICAL REALITY

(a) Why it failed: politics in the First Republic
Anyone who has read the basic descriptive and interpretive literature on Nigerian politics could (as the introduction to Chapter 5 illustrates) suggest major characteristics and patterns in political interaction of the 1951-66 period. However, the university students have not, for the most part, read

that literature.[4] The weight that the students assigned to the various general forces at play in Nigerian politics, and in particular their diagnosis of what went wrong with the First Republic interested us, not as a source of new knowledge about past politics (it must be borne in mind that the majority of the present generation of university students were in the last years of primary school when the last elections were held in Nigeria), but as an insight into the students' general evaluation of politics, and the implications for future participation.

The students were questioned on the weaknesses of the first Nigerian Republic and on how politicians won support from people. They were asked to rate a series of problems "of most African countries". In each case lists of relevant alternatives evolved through pre-testing were provided. Both relative (competitive) ranking and simple choice techniques were used. The results produced by the different questions show considerable consistency. In every formula, ethnicity ("ethnic bitterness", "ethnic and regional loyalties as opposed to national ones", or simply "ethnicity") was ranked far ahead of other alternatives, *both as a characteristic and a problem* of Nigerian politics.[5] This result is unsurprising to any observer of Nigerian politics and the literature on it, but it is also a highly significant finding. It is the opposite of the unity ideal which found so central a place in our discussion of value structure.

Table 64 shows four major categories of problems we put to the students, which can be labelled as: ethnicity, leadership and corruption, incivility, and neo-colonialism. In both the specifically Nigerian formulation and the general "African" one (designed to check for wishful thinking and answering on the "Nigerian" question) the faults of leadership were ranked second after ethnicity. Corruption was seen as a problem in government and society as well as in politics, but it was associated primarily with politicians and only secondarily with civil servants. There was some variation between Nigerian and African contexts in the third most important factor, but this is more easily explained by differences in formulation than by other factors. Each question included what can be called an incivility alternative. In the question relating to Nigeria (Table 64A) this alternative ('unrestrained use of power against opponents') was placed clearly in the middle rank, while in the African question (Table 64B) 'lack of tolerance and fair play' was ranked lowest. Nigerian students may have heard first-hand stories, or perhaps experienced personally, political suppression in Nigeria, but the simplest explanation is that the Nigerian formulation ("unrestrained use of power against opponents") may have had more impact than the less positive formulation in the African question ("lack of tolerance and fair play among political activists"). In both cases, it is interesting to note which factor students considered *least*

Table 64. Salience of Political Problems

A. *"What were the greatest weaknesses of the First Nigerian Republic? (Choose three)"*

Alternatives	ABU, 1971:* Percentage making alternative†
Ethnic bitternesses:	77.7%
Financial corruption:	50.4%
Poor calibre of politicians:	41.0%
Unrestrained use of power against opponents:	34.7%
Lack of ideology:	33.7%
Constitutional balance between the Regions:	22.3%
Failure to promote rapid economic growth:	12.7%
Failure to retain sympathy of educated elite groups:	7.1%

* The same question was administered at Ibadan and Ife with similar results, except that "unrestrained use of power . . ." was marked by higher percentages (51 and 58).
† Each student could choose up to three alternatives; percentages add to more than 100.

B. *"Rate the following as problems of most African countries. (Number in order of importance)"*

Alternatives*	ABU, 1972†		
	Modal ranking	Percentage of first rankings	Percentage of last rankings
Ethnic and regional loyalties, as opposed to national ones:	1	36.2%	7.4%
Corruption among politicians:	2	18.8%	4.4%
Corruption among civil servants:	3	10.5%	8.5%
Interference and exploitation by developed countries:	6	18.8%	25.8%
Lack of educated administrators and technicians:	6	10.9%	24.7%
Lack of tolerance and fair play among political activists:	6	4.7%	29.2%
		99.9%	100.0%

* Order of alternatives rearranged to reflect responses. See Appendix 2.
† This question was also administered at ABU (1970); Ibadan (1971, 1972) Lagos (1971, 1972) and Nsukka (1973). Ethnicity and corruption were always ranked highest as problems.

important. In the "most African countries" context (Table 64B), "lack of educated administrators and technicians" was ranked low, only slightly ahead of the incivility alternative. Given that the students value administrative and technical skills very highly indeed (as we have noted above), this result serves to emphasise the primary importance of the political and social problems raised by the other alternatives (above all disunity) and the secondary value of modernizing and developmental change for which educated administrators and technicians are required. Still more interesting is the ranking assigned to the neo-colonial alternative, which received little support from most of the students; more than 50 percent placed the alternative in the lower half of rankings, and 25 percent ranked it in last place. Nearly 20 percent of the students considered 'interference and exploitation' the *most* important problem, and 25 percent of the students ranked it in either first or second place. The responses to this alternative indicate a tendency toward polarisation.

In the Nigerian context (Table 64A) the low ranking given to 'failure to promote rapid economic growth' was one of the indications which suggested to us that Nigerian university students are much less obsessed with economic development and the performance of political leaders in promoting it than first world literature on the third world often implies. It is interesting that the structural explanation of the failure of the First Republic, "constitutional balance between the regions", received a low ranking, yet most political scientists familiar with Nigerian politics would rate this very high. The students ranked the particular qualities of politicians and their actions (corruption and suppression of opposition) far ahead of the more basic structural problem. One might hypothesize that the students tend to personalize and to overlook the structural dimension. Finally, we were struck by the extremely low relevance rating given by the students to their own group-stratum: the great majority of the students did not consider 'failure to retain sympathy of educated elite groups' as among the most important of the First Republic's weaknesses. This is probably an indication that the students thought that the educated groups as *elites* did well out of independence and were reconciled as *elites*.[6] If individuals were unreconciled it was as citizens worried about the country and their own communities within it.

It is interesting to juxtapose the problem-oriented view above, where students were asked to make value judgements, with a more descriptive view. Table 65 summarizes the students views on factors contributing to political support. Ethnicity, which was ranked first as a problem by the strong majority of the students, was also considered the most important factor in political support. Two other factors confirm the significance for the majority of students of the home community. Making partial exception for the Hausa-Fulani, Kanuri, Bini and Yoruba systems of nobility, titles, status and power, "traditional connections" are in general specific to home communities and not transferable. The high ranking attached to the ability to provide amenities for local communities and the low ranking given to "national reputation" still more obviously emphasize the significance of

Table 65. Political Support

'In Nigerian elections what do you think contributed most to a politician's ability to gain support from people?'

Alternatives*	Modal ranking	ABU, 1971† Percentage of first rankings	Percentage of last rankings
Ethnicity:	1	52.6%	2.8%
Traditional connections:	2	16.9%	4.1%
Amenities for local communities:	3	10.3%	3.5%
Personal wealth:	4	9.3%	10.4%
National reputation:	5	9.3%	24.3%
Ideology:	6	1.7%	54.9%
		100.1%	100.0%

* Order of alternatives rearranged to reflect responses. See Appendix 2.
† Results obtained at Ife (1973) were similar except that "national reputation" and "amenities..." were marginally higher.

home communities as primary units of political support. National reputation was ranked by most students behind "personal wealth". Finally, the general consensus that ideology was the least important factor in determining political support in the First Republic is consistent with our findings elsewhere. "Ideology", which evoked among the students both notions of principled social action and unity on wider than communalist bases, was regarded as effectively non-existent in the past (and perhaps the present), and was one of the factors most wished for in future Nigerian politics. Similarly, ethnicity was seen as the most pressing characteristic and problem, while its converse, unity, was the most important social and political aspiration.

These findings indicate that we as political scientists, can learn from the students, and they can learn from us. Their de-emphasis of ideology as a factor in politics and the related emphasis on home-community factors counteract earlier academic views which tended to accept the self-images presented for national and international consumption by the Nigerian parties themselves, with their organizational charts and ideological documents.[7] The students quite spontaneously adopted the approach which professional students of African politics have found more slowly and painfully: emphasis on the micro and the communal, on levels and arenas and on the relations (or lack of them) between centre and periphery. The answers also suggest, however, a tendency (exception being made for the focus on the social factor of ethnicity) to focus on the character of the men and groups and what they *do* (corruption, misuse of power) and to overlook underlying structural factors. This suggests the value of a deeper examination of students' views of groups in the society, and likewise an examination of the role and possibilities of leadership.

(b) Groups in the society: their contribution and their nationalism
A number of socially and politically significant categories can be distinguished in Nigerian society. A general characteristic of the society is the weakness of interest group *organization* within the potential scope offered by such categorized distinctions, with the exception of ethnic, kinship and town-district type organization as well as a few professional groupings. The weakness of organization around other shared interests is partially explained by, and in turn helps to explain, the strength of communal organization. Thus, the strength of home community and/or "tribal" affiliation both helps to explain, and is enhanced by, the weakness of trade union organization.[8] Noteworthy but few in number are the occupational groups whose interest group potential not only develops from but is seen to develop from an institutional structure within the post-colonial state, for instance, the military.

The group divisions shown in Table 66 seem to us to be the most relevant for Nigeria since independence. This ignores the infinite complexity of group definition and interaction at a lower level of generalization, deriving especially from the particularistic elements of history and situation of the country's myriad communities. Major levels of ethnic and regional group allegiances have been discussed in Chapter 3. Modern post-colonial society, however, is much simpler. There are the broad occupational categories of administrator, technician, politician, businessman, worker, farmer-peasant, and, not least, student, a separate if transitional occupation and status.

We were interested in students' evaluations of elements of group character and contribution to the state. Some results are summarized in Table 66. These questions brought out an "esteem order" ranking which was produced in a number of questionnaire administrations and was confirmed by related questions. The students consistently ranked technical skills (engineering and medicine were mentioned as examples) and their possessors highest in terms of being important, and making the greatest contribution to the country and to development. Next, with equal consistency, were the administrative skills. Politicians were ranked very low, both in terms of the importance of their skills, and in terms of their actual contribution to society. Military officers who were emphatically not desired as future leaders (see Table 71) were nevertheless considered by most of the students to have made a positive contribution to society. The positive view of the military is largely explained by its contribution to the

Table 66

*Groups in the Polity**	
Which groups:	*Rank Orders:*
1. Are most important to development in terms of the skills they possess:	Technically skilled Administrators Businessmen Politicians
2. Have made the most positive contribution to society:	Technicians and professionals Senior civil servants Military officers Businessmen Political leaders Students
3. Have the strongest sense of nationalism:	University students Military officers Senior civil servants Secondary school students Businessmen Town workers Farmers
4. Are most important to conciliate for regimes to stay in power:	Educated elite groups Traditional leaders Town working classes Peasants
5. Are most influential in home communities:	Traditional leaders Secondary and university graduates Middle level groups (clerks, traders, contractors, etc.)

* See Appendix 2 for questions on which this summary is based.
† Rank orders derived from mean ranking accorded each alternative in ABU results. Other university samples do not vary significantly.

preservation of Nigeria as a social and political unit, but it also emphasizes the low regard for political leaders. The military has made a contribution in Nigeria and in other African countries by putting an end to corrupt and oppressive political regimes.[9] Businessmen and business skills (even when the impressive adjective "entrepreneurial" was added) were ranked consistently almost as low as politicians in terms of their contribution and their significance for development. We were initially puzzled by the low ranking the students gave to their own group in terms of contribution to the society (less than 5 percent thought students had made "the most positive contribution"). Exploring this in informal discussion, we found that the students almost uniformly placed a literal interpretation on the question, and were forced to rank students lowest because they were by definition not yet senior enough in the society and its structures to have been able to make a contribution.

There were interesting shifts in rankings when groups were compared in terms of sense of nationalism (Table 66. Number 3). The vast majority rated university students highest among the groups. Military officers were a poor second, followed closely by senior civil servants. There was some ambivalence with regard to the military. Despite a topical impatience with military rule in Nigeria (which has been almost annually apparent in student demonstrations) the students generally accepted the military's own self-image as a peculiarly "national" institution. The senior civil servants, the men of the all-embracing administrative state, were accorded a somewhat lower ranking on national-mindedness. Farmers, the men of the villages, were, unsurprisingly, ranked lowest by the majority. Town workers were generally ranked low suggesting that for the students the town workers tend to be intruders on the national scene.

Still more interesting is the extreme gulf between university students and secondary students in terms of their sense of nationalism. While university students ranked themselves first of the seven alternatives they ranked secondary students below both military officers and senior civil servants (who have university education or its rough equivalent). Given the miniscule present proportion of graduates and senior elites with equivalent education, and considering the great value students placed on Nigerian unity and national-mindedness, it would be a dismal prospect if only the university educated had any claim to being "true Nigerians". Contrary evidence is provided by another question in response to which the great majority of the students said that they personally began to think in national (Nigerian) terms at the secondary level (and not earlier or later): (see Table 30). We cannot judge whether the students see themselves individually in a different light from secondary students; at the moment we can only note the uncertainties without resolving them. The question format (competitive ranking), while showing that secondary students were ranked *lower* than the first three groups, does not permit us to say *how low* that ranking was, or *how much* lower still the remaining three groups were.

Recognising these elements of uncertainty, however, it is possible to say three significant things about "sense of nationalism". First, the university students saw themselves as the standard bearers of nationalism. There was an unusual measure of consensus among the students on this point. In this context we should also note the contrast between those (the educated elite) whom the students believed had to be conciliated by a regime interested in remaining in power and those (the traditional leaders) whom they regarded as exercising most influence in the communities (Table 66). On national issues the communities are obliged to work mainly through the educated groups and government itself must deal with and conciliate the latter more than the traditional leaders. Second, the results suggest that "sense of nationalism" for the students is related both to high education and their role in the institutions of the post-colonial State. Urban groups not associated with those structures (businessmen and workers) and the farmers outside the urban sector were rated low by the students. Third, however, these results present a gloomy picture, if one accords "sense of nationalism" the same value as the students. The majority of university students have recently emerged from secondary school, and they must know what secondary school boys are like. The sharp contrast between the sense of nationalism attributed to university and secondary school

Table 67. Civil Servants and National Outlook

'What proportion of civil servants in most African countries are capable of putting national interests ahead of their own interests and family loyalties?'

	ABU. 1970	Ibadan. 1972	Lagos. 1972
Almost all:	0.6%	3.2%	0.8%
Most, but by no means all:	10.8%	2.6%	12.0%
Relatively few:	88.6%	94.2%	87.2%
	100.0%	100.0%	100.0%

Table 68. University students and National Outlook

A. *'Do you think that the generation of university graduates which is emerging from the universities now has a more national outlook than those of ten years or more ago?'*

	ABU. 1973	Ibadan. 1972	Nsukka. 1973
More national in outlook:	56.7%	57.9%	47.8%
Less national in outlook:	24.1%	24.3%	32.4%
About the same:	19.2%	17.8%	19.8%
	100.0%	100.0%	100.0%

B. *'Do you think that most students tend to form their closest friendships among students from the same area of Nigeria?'*

	ABU. 1970	Ibadan. 1972	Lagos. 1972
Yes:	82.3%	77.7%	81.2%
No:	17.7%	22.3%	18.8%
	100.0%	100.0%	100.0%

students suggest that the former's sense of nationalism must, if only by reason of its newness, be fragile. Evidence produced by other questions indicates that the groups rated relatively high in this context were ranked much lower in absolute terms. Thus, the students ranked senior civil servants among the highest groups in Table 66 but they were overwhelmingly cynical in response to a general question about the proportion of African (read Nigerian) civil servants who put the national interests ahead of their personal and family ones, as Table 67 shows. And as was indicated in Chapter 3 the students acknowledged that their own friendships at university followed home area patterns (see Table 68B). Thus the high point (university students) on the relative scale reproduced in Table 66, number 3, is not in fact very high in absolute terms. A slightly more positive picture is presented by the responses to the question reproduced in Table 68A. Even here, however, little more than half the students (and a little less than half at Nsukka) felt that the decade since independence had produced a greater sense of Nigerianism among university graduates; in fact about one quarter felt that change had been retrogressive.

Taken as a whole, the responses to the above questions may show the continuing impact of the colonial experience. The value placed on groups and their skills is that of the colonial administrative quasi-state in which the technician and the administrator reigned supreme. In this value system both the politicians and the businessman lack legitimacy. It is probable that they are seen as serving themselves rather than society. Only a minority of the students gave evidence of adherence to the liberal concept of economic growth through the cumulation of individual entrepreneurial efforts. Those who occupy roles in the institutions of the supreme State, the civil service and the military, are considered to have a higher (in relative terms) sense of the national against the parochial. The students' belief of the weakness of national identity, even among those groups rated highest in competition with other groups, illustrates another aspect of the heritage. An artificial colonial political unit, created and run by an alien elite, with no systematic and conscious effort (until the very end) to create new social and political orientations relating to the level of all-Nigeria has meant that "nation-building" is a task for independence. Since the creation of such new orientations is in large part dependent on the efforts and teaching of men and women who are themselves products of parochial political cultures, it is not surprising that more than a decade after independence there is still far to go.

(c) Leadership: problem or solution?
The political leaders of the First Republic were associated by most of the

students with ethnicity as well as corruption and use of power to suppress opposition. These factors, together with the "calibre" of the politicians themselves, were seen as the major explanations for the erosion of support for the personnel and processes of the First Republic.

The importance of the leadership variable suggested three lines of inquiry to us: the abstract problem of relative focus on leaders versus structures; the scope of possible achievement given *good* leadership; and the more specific preferences of the students for types of leaders in a future democratic republic. The first (abstract) problem was formulated as shown in Table 69. More than two-thirds of the students put "men" ahead

Table 69. Successful Political Systems

'*What most determines the success of political systems?*'

	ABU, 1971	Ife, 1973
Good constitutional arrangements and structures:	27.2%	15.5%
Able and upright leaders:	72.8%	84.5%
	100.0%	100.0%

of "laws". The minority opting for structures was about the same proportion as that which opted for the constitutional-structural alternative in explaining the failure of the First Republic (Table 64A). Our own contact with the students has tended to confirm this focus on the quality of men and their actions, as opposed to the structural arrangements of a political system.

With respect to the second problem, the scope of *possible* achievement by good leadership, we posed the question reproduced in Table 70A. This somewhat cumbersome formula was designed to throw light on the students' outlook on the future of Nigeria, by testing their abstract predisposition to put faith in a leadership solution to Nigeria's problems, and by questioning how intractable they considered those problems to be. 50 percent or more of the students inclined to the leadership solution (and thus a hopeful outlook).

We tried to explore this further by making a comparison with the Chinese regime, as shown in Table 70B. When the solution to problems was linked to a high level of "transformation" and the experience of a different people (the Chinese) the proportion admitting the possibility dropped: only slightly more than one third envisaged the possibility of the suggested level of transformation in Nigeria. On the other hand, nearly

Table 70. Leadership and the Enduring Problems of Nigerian Society

A. *'If a leadership were inspirational, upright and efficient, do you think that it could overcome the inertia, selfishness and divisions that exist in Nigerian society, or would these problems resist in this generation the best leadership efforts?'*

	ABU, 1973	Ibadan, 1973	Nsukka, 1973
Leadership could overcome the problems:	57.3%	54.1%	49.8%
Problems would mostly remain, no matter how good the leadership:	42.7%	45.9%	50.2%
	100.0%	100.0%	100.0%

B. *'Do you think it is possible to transform Nigerian society as thoroughly as the Chinese Communists seem to have transformed their society?'*

	ABU, 1973	Ibadan, 1973	Nsukka, 1973
It is possible:	38.6%	41.8%	37.5%
It is not possible:	61.4%	58.2%	62.5%
	100.0%	100.0%	100.0%

'Whether or not you think it is possible do you think it is desirable?'

	ABU, 1973	Ibadan, 1973	Nsukka, 1973
Yes:	60.4%	59.3%	56.9%
No:	39.6%	40.7%	43.1%
	100.0%	100.0%	100.0%

two-thirds saw such a transformation as *desirable*, whether or not it was *possible*.

The two questions presented in Table 70 permit us to make some general observations, but they also raise more questions than they answer. The responses suggest that the majority of students were oriented toward men rather than structures. The fact that members of Nigeria's intellectual elite hold this view hints (it cannot be taken as more than a hint) that a future constitutional document establishing a second Nigerian civilian system may be planted in infertile soil. The results also suggest, however, a pre-disposition to respond to good leadership among a strong proportion of the students. A larger number than expected refused to believe that Nigeria's problems and weaknesses were intractable and permanent. Even when the question was posed in terms of the Chinese revolution, with the obvious effect of narrowing the range of positive responses, a little more than one third affirmed the possibility of revolutionary transformation.

The third problem concerning leadership was that of general preferences with regard to likely political leaders in the next civilian regime (see Table 71). The students were invited to respond to new leaders as well as the old

Table 71. Future Political Leaders

'When military rule ends in 1976,* what kinds of political leaders would you like to emerge? (Number in order)'.

Alternatives†	Modal ranking	ABU, 1973‡ Percentage of first rankings	Percentage of last rankings
Participants moved by ideology	1	40.0%	3.3%
Politicians more educated than those in the past	2	30.0%	2.0%
A new set of political participants	3	20.8%	1.6%
Champions of community rights	4	7.1%	8.3%
Military officers who run for public office	6	1.3%	41.3%
Members of the former political parties	6	0.8%	43.6%
		100.0%	100.1%

* This question was (after its use) overtaken by events: as noted in Chapter 1, transition to civilian rule was (on 1st October 1974) postponed indefinitely.
† Order of alternatives rearranged to reflect results. See Appendix 2.
‡ Nearly identical results were obtained at Ibadan (1973) and Ife (1973).

politicians, the "communal champions" of local community rights and "military officers who run for public office". The majority of students responded most positively to the idea of political leaders "moved by a sense of ideology". Politicians "more educated than those in the past" and, simply, a "new set of political participants" followed closely. Nearly one fifth of the students ranked communal champions very high, whereas the overwhelming majority of students ranked the old politicians ("members of the former political parties") and military officers turned politicians lowest. These groups, who have ruled the country up to now, were ranked high in the list by only a tiny minority. The students clearly responded to newness, education, and ideology. To the extent that the university students are influential and their attitudes characteristic of a wider elite stratum in Nigeria, these findings bode ill for the older generation of politicians as they do also for soldiers who might want to exchange the bayonet for the ballot box. However, practical circumstances in future politics might well alter the attitudes that the students expressed here.

On the question of future politics we asked the students a question at the most general level (Table 72A). Slightly more than half the students were optimistic at this level of general outlook. About one third felt that there would be no improvement, which, given what we know of their evaluation of the past, must be characterized as pessimism. This pessimism is reinforced by the belief on the part of the majority that ethnicity, the source of so much division in the past, would be the main factor in electoral politics in the future (see Table 72B). A very small minority thought that the politics of the future would actually be worse than in the First Republic.

Evaluating the data dealt with in this section, we can see both positive and negative aspects. On the negative side, the suggestion of concern with leadership and men to the exclusion of structures and constitutions seems to bode ill for the development of elite support for constitutionalism. On the positive side, there is an apparent readiness to respond to a leadership

Table 72. Future Politics

A. *'Do you think that the politics of the future in Nigeria will be better or worse than the politics of the First Republic?'*

	ABU, 1973	Ibadan, 1973	Ife, 1973
Better:	55.3%	59.7%	56.3%
About the same:	31.8%	28.8%	36.4%
Worse:	12.9%	11.5%	7.3%
	100.0%	100.0%	100.0%

B. *'After transition to civilian rule in Nigeria,* what factors will most influence the majority of voters? (Number in order of importance)'*

Alternatives:†	Modal ranking	ABU, 1973‡ Percentage of first rankings	Percentage of last rankings
Ethnicity:	1	51.8%	17.5%
Political personalities:	2	17.4%	15.4%
Amenities:	3	14.2%	22.8%
Ideology:	4	16.7%	44.3%
		100.1%	100.0%

* This question was employed when transition to civilian rule was expected in 1976.
† Alternatives have been rearranged to reflect results; see Appendix 2.
‡ Results at Nsukka (1973) and Ibadan (1973) were similar except that in both cases a stronger minority of students ranked ideology in first place. The modal pattern was the same at all three universities.

that transcends the past and present realities. This readiness together with the expressed willingness (admittedly, in the abstract) to sacrifice for the general good suggests the possibility of a more positive future. The students may turn out to be better and more "national" citizens than they themselves believe.

3. POLITICS AND PARTICIPATION: THE RESIDUAL DEMOCRATS

We are now in a position to take up what is thematically the most important issue of this chapter. In the preceding chapter we argued that the question of democracy in Nigeria can be regarded as "the most significant element of unfinished business in the process of becoming an independent State", but that, given the failure of the First Republic and the uncertainty of the present, the future of democracy remains problematic. We can now add to the historical discussion attitudinal data relevant to the problem of democracy.

The most basic question we asked elicited attitudes toward the logical precondition of democracy: whether or not the students believed that the "masses", participating through elections, were capable of making rational choices. We feel that probably no other item within our survey project has more individual significance, and we therefore present the results in more than the customary detail. Table 73 indicates the very considerable stability which we encountered in all our administrations. Consequently, we can confidently say that only between one-fifth and one-quarter of Nigerian university students affirmed what can logically be considered an essential precondition of democracy. The students (that is, approximately three-quarters of them) implicitly convicted themselves of a form of elitism

Table 73. Political Awareness

'Do you agree or disagree with the following statement: "The masses in African countries are not yet capable of making rational choices in elections for national political offices".'

	Successive Administrations:						
	ABU		Ibadan		Lagos		Nsukka
	1970	1973	1971	1972	1971	1972	1973
	%	%	%	%	%	%	%
Agree:	79.6	74.6	73.4	78.1	73.3	72.7	82.1
Disagree:	20.4	25.4	26.6	21.9	26.7	27.3	17.9
	100.0%	100.0%	100.0%	100.0%	100.0%	100.0%	100.0%

in the process. While we did not ask the question, we have no reason to doubt that if asked whether university graduates were capable of making rational electoral choices, the responses would have been almost unanimously affirmative. More light is cast on students' elitism by questions treated below; but at this point the significance of the appended phrase "for national offices" in the question reproduced in Table 73 should be noted.[10] The students were asked to evaluate the ability of the men of the farms and villages to understand and act in the context of *national* events. We do not think that the students were expressing a general contempt for the intellectual abilities of the uneducated farming masses. Other questions, dealt with in Chapter 3, make clear that the great majority of the students retain an attitude of respect and ties of affection toward their parents, relatives and the elders of the farming communities from which so many of them come. In conversation students will frequently remark, sometimes with evident regret, that they, by reason of their concentration on school learning and their many years "abroad" from home areas, are only partially competent within the culture and traditions of their communities. We believe that the results would have been very different indeed, had we asked whether the masses were capable of making rational choices about leaders and policies in their own local communities. Outside the local community, however, the "masses" are removed from their proper sphere. The business of pan-Nigeria is the business of "elites" as the term is used by Nigerians, and, above all, of the most highly educated: the university graduates. Inevitably, in consequence, the students' attitude toward democracy remains ambivalent. The hypothesis that educated elites elsewhere in West Africa tend to share this basic lack of faith in mass participation, along with the contrary less clear attractions *toward* democracy, seems to us to explain a good deal about West African political trends. In particular it helps to explain the weak defense of fair electoral procedures.

The ambivalent attitude towards democracy is illustrated more clearly by the question presented in Table 74.[11] The basic pattern requires little discussion. "Honest government in the interests of the people" received by far the most support. In the Lincolnesque formulation which is popular among Nigerian political journalists, this is "government *for* the people." Civil liberties performed well, especially when combined with "free press" (see Table 74 note ‡). Constitutional structures implying the concept of balanced forces performed rather badly, again suggesting the absence of a preoccupation with constitutions and constitutionalism among the majority of students. Most interesting and significant, however, is the low ranking given by most of the students to competing parties and politicians.[12] Yet this is the truly essential structural component of democracy in the form

Table 74. Factors in Democracies

'Which do you think are most essential if a political system is to be called "democratic"?'

Alternatives*	Modal ranking	ABU, 1971† Percentage of first rankings	Percentage of last rankings
Honest government in the interests of the people	1	56.4%	8.1%
Maintenance of civil liberties	2-3	10.4%	8.1%
Constitutional structures respecting the balance of power	2-3	11.6%	16.5%
Free press‡	5	8.9%	26.7%
Competing politicians and political parties	5	12.7%	40.7%
		100.0%	100.0%

* Order of alternatives rearranged to reflect results.
† Ife (1973) produced similar results: Ife students were marginally more likely to give maintenance of civil liberties' a higher rank, and to give 'competing politicians and political parties' a very low one.
‡ The addition of free press is a weakness in the question format since it could properly be associated with "maintenance of civil liberties". Inclusion as a separate item was necessary because it represented a topical issue at the time of administration. Had it not been included, "Maintenance of civil liberties" might have attracted more high rank assignments, while the last-place rating of "competing politicians and political parties" would probably have been still more conclusive.

bequeathed by British colonialism and the most likely form of a future Nigerian democracy. About 40 percent of respondents ranked this as the *least* essential factor. The majority of students regarded "democracy" as essentially *good* government and government *for* the people; they would perhaps be easily satisfied by a system which was labelled democratic and was broadly consultative but did not include competition by parties in elections. One would definitely not expect the majority of students to defend free electoral competition when threatened, for example, by the imposition of a single-party system.

The picture presented above, however, can be maintained only so long as examination of the results is limited to the views of the majority. Complexity is added to ambivalence as we find that the variation in responses was much higher than that normally encountered. The "competing politicians and political parties" alternative in particular showed a tendency toward bimodality which is concealed by the presentation in Table 74. Thus, while 40 percent ranked this alternative last, *about one-third ranked it either first or second.* "Constitutional structures" was distributed unusually evenly among the possible rankings, again with a noticeable tendency toward bimodality. Even "honest government in the interests of the people", ranked first by an overwhelming majority, was ranked last or next-to-last by some 15 percent. Consequently it is more difficult here than elsewhere to characterize the students as a whole. Where democracy is concerned we feel that the student body tends toward ambivalence and division.

We explored and tested this idea further, firstly by posing the problem of the relationship of democracy to economic development, and secondly by testing evaluations of democracy against other values. The formula we used (early in our series of surveys) to pose the problem of the relationship of democracy to economic development rested on two assumptions. We assumed that the idea of authoritarian development contrasted with democracy would be meaningful to the students, and we assumed that they placed a high independent value on economic development. The problem was posed both in terms of a factual judgement and a value judgement, as shown in Table 75.

At least half of the students responded in the affirmative to the question of fact (Table 75A) with the exception of those at Ibadan, where

Table 75. Democracy and Development

A. *'Do you think that in general authoritarian governments dominated by public servants are better able to bring about rapid economic development than democratic governments dominated by politicians?'*

	ABU		Ibadan		Lagos		Nsukka
	1970	1973	1971	1972	1971	1972	1973
	%	%	%	%	%	%	%
Yes:	61.3	60.8	39.2	37.3	54.0	48.9	50.4
No:	38.7	39.2	60.8	62.7	46.0	51.1	49.6
	100.0%	100.0%	100.0%	100.0%	100.0%	100.0%	100.0%

B. *'Which do you think is better for a developing country (if the choice has to be made)?'*

	ABU, 1970	Ibadan,* 1972	Lagos,* 1972
An authoritarian government with a strong commitment to economic development:	63.5%	66.9%	66.9%
A democratic government closely connected with the masses but not so committed to economic development:	36.5%	33.1%	33.1%
	100.0%	100.0%	100.0%

* Other administrations at Ibadan (1971) and Lagos (1971) provided nearly identical results.

the results were approximately the reverse of those at ABU. The fact that the Lagos and Nsukka results did not bear out this trend argues against a regional (southern) tendency to be more suspicious of claims made in favour of authoritarian government. Once again, we think the greater variability of results when the question of democracy is raised suggests a high level of ambivalence. Similarly, the majority favoured authoritarian government committed to more rapid economic development in the value judgement (Table 75B). Interestingly, the Ibadan students, while more likely to reject the factual claim, were at least as likely to make the value judgement in favour of authoritarian government. These results again suggest the weakness of allegiance to the *idea* of democracy and indicate that a strong majority could be brought to accept and support "dictatorship for development" (whether revolutionary or frankly bureaucratic). Yet we know that the students themselves are far from being committed to economic development as a first priority.

If we have to come to question the assumption that these highly educated elites are intensely concerned with the problem of economic development, we likewise have come to doubt that the basic problem posed, democracy/slow development versus authoritarian government/fast development, is one which occurs naturally to the students. Modification of the assumption—that economic development is highly valued—makes democracy seem much less valued still. Modification of the problem, however, suggests that the students may not themselves posit conflict between democratic participation and efficient use of society's resources for development, and this in turn tends to increase potential support for democracy when it is seen as an independent question. Despite the weaknesses of the above formulae, the results achieved are borne out by the responses to the question in Table 76.

Table 76. Government in Developing Countries

'*Which is more important in a developing country? (Mark one alternative . . .)*'

	ABU, 1973	Ibadan, 1973	Nsukka, 1973
Governing elite elected in free and fair elections:	36.5%	61.5%	47.7%
Competent governing elite:	63.5%	38.5%	52.3%
	100.0%	100.0%	100.0%

Some further light is cast on relative evaluations of democracy by a series of two-way contests posed in value terms, which are summarized in Table 77.

Table 77. Democracy vs. Other Values

'Which is most valuable or important?'

Alternative pairs:	ABU, 1973	Ibadan, 1973	Nsukka, 1973
A. Economic development:	61.8%	47.8%	45.6%
Democratic form of government:	38.2%	52.2%	54.4%
	100.0%	100.0%	100.0%
B. Democracy:	30.7%	36.6%	45.4%
Political stability:	69.3%	63.4%	54.6%
	100.0%	100.0%	100.0%
C. Democracy:	8.4%	16.3%	15.4%
National unity:	91.6%	83.7%	84.6%
	100.0%	100.0%	100.0%

The first pair is a repetition, in different format (and in a later set of administrations), of the problem posed in questions discussed above. The pattern of responses is similar: slightly less than two-thirds of ABU students saw themselves as "developers" and a little more than one-third as "democrats." At Nsukka and Ibadan fewer than 50 per cent of those answering considered themselves as "developers", and the proportion of "democrats" was marginally higher. Support for democracy among the ABU students was slightly weaker. We then proceeded to measure democracy against the two values already found to be the most basic of all: stability and unity. The results are predictable: democracy did not perform nearly as well as it did against the less valued "economic development." However, the responses emphasise more strongly than before the persistence of a democratic minority. We know that political stability was valued very highly by the overwhelming majority, and yet one-third or more were willing to rank democracy higher (Table 77B). Even in competition with 'national unity' democracy was supported by between 8 and 16 percent of the students.

A final comparative question, of significance to the question of democracy as well as other important questions, is presented in Table 78. It is evident that of the alternatives offered, "system of electoral democracy" was the most dispensable inherited institution for the largest number of students. Again, however, between one-quarter and one-third of the students evinced strong support for the inherited democratic institutions, nearly half could be characterized as ambivalent, one-third felt that the democratic institutions had no value at all. Once again, the heritage of the administrative state (public administration and modern law) is evident.

Table 78. Institutions

'Which of the institutions with which Nigeria began independence do you think continue to have value for Nigeria as an independent country?'

Alternatives:*	ABU, 1973†			
	Much	Some	None	Total
Education system:	48.3%	41.1%	10.6%	100.0%
System of public administration:	44.2%	48.7%	7.1%	100.0%
System of modern law:	39.3%	52.4%	8.2%	99.9%
Economic system:	36.6%	51.3%	12.1%	100.0%
System of electoral democracy:	27.3%	41.3%	31.4%	100.0%

* The order of the alternatives has been rearranged to reflect the responses. See Appendix 2.
† This question was administered at ABU (Spring, 1973) and at Ibadan (1973) and Nsukka (1973). The same basic pattern of responses was received in all administrations. But an apparent if slight regional variation is suggested by the fact that students at the two Southern universities are still more likely to accord "educational system" a "much" rating than ABU students (in either of the ABU administrations).

Having become, through collection and analysis of the preceeding responses, relatively sure of the situation, the authors posed in the final survey a highly specific and highly practical choice—and received a surprise. Looking at the present Nigerian situation, and surveying such public discussion of the structure of future politics as has so far appeared, we outlined three major structural alternatives which we thought were relevant: full democracy; diluted or indirect democracy; and frankly elitist and technocratic non-democracy. The question

Table 79. What, then, is to be done?

'Many people assume that the masses of the people are not able to choose rationally in elections for national office. If one assumes that that is true, which of the following do you think is best?'

	ABU, 1973	Ibadan, 1973	Nsukka, 1973
Nothing to suggest; in a democratic system we must take the risk of letting the people choose:	41.1%	61.7%	43.8%
Finding some form of indirect election so that the final electors are sensible and informed:	43.7%	28.5%	40.6%
A group of technocrats (able, skilled, and upright men) be permitted to rule without democratic participation:	15.2%	9.8%	15.6%
	100.0%	100.0%	100.0%

was made more interesting and more stringent by prefacing it with the premise that we know to be accepted by the considerable majority of any representative group of Nigerian university students: that the masses are not capable of choosing rationally. Given this formulation we expected an elitist (technocratic) response from a sizeable proportion of the students; and we expected a very weak democratic response. In fact, as Table 79 makes clear, relatively few of the students (at this point of time, at least) were in favour of indefinite undemocratic technocracy. A sizeable group preferred the compromise but we were surprised by the size of the vote for democracy, in full recognition of the weak assumptions and the cost to be paid. Taking the first two alternatives together, nearly four-fifths, confronted with this practical choice, opted for some form of democracy. Nearly half of those answering (at Ibadan nearly two-thirds) were apparently willing to take a chance on full democracy. Despite suggestions encountered elsewhere, and suppositions one might make on the basis of their role and society, the students did not consider themselves political technocrats. Keeping in mind the various sources of their ambivalent attitude toward democracy discussed above, we might describe them as *residual democrats* when the practical choices have to be made—and that is, after all, what is most important.

It is difficult to explain this somewhat surprising ending to our inquiry on democracy. We cannot say whether it is the effect of socialization through formal education as our research excluded any attempt to study prior socialization in the schools. Nor can we say with any certainty whether it is mainly *topical,* i.e. dislike of the present situation of authoritarian government. This could only be ascertained by repeating the question at a later point in time after a period of democracy. We can, however, make one suggestion which is complementary to these two possible sources of explanation. We have elsewhere (in Chapter 3) emphasized the close ties of identity and affection with the people of the home communities—for the most part, the rural towns and villages. It is these people, by and large, who are shut out of the modern system of government and politics in Nigeria which is run by, and in many ways for, the educated. The parliamentary democracy which Nigeria has experienced is alien in origin. Yet, paradoxically, it provides a means of bringing the rural, 'traditional' people into participation in the modern system. And despite the sharp structural dissimilarities, it undoubtedly evokes the sense of communal participation which is a feature of most village traditions in Nigeria. On the other hand, traditional Nigerian cultures contain little or none of the aristocratic "tyranny of the mob" tradition of thought which tends to undercut support for democracy in the Western tradition. In the Nigerian context, the main corresponding counter-democratic factor would be the close association of democratic politics with ethnicity.[13] The residual support for democracy held by large proportions of the students implies also a tacit acceptance of ethnicity, despite their abstract abhorence of ethnicity as anti-unity. This is simply another feature and illustration of the prevalence and inevitability of ambivalence and contradiction in a post-colonial situation.

4. CONCLUSION

Little further summarising is necessary. We have seen that the students' perceptions of past political experience emphasized ethnic division and corruption and the fallibility of the leaders. In value terms they condemned these phenomena, but their perceptions also emphasized the communal essence of Nigerian politics—and not necessarily with condemnation. We have argued that the students' answers show a relative lack of interest in the structural aspects of Nigerian political problems, tending instead to focus on the social (ethnicity) and the personal (leadership factors). This lack of interest in what might be called the constitutional dimension is paralleled by a greater interest in the *effect* of democracy (government *for* the people) than in democracy's structural basis (electoral and party systems, in particular). Findings on the roles of principal occupational groups in the polity relate to patterns of thought and value discussed in other chapters. Technical and administrative skills were valued higher than business and political ones. Military officers were given credit for strong nationalism, and for having made a significant contribution up to the present, but were emphatically not desired as participants in a future system of electoral politics.

The overall picture of student views on democracy is one of deep ambivalence. The students *were* (inevitably) elitist where status is defined in terms of educational qualification. The majority ranked competence in governing ahead of legitimacy in terms of election. They doubted the basic premise in democracy: that the masses are capable of rational electoral choices. For the majority, "democracy" was loosely, perhaps even negatively, connected with the structural features essential to democracy in the Western form. Politicians and political skills were not highly valued. However, there was also a considerable degree of support for democracy. The students are for the most part linked emotionally to the people. They are populist in this sense, even if without a populist faith in the wisdom of the people. They are technocratic in terms of their personal ambitions and in terms of the values they place on skills and functions, *but they are not for the most part political technocrats*. When they made the final practical choice surprising numbers supported democracy whether complete or indirect.

THE DYNAMICS OF POLITICS IN NIGERIA   163

We must finish by pointing to the probable circumstantiality of any one position adopted by the various proportions of students with regard to the overall problem; our inquiry shows clearly the ambivalence that exists. There is considerable support among university students for a return to electoral democracy, but we think it likely that the structure of ambivalence that underlies this (or any) practical and general position means that that position is prey to circumstances. At the moment democracy benefits from its own absence, and from the general unpopularity among the students of the military regime. These factors undoubtedly help shift the "balance of ambivalence" toward support. But one must keep in mind the negative value patterns, in particular, the strong association of democracy with ethnic division and with corrupt and ignorant politicians. If circumstances should render these associations more relevant, then the "balance of ambivalence" could shift massively in the other direction, with probably only a very small hard-core minority of true democrats remaining to support democracy.

FOOTNOTES

1. A. Almond and S. Verba, *op.cit.,* pp. 2-3.
2. As noted in Chapter 1, General Yakubu Gowon, the head of the Nigerian Military Government, announced on 1st October, 1970 that the military planned to hand back power to a civilian government in 1976. But on 1st October, 1974 General Gowon announced that the military government did not consider that the country was ready for politics, and so the transition to civilian rule was to be postponed indefinitely. He made it clear however that the military government still saw itself as temporary: 'I want to make it abundantly clear . . . that we have not abandoned the idea of return to civilian rule.' One of the first acts of the military government that replaced General Gowon's was to declare that civilian rule would be restored in 1979.
3. It also seems to us that a creeping fear of praetorianism, repeated military interventions in politics, lies behind much Nigerian thinking about the future. However for a hopeful Nigerian analysis and statement, see B. J. Dudley, *Politics and Crisis in Nigeria* (Ibadan: Ibadan University Press, 1973), pp. 239-258.
4. An important reflection of the fact that decolonization is incomplete in Nigeria is that primary and secondary syllabi are still in the process of being revised to employ teaching materials that deal with Nigerian history and society. Many innovations are too recent to have benefited the present generation of university students. We find in teaching that few of the students have read the basic material available on Nigerian politics and they tend to have only a shaky grasp of national-level Nigerian history. At the same time most are much more intensely interested in and knowledgeable about the politics of their home areas and home states than are equivalent groups in Britain or the U.S.A.
5. There are two important exceptions to this: all the students at Nsukka—and not the Ibo students only—indicated 'corruption among politicians' as the first African problem, and the Hausa students at ABU put 'interference and exploitation by developed countries' in first place.
6. This is borne out by the results of the question on disappointment of groups with independence: see Table 53.

7. Political scientists have not always agreed on the nature of ideological formulations in Nigerian political activism. For example, Richard Sklar interprets Chief Obafemi Awolowo's swing to the left in 1961-62 as a genuine ideological shift in outlook; see R. Sklar, "Nigerian Politics: The Ordeal of Chief Owolowo, 1960-65" in G. M. Carter (editor), *Politics in Africa* (New York: Harcourt, Brace and World, Inc., 1966), pp. 129-132; whereas John Mackintosh interprets the same shift as purely tactical; see J. P. Macintosh, *op.cit.*, pp. 427-460.

8. On trade union organization and politics, see Cohen, *Labour and Politics in Nigeria, 1945-71* (London: Heinemann, 1974).

9. For an excellent study of the Nigerian military, see R. Luckham, *The Nigerian Military: A Sociological Analysis of Authority and Revolt 1960-67* (London: Cambridge University Press, 1971); also N. J. Miners, *The Nigerian Army 1956-66* (London: Methuen, 1971). Luckham decribes the military officers' self-image, especially pp. 109-130. Luckham refers (p. 125) to officers' disquiet at their lack of prestige among elite reference groups. P. Day, *op.cit.*, pp. 333-46, found 'army officer' ranked eleventh in a series that saw doctors, university teachers, agricultural officers and clergymen among others put before them in prestige order.

10. It seems to us important to stress the factors mentioned in the text because the charge of 'elitism' is often levelled in an unqualified way against both students and graduates. The Udoji Commission writes: '(A) . . . critical aspect of human relations in Nigeria may be referred to as elitism. . . . The entire education system of the nation seems to be designed to uphold and reinforce this elitist philosophy: to sort out by stages the most worthy, who are crowned with the laurels of "success" certified by diplomas and degrees, from the less worthy . . . crowned with the dunce-cap of "failure".' Public Service Review Commission 1974. *Main Report*, p. 4.

11. The lack of a clear pattern in the responses on democracy draws attention to a feature of survey work that may well be operative here. Converse has analysed data collected by the Survey Research Centre as a result of interviewing the same American sample three times, with an interval of about two years between each interview. Faced with certain items 'only about 13 people out of 20 manage to locate themselves even on the same *side* of the controversy in successive interrogations, when 10 out of 20 would have done so by chance.' Commenting on Converse's views and findings, Brian Barry says: 'It might perhaps be argued, desperately, that this simply reflects the fact that people 'change their minds' with great frequency on these issues, but it is much more likely that many do not have a 'mind' on them at all; in other words, they do not think about them at all except when being interrogated, and then respond virtually at random. . . . the variation in responses was greatest for the items which were furthest removed from personal experience and where it was most difficult to see the personal implications of the issue: foreign policy questions and the one about private versus public initiative in electricity and housing. The greatest stability occurred on questions about Negroes (school desegregation and the anti-discrimination pattern . . .), followed by one on government responsibility for maintaining full employment. This pattern supports the view that changes in response are more a matter of what Converse calls low 'centrality' of the issue than anything normally described as a 'change of mind'. B. Barry: *Sociologists, Economists and Democracy* (London: Macmillan, 1970), pp. 127-28. We do not think that democracy is a matter of low 'centrality' for the students—though the actual political apparatus of parties, etc., that went with it in Nigerian politics may well be. But we think that the fluctuations in the answers about democracy suggest how little the matter has been thought through by the students.

12. The students automatically, if unconsciously, observe Post's injunction to 'distinguish between two levels, that of the national debate, with its policy papers, newspaper articles, and keynote speeches, and that of the constituencies, where the issues involved were reinterpreted until the contest became different in almost every place.' K. W. J. Post, *op.cit..* p. 435.

13. The politicians are not blamed for creating ethnic divisions by the majority of the students. A hypothesis, deriving from one of the present authors' memories of elite comment during the politics of the First Republic, was that students might be happy to think that ethnic bitternesses were *created* by politicians as they strove to mobilize support for personalistic ends—just as occasionally some Nigerian speakers achieve an anti-colonial rhetorical flourish in asserting that ethnic antagonisms were consciously and systematically created by the British and have no other origin. Only one-third of the students said that politicians *created* tribalism; two-thirds said they primarily *used* existing sentiments.

7 University Students and the Nigerian Future

This chapter draws together conclusions derived from the data presented in the preceding chapters. We have permitted ourselves to interpret more freely here than we did in the body of the study. We consider four main issues: social privilege and access to university education; regional inequalities; the uneven benefits of decolonisation; and the elements of a common culture among the students.

1. *SOCIAL PRIVILEGE AND ACCESS TO UNIVERSITY EDUCATION*

Our data does not indicate that at present children of well-to-do families are dominating access to university education, but they do take up a disproportionate share of available places and their absolute numbers are growing all the time. They are more competitive than candidates from poorer families because they are more assured of admission to secondary schools (and to good secondary schools) and of more effective parental support. There are suggestions in our data—we do not want to put this point more strongly than that—that their proportionate numbers are also slowing increasing. Already higher occupational groups are much better represented among the women students than among the men. As things are, however, the rapid and continuing spread of the secondary and university systems has continued to give male candidates from poorer, especially farming, families the possibility of making their way to university.

Two new factors may alter the existing patterns. First, the system cannot go on expanding indefinitely at its present rate. As expansion slows, more competitive candidates from well-to-do families will edge out candidates from poorer families, and so existing proportions will begin to change. Second, there is evidence from various sources that children from better off families have begun to reach university age in very much larger numbers than in the past. The explanation of this increase is that public servants and professionals in their late 40's, whose children are now of university age, form the beginning of a bulge of well-paid and highly educated Nigerians who benefited from the first policies of rapid indigenization in the public service and equivalent posts and occupations.[1] This factor, which implies the rapid and continuing increase in the absolute numbers of candidates from the well-to-do families, would operate to change existing class proportions among students even if the rate of university expansion did not slow down. In any case, the future may well see children from the already privileged groups not only dominate university entrance in the fairly near future but also form the beginnings of a hardening social class system where none has hitherto operated to any substantial degree.

2. REGIONAL INEQUALITIES

We dealt in Chapter 2 with the regional and state imbalances in university recruitment. Not only are these imbalances of serious magnitude at present but the gap between the northern and southern States is widening in absolute numbers rather than being bridged. A practical consequence of the continuing imbalance is that the Federal public service will remain overwhelmingly southern (it is already over 90 percent southern). This disproportion inevitably causes resentment in a country where top jobs (and for that matter nearly all jobs) are seen as 'spoils' in a distribution system. Moreover, the scarcity of northern skills at the centre reduces Federal understanding of northern problems. One means of altering present recruitment trends, particularly in the event of a slower rate of university expansion, would be to introduce a quota system of admissions that would favour the underrepresented areas. Such a system would, however, encounter great hostility from the more socially mobilized (mainly southern) communities and from the more well-to-do social classes poised to send their children to university. People know that not just university places are at stake, but also jobs, income and influence. The battle fought over university places today foreshadows the battle to be fought over posts in the Federal and State services tomorrow.

3. UNEVEN BENEFITS OF DECOLONIZATION

Indigenization policies, coupled with educational expansion and large governmental revenues, have over the last two decades been producing large numbers of privileged persons who nonetheless form only a minute proportion of the country's total population, or, for that matter, of the country's population with some formal education. These people offer a glaring contrast to the underprivileged majority. The majority of the educated elite, including the students, have roots in the rural communities. Nearly all the children of these elite members will be brought up away from their parents' rural communities of origin and will inevitably have weaker roots in those communities. In any case, that individuals are attached to their communities of origin does not necessarily mean that rural communities in general will be given priority in public policy. There are many reasons for thinking that the present ruling elites (whose background is much the same as that of the students) are as attached to their communities of origin as the students are. Yet only a minor share of governmental revenue is spent on agriculture, which is the main occupation and source of livelihood of these communities. Urban-related projects and the salaried classes constitute more visible and pressing priorities for government spending. A generation hence when rural attachments have grown weaker and urban problems and pressures more urgent there is likely to be the temptation to neglect the rural groups more than ever, unless the latter find some leadership and means of political organization that makes use of their superior numbers.

The students did not manifest a concern for the lower paid workers and the urban poor that remotely matched their attachment of sentiment to the farmers. Yet the workers' urban location, poor living conditions and awakened social sensitivities leave them much more exposed than the farmers to sentiments of relative deprivation. As the contrast between the privileged situation of the senior administrators and the wretched living conditions of the workers deepens and as sentiments are in all likelihood exacerbated by the conspicuous consumption of private entrepreneurs benefiting from the general new found wealth it seems unlikely that social confrontation can be avoided. Only extreme sensitivity to the anomalous situation of the lower paid workers, excluded from wealth but close enough to it in various ways to appreciate it, as well as able political leadership and good management of the economy can reduce tensions.

The issue of social class differentials discussed in the previous paragraph leads to a more central aspect of the question of decolonization. The highly educated elite groups in the African countries have come under a fair share of criticism: it is argued that they have simply stepped into the shoes of colonial masters and have perpetuated established salary structures and privileges, that they are removed from the masses of the people, that they live in opulence but perform only parasitical roles and that they act as intermediaries in an international system of neo-colonial exploitation. These Fanonesque charges focus on the attitudes of the post-independence elites in the maintenance of the previously existing administrative, educational, legal and economic structures.

A number of our own findings lend some support to this criticism. There is a general acceptance of the structural *status quo* in the wake of colonization. To the extent that our students samples can be taken to be representative, and to the extent that the highly educated remain in control of events, we predict that divergence from the colonial heritage will be cautious and non-revolutionary. In this sense it seems fair to say that the great majority of students are conservative. Their conservatism does not rule out opposition in cases where they perceive their interests threatened or their ambitions frustrated. But it means establishmentarian rather than radical rule once the control of government has changed. The experience of Ghana and Sierra Leone as well as Nigeria illustrates this kind of continuity in West Africa. In other words, governments may be opposed or toppled but the educated elite continue to administer, salary and other differentials are maintained and urban-biased development goes on. Only the eventual need to conciliate the socially mobilized urban groups may force a modification of conservative policies and bring a radical ideological element into Nigerian politics that the majority of politicians and administrators would be unlikely to introduce on their own initiative.

In considering possible decolonization patterns in Nigeria, there are, however, considerations that remove some of the stigma involved in labelling groups such as the students conservative. First, the structure of administrative and technological skills (as distinct from the structure of incomes) in government and administration in post-colonial Nigeria is much the same as in any modern State. Second, radical alternatives in terms of practical patterns of political and social reform are far from being as discernible in contemporary Nigeria and other developing countries as facile criticisms of existing structures would suggest. At the same time parts of the survey data and other evidence adduced in this study suggest the possibility of an upper intelligentsia that closes ranks, consolidates its position, maintains colonial-inherited structures and differentials and subordinates the pace and shape of socio-economic development to its own interests. However, an analysis of Nigerian (and African) politics also suggests the possibility of a take-over during labour strife and social upheaval by disgruntled middle level persons (Uganda, Central African Republic and Equatorial Guinea may prove to be more typical than they presently appear). In short, those observers who resent the privilege of the present educated elite groups and the likelihood that their privileges will be handed on to their children have a case, but the most probable alternative to the government and administration of the educated intelligentsia is—speaking somewhat figuratively—a take-over by the sergeants and control by the clerks.

4. OUTLOOK AND FORMATION: THE ELEMENTS OF A COMMON CULTURE

Viewed in functional terms the single most important role of the universities is to provide personnel for the institutions of government, education and the economy. The universities are thus linked to institutions that belong to the country as a whole and to processes that transcend social particularisms within the country. The students accepted the broad logic inherent in university education and they considered themselves characterized by a stronger and more consistent sense of nationalism than other major occupational groups, including the military. Yet they remained sharply aware of the strength of particularistic loyalties, not only in the country but also within themselves. For this reason the students can be said to see the universities—and what they perceive is probably accurate—as the main, if flawed, institutions for building and consolidating loyalty to the Nigerian nation.

There is an element of ambivalence in the students' attitudes to the culture acquired through formal education. We found some evidence of nostalgia for the less modern life of the peasant communities. Yet the majority of students also agreed that their university period was a relatively happy one and they viewed their future positively. The students adopted a negative stance with regard to their university syllabuses, which they considered unnecessarily alien. Many were also unsure that they had a proper mastery of either English, the language of their instruction, or of their first language. The overall impression is that the students' main problems at university are practical: examinations, fees, family difficulties.

We were able to distinguish few reactions of existential anguish among the students. We acknowledge that survey research is not well geared to uncovering such reactions, but there did not appear to be much cultural anguish (as distinct from worry over problems of personal advancement and success) in the biographical accounts written for us by the students. There may indeed be more anguish in student sensitivities than foreign observers like ourselves can easily discern or than the students themselves are entirely conscious of. But we suspect that if there is any anguish, it is integrated in this generation of students into attitudes that are dominantly pragmatic: they are hurrying in 'out of the rain', and in their hurry they are mainly concerned with practical achievement. In this respect the public attitudes of the students are similar to their more personal attitudes. If they are ideological in any way, it is mainly in being pragmatic. In their general approach they accept what works, whether in the university system or in the wider political and social system. They are not unaware that these systems work to their particular advantage. But they also probably see them as all that is realistically possible in the country.

Implicit in the generalizations that we have been making is an important observation that emerges from our empirical data: there is only relatively light variation in attitudes on most issues between subgroups within the population of university students. Especially striking is the uniformity on most issues between the samples at each of the universities, despite the traditions of political division and socio-economic differentiation between areas. This is also broadly true in terms of ethnic, religious, age and academic groups, and, for that matter, of groups distinguished according to fathers' occupation and income. The impact that such variables seem to have on attitudes is generally slight, modifying only marginally the major patterns.

The uniformity that we have observed suggests the conclusion that many elements of a common elite culture already exist among educated Nigerians. Since our data relates to students, we can only put forward this conclusion as a hypothesis that requires verification in a full elite survey. If such a common or national culture exists—and we tend to think that it does—it provides some basis on which the integration of the peoples can be constructed. We venture to say that in their outlook and values educated Nigerians are further towards social integration than they themselves may realize.

Explaining the relative uniformity of outlook that has been found among the students is essentially a problem of socialization which is beyond the direct scope of the present study. Yet we would like to end our own study with a brief set of hypothetical and converging explanations of the phenomenon. First, in spite of the variations in language, social structure and religious belief among the indigenous cultures of the Nigerian peoples, these cultures tend to produce a broad likeness in the basic attitudes of their members. This effect is hardly surprising in view of the similarities in technology (manual farming and mainly local markets) and social organization (lineage structures and/or extended family relations and village communities, even in large towns) among the peoples. Second, the schools system, despite differences in sponsorship (government or mission), has been remarkably uniform throughout the country in curriculum, examination methods and discipline. Third, and probably most important for the wider political and social attitudes that we have been probing, is the shared relationship to the structures and processes of modern Nigeria—social occupations and economic rewards; bureaucracy with its colonial heritage and contemporary functioning, inter-ethnic and inter-class relations, political experience during three phases (colonial, civilian/democratic, and military) and international communications and relations. These provide the context within which the students expect to operate and set the values that appear both to further the good of the peoples and to legitimize the privilege of the intelligentsia.

FOOTNOTES

1. The age patterns of Nigerian professionals is discussed in a manpower survey carried out in 1966. In that year 54.1 percent of the total of registered professionals were under 36 years of age (in 1964 the percentage was 64.1). The greatest concentration of registered professionals in 1966 was within the age group of 31-35 years which accounted for 31.9 percent of total registration: see *Nigeria's Professional Manpower in Selected Occupations 1966* (Lagos: National Manpower Board, 1967), p.9.

Appendix 1: Information on the Samples

INTRODUCTION

This study draws on data produced by three distinct questionnaires (or combinations of them) administered to a number of different samples. The succession of the questionnaires is explained in the introductory chapter; the complete text of the questionnaires (with notes as to which samples they were used in) will be found in Appendix 2. The purpose of the present Appendix is to supplement the information on the samples which was given in the introductory chapter.

According to the use we have made of them our samples fall into three categories: one probability sample (ABU, 1973) is treated as fully representative of the student population from which it is drawn (the ABU main campus student body) and provides the main foundation of the study; two non-probability samples (ABU, 1970 and ABU, 1971) are drawn on both for analysis of attitudinal and personal background (social characteristics) variables; nine non-probability samples which, with the exception of ABU 1973A, were done at four of Nigeria's other universities are referred to as explained in the intrductory chapter. Further information is provided below about the samples in each of these categories.

1. THE ABU PROBABILITY SAMPLE, 1973

This sample is the main basis of our study. At the time this probability sample was undertaken (employing the composite questionnaire numbered V in Appendix 2) we had carried out and analysed the results of the two non-probability samples at ABU (discussed below) and several of the non-probability samples done at other Nigerian universities (listed below). Analysis and comparison of the results produced by these samples at ABU and at the other Nigerian universities had convinced us of their general reliability. Technically, however, the results retained the element of uncertainty deriving from the fact that the samples were not technically

APPENDIX 1: INFORMATION ON THE SAMPLES

random within the whole student populations, and while they shared some of the elements of quota, cluster, and stratified sampling, they could not properly be considered any of these.

We decided, therefore, in order to put our basic ABU data on the most solid technical basis possible, to consolidate the most productive items tested in our previous questionnaires into a single questionnaire, and to administer this to a probability sample representative of the ABU student body. We decided on a systematic unstratified random sample of all degree programme students on the ABU main campus,[1] aiming at a sample of completed questionnaires of at least 10 percent of the relevant population. To this end, a name and address list of all students was obtained from the university administration. While the ABU total student enrolment was (during the 1973/74 Session) put at 6,050, elimination of the non-degree programmes (pre-university and diploma programmes) and the programmes carried out off the main campus (especially those at the Institute of Administration in Zaria and Abdullahi Bayero College in Kano) reduced the number to 2,795. From the students in this core category, using an interval method, a sample of 362 names was drawn. These were divided up (again using a randomizing method) among paid student research assistants. The student assistants were given uniform training and instructions. They found the students on their lists, explained the project, left the questionnaire and returned to collect the completed questionnaire. A female student assistant dealt with the female students in the sample.

Administration took place during the first two weeks of December, 1973, with some call-back work done in January, 1974 (after the Christmas holiday). Of the original 362 names in the sample, 20 were eliminated because they were not (for one reason or another) presently in the university, or because they were not (records to the contrary) in main-campus degree programmes. The sample from which our assistants attempted to obtain completed questionnaires was thus reduced to 342. The majority of these returned the questionnaires promptly with a single return call. Return calls were limited to three with a few exceptions. Completed questionnaires received totalled 286, a return rate of 83.6 percent (and slightly more than 10 percent of the student population concerned). Flat refusals reported to us totalled only 14 (4.1 percent). Some of the other students who did not return questionnaires might be classed as refusals by the method of infinite procrastination, but the majority of the remaining members of the sample were not found; among them were probably some additional students who had withdrawn from the university. Since the return rate was satisfactory as a result of the work of our student assistants alone, we cancelled plans to make personal

APPENDIX 1: INFORMATION ON THE SAMPLES

approaches ourselves to the 'recalcitrants' (since this would have carried the danger that the results produced by this pressure might be biased).

Some major characteristics of the sample are as follows:

Table 1 *The ABU 1973 Sample*

Year at ABU	Number	Percentage	Sex of student	Number	Percentage
First year	115	40.2%	Male	249	87.1%
Second year	96	33.6%	Female	35	12.2%
Third year	72	25.2%	(No response)	(2)	(0.7%)
Fourth or fifth year	2	0.7%			
(No response)	(1)	(0.4%)			
	286	100.1%		286	100.0%

Type of Study	Number	Percentage	Student's Religion	Number	Percentage
Humanities Faculties	153	53.5%	Muslim	71	24.8%
Sciences Faculties	124	43.4%	Christian	205	71.7%
(No response or 'other')	(9)	(3.1%)	Animist, agnostic, atheist	9	3.1%
			(No response)	(1)	(0.3%)
	286	100.0%		286	99.9%

Students' Home State

Northern States	Number	Percentage	Southern States	Number	Percentage
Benue Plateau	39	13.6%	East Central	14	4.9%
Kano	13	4.5%	Lagos	1	0.3%
Kwara	74	25.9%	Mid-Western	13	4.5%
North Central	25	8.7%	Rivers	6	2.1%
North Eastern	45	15.7%	South Eastern	8	2.8%
North Western	20	7.0%	Western	20	7.0%
(No response or non-Nigerian)	(8)	(2.8%)			

In these characteristics, the sample approximates (allowing for the exclusions of faculties noted above) official data available on the student body. The apparent bias toward first year and away from third year in fact is a reflection of the very rapid growth in ABU enrolment. The sample thus permits us to generalize with a high degree of confidence on the ABU degree programme student body as a whole. It is also noteworthy that the attitudinal data produced compared closely with that produced by our earlier non-random samples, thus strengthening our faith in those findings. This sample is referred to in the text as 'ABU, 1973'.

2. THE ABU, 1970 AND ABU, 1971 NON-PROBABILITY SAMPLES

Our first questionnaire (reproduced as questionnaire I in Appendix 2) was designed, pre-tested and revised during the first months of 1970. During May and June, 1970, 432 usable questionnaires were obtained; a further 63 were obtained the next autumn (1970) (care was taken to avoid overlap with the earlier group) giving a total number of completed questionnaires of 495.

APPENDIX 1: INFORMATION ON THE SAMPLES

Our second questionnaire (reproduced in Appendix 2) was designed, pre-tested and revised during the autumn months of 1971 and administered in November and December of that year and 419 completed questionnaires were obtained. Using the university's structure of courses to construct these samples it was possible to avoid overlap between respondents in each case (see below), which made it possible to combine the ABU, 1970 and ABU, 1971 samples for analysis of background variables, producing a total sample of 914. The samples are not combined for purposes of attitudinal analysis. The size of the combined sample (which included nearly half the students in the programmes dealt with) compensates for its non-probability basis. And the consistency of results of each of the samples on attitudinal variables with the results of the 1973 probability sample (and with non-probability samples done at other universities) has led us to have confidence in their reliability, despite their non-probability basis.

After an initial and unsatisfactory experiment with handout-and-voluntary-return, we used in-class fill-in for both these samples, constructing the sample by using the structure of courses of study. ABU makes wide use, especially in Part I, of large lecture courses which bring together most, sometimes all, of the students in a given faculty (e.g., Science, or Arts and Social Sciences), thus affording a good one-year cross-section of students in that faculty. The structure of ABU's courses of study likewise has the advantage (from the present standpoint) of affording little choice to individual students. By comparison with universities in the U.S.A. the various degree programmes tend to be rigid and self-contained, and students usually take classes only in their own year and own faculties. Memberships of a large proportion of ABU's classes are thus mutually exclusive, which made it possible to avoid overlap.

We were generally successful, using this method, in obtaining adequate numbers of the various sub-populations (such as women students, southerners, the various years at university, the major field-of-study categories, and the major ethnic groups) to be able to analyse the impact of such variables on attitudes. Both the samples were weighted towards the non-science fields, but included control groups of science students of adequate size. The same is true of year-at-university with Part I (first year) heavily over-represented but with adequate representation of second and third year to permit analysis of the impact of this variable. Our analysis of the results of the two questionnaires (using extensive two and three variable cross-tabulations) showed in fact that the field-of-study and year-at-ABU variables had surprisingly little impact on opinion, even in cases where one would have expected a link between studies and opinions. As is indicated at various points in the study variables such as ethnicity, home State and sex were more important in terms of affecting opinions. These latter variables were not significantly affected by the patterns of over- and under-representation in the samples as a whole. These facts undoubtedly help to explain why these two non-probability samples produced results consistent with the probability sample.

Some characteristics of these two samples are shown in Table 2.

Table 2. The ABU 1970 and 1971 Samples

Year at ABU	Questionnaire I (1970)	Questionnaire II (1971)	Religion	Questionnaire I (1970)	Questionnaire II (1971)
Pre-Degree	7.9% (39)	22.2% (93)	Muslim	30.5% (151)	33.4% (140)
First year	48.1% (238)	52.5% (220)	Christian	66.1% (327)	61.1% (256)
Second year	24.7% (122)	24.8% (104)	Animist, Atheist, Agnostic, other	1.6% (8)	3.4% (14)
Third year	14.9% (74)	*	(No response)	1.8% (9)	2.1% (9)
Other, did not provide information	4.4% (22)	0.5% (2)	Total	100.0% (495)	100.0% (419)
Total	100.0% (495)	100.0% (419)			
Sex			Type of Study		
Male	91.5% (453)	91.4% (383)	Faculty of Arts and Social Sciences	60.2% (298)	43.4% (182)
Female	7.7% (38)	8.1% (34)	Other non-Science	16.0% (79)	20.3% (85)
No response	0.8% (4)	0.5% (2)	All Sciences	19.8% (98)	33.4% (140)
Total	100.0% (495)	100.0% (419)	Other, No response	4.0% (20)	2.9% (12)
			Total	100.0% (495)	100.0% (419)

Students' Home State

Northern States	Questionnaire I (1970)	Questionnaire II (1971)	Southern States	Questionnaire I (1970)	Questionnaire II (1971)
Benue Plateau	16.2% (80)	17.4% (73)	East Central	1.4% (7)	1.9% (8)
Kano	5.7% (28)	6.0% (25)	Lagos	0.4% (2)	0.5% (2)
Kwara	16.6% (82)	18.6% (78)	Mid-Western	6.1% (30)	6.2% (26)
North Central	9.5% (47)	7.6% (32)	Rivers	2.6% (13)	4.5% (19)
North Eastern	10.9% (54)	16.0% (67)	South Eastern	4.6% (23)	2.6% (11)
North Western	7.5% (37)	11.9% (50)	Western	14.3% (71)	5.5% (23)
No response	4.2% (21)	1.0% (4)			
Non-Nigerian	—	0.2% (1)			
Totals	100.0% (495)	99.9% (419)			

* The third year was avoided in the 1971 survey to avoid overlapping with the first (1970) sample.

3. THE OTHER NON-PROBABILITY SAMPLES

As we developed our questionnaires and analysed our ABU data, when the opportunity presented itself we also asked colleagues at other of Nigeria's universities to give our questionnaires to classes of students. We were interested in the extent to which opinions among student groups at the southern universities, sharply differentiated from ABU in terms of recruitment patterns, would diverge from the ones found at ABU. In the event, with few exceptions we found a remarkable pattern of similarity in the distributions of responses obtained at the various universities. This general similarity of results suggested two related conclusions: that there was less variability between the university student populations and within each than might have been predicted; and that the non-probability samples done at the other universities, even where they consisted of only 100 students drawn from a single class, were producing results which were at least roughly indicative of patterns of opinion in the whole student bodies concerned.

We therefore decided to present results from these samples in the study. The various samples, their "N", their date, the questionnaire involved, and the mode of reference to them, are shown below. Among them, the most important are the Ibadan 1973 and Nsukka 1973 samples. Both these employ composite questionnaires paralleling that used in the ABU 1973 probability sample. While both are non-probability samples, each has more strength than the other non-probability samples, the Ibadan sample in terms of roughly balancing science and non-science subjects and the Nsukka sample in terms of number (N=566).

Table 3. Non-Probability Samples

University	Session	Questionnaire Employed	"N"	How referred to in Text*
Admadu Bello	1972-73	Questionnaire III	225	ABU 1973A†
Ibadan	1970-71	Questionnaire I	140	Ibadan 1971
	1972-73	Questionnaire I	162	Ibadan 1972
	1973-74	Questionnaire IV (composite)	197	Ibadan 1973
Lagos	1970-71	Questionnaire I	109	Lagos 1971
	1971-72	Questionnaire I	133	Lagos 1972
Ife	1972-73	Questionnaire II	98	Ife 1973
Nsukka	1972-73	Questionnaire II	68	‡
	1973-74	Questionnaire V (composite)	566	Nsukka 1973

* Dates used refer to calendar year within which the administration fell.
† Questionnaire III was used only in this administration; its questions were incorporated into the composite questionnaires used in the first term of the 1973-74 Session.
‡ We decided as a matter of arbitrary principle not to report samples smaller than about 100: hence this Nsukka sample is not referred to in the text.

APPENDIX 1: INFORMATION ON THE SAMPLES

FOOTNOTE

1. This included students of the Faculties of Arts and Social Sciences, Science, Education, Engineering, Veterinary Medicine and Medicine (Pharmacy). The main exclusions were ABU's predegree programme, the School of Basic Studies (1,085 students), and the programmes carried out at ABU's other two campuses, the Institution of Administration (865 students) and Abdullahi Bayero College in Kano (853 students).

Appendix 2: The Questionnaires

QUESTIONNAIRE I

Personal Data

We will appreciate it if you will provide the following information, none of which will affect the anonymity of the survey.

Age _____   Home division _____
Sex _____   Present year at ABU _____
Marital status _____   First language _____

Indicate the size of your home community *(Mark one):*
 ___ Less than 500 inhabitants
 ___ 500-1,000
 ___ 1,000-10,000
 ___ More than 10,000

Indicate the type of primary and secondary schools, T.T.C. etc, you attended *(mission, government, etc.):*
 Primary _____
 Secondary (T.T.C., etc.) _____

Of what religion are you (if Christian, what denomination)? _____
What is your father's occupation? _____
Please estimate your father's average annual income:
 ___ Subsistence farmer   ___ £200-600
 ___ Less than £50   ___ £600-1,000
 ___ £50-200   ___ More than £1,000

Please indicate the level of education of your parents:
 Father _____ Mother _____

If you have held a full-time job *before coming to ABU* please indicate its nature. _____

If, since coming to ABU, you have held a full-time job during the summer holidays, please indicate its nature. _____

What is your major subject at ABU? _____
In what other two fields have you (or, do you plan to) take the most classes?
_____ ; _____

What career do you plan to go into after graduating from ABU? (Be as specific as you can; if at this point you don't know, write "don't know".)

APPENDIX 2: THE QUESTIONNAIRES

Opinion Survey

1. Which are most important in achieving rapid economic development? *(Number the five alternatives in order of importance.)*
   - ____ Comprehensive governmental economic planning
   - ____ Sacrifice by all sectors of society
   - ____ Aid from developed countries
   - ____ Technical competence on the part of government leaders
   - ____ Mobilization of the masses

2. Which three *non*-African countries do you admire most?

   _____

   _____

3. Which three African countries do you admire most?

   _____

   _____

4. How fast do you expect that Nigeria's economic development will progress in the next twenty years? *(Check one.)*
   - ____ Very rapidly
   - ____ Rapidly
   - ____ Moderate speed
   - ____ Slowly

5. Do you think that a full-time career for a wife can be compatible with being a good wife and mother?
   - ____ Yes
   - ____ No

6. Does your education tend to reduce the understanding between you and your parents and other members of your immediate family?
   - ____ Yes
   - ____ No

7. Do you think there tends to be a conflict between getting foreign aid from developed countries and national independence? *(Check one.)*
   - ____ Almost always
   - ____ Sometimes
   - ____ Rarely

8. Why do people resent being governed by those who belong to other ethnic groups? *(Number in order of importance.)*
   - ____ They will not get a fair share of amenities
   - ____ They simply do not trust strangers
   - ____ They feel it degrading and contrary to their dignity
   - ____ Other (Insert, and number in order) _____

APPENDIX 2: THE QUESTIONNAIRES

9. Do you think that in filling jobs requiring university degrees there tends to be too much emphasis placed on the place of origin of applicants?
   ____ Yes
   ____ No

10. Which do you think is likely to have a happier life? *(Number in order.)*
    ____ African peasant living in a traditional culture
    ____ Western industrial worker
    ____ High African civil servant
    ____ High African political leader

11. Men who are university graduates tend to select their wives (if they are not already married) according to which criteria? *(Number in order of importance.)*
    ____ Love
    ____ Money
    ____ Attractiveness
    ____ Same ethnic group
    ____ High education (including university degree)
    ____ High education (but a little below the university level)
    ____ Same religion
    ____ High traditional status

12. Women who are university graduates tend to select their husbands according to which criteria? *(Number in order of importance.)*
    ____ Love
    ____ Money
    ____ High status of man
    ____ Security of husband's position
    ____ Same ethnic group
    ____ Feeling that husband will treat her well
    ____ Same religion
    ____ High traditional status

13. Do you agree or disagree with the following statement: "The masses in African countries are not yet capable of making rational choices in elections for national political offices."
    ____ Agree
    ____ Disagree

APPENDIX 2: THE QUESTIONNAIRES   183

14. Which are most important for a developing country? *(Choose three.)*
    - ____ National unity and patriotism
    - ____ Efficient civil service
    - ____ Abundant economic resources
    - ____ Integrity in all ranks of society
    - ____ Respect for authority
    - ____ Modernizing and technical skills

15. Out of the following, mark the *two* mottoes which you like best.
    - ____ No condition is permanent
    - ____ Those who envy me are those of my own house
    - ____ Don't spoil my joy, Lord
    - ____ Life is war
    - ____ Love all, trust few

16. List in order of importance the groups which most influence opinion in your home community.
    - ____ Secondary and university graduates
    - ____ Middle level groups (clerks, traders, small contractors, etc.)
    - ____ Traditional leaders
    - ____ Other: _____ (Write in, and number)

17. Would you prefer a job in your home state to one in a different part of the country? *(Mark one answer.)*
    - ____ Yes
    - ____ No

18. Do you think that in general authoritarian governments dominated by public servants are better able to bring about rapid economic development than democratic governments dominated by politicians?
    - ____ Yes
    - ____ No

19. Suppose you wished to express feelings of affection to someone; would you prefer to do it in English or in your first language?
    - ____ English
    - ____ First language

20. Which of the following skills are most important for a developing country? *(Number in order.)*
    - ____ Political skills
    - ____ Administrative skills
    - ____ Technical skills (engineers, doctors, etc.)
    - ____ Business and entrepreneurial skills

21. What are the three most common sources of tension, unhappiness and worry among uneducated people who live in your community?
   _____
   _____
   _____

22. Number the following values in order of importance:
   ____ Equality
   ____ Law and order
   ____ Freedom
   ____ Economic growth

23. How should a government act about ethnic loyalties? *(Check one.)*
   ____ Ignore them
   ____ Abolish them
   ____ Conciliate them

24. What are the best uses of money, when people make more than enough to satisfy their immediate material needs? *(Choose three.)*
   ____ Help members of the family
   ____ Help other people in need
   ____ Save, to assure security for the future
   ____ Save, to amass capital for investment
   ____ Live a full and exciting life

25. Name three elements of Western culture which you most like.
   _____
   _____
   _____

26. Name three elements of Western culture which you most dislike.
   _____
   _____
   _____

27. What do you think are the most important motives of European expatriates who work in independent African countries? *(Number the five alternatives in order of importance.)*
   ____ High salaries
   ____ More social prestige than they would get at home
   ____ Desire to be of service
   ____ More professional advancement than they could get at home
   ____ They find the life pleasant

28. What kind of career advancement do you expect that people graduating now will tend to experience? *(Mark one.)*
    ____ Rapid
    ____ Moderate
    ____ Slow
    ____ Very slow

29. If they had the choice, which one of the following situations do you think most members of most 'ethnic' groups would choose?
    ____ Form minority in rich state
    ____ Have own state, even if economic advantages are less

30. Which is the better way to bring about major social changes which are bound to come about sooner or later?
    ____ Rapid change, which "gets it over with," but at the cost of some disruption of the lives of individuals and groups
    ____ Evolutionary change, which is less disruptive but moves slower

31. Do you think that there is disappointment with the results of independence among the following groups? *(Mark the appropriate word beside each group.)*
    1. High civil servants   __ Much   __ Some   __ None
    2. University students   __ Much   __ Some   __ None
    3. Lower civil servants   __ Much   __ Some   __ None
    4. Big businessmen   __ Much   __ Some   __ None
    5. Small businessmen
       and traders   __ Much   __ Some   __ None
    6. Common people   __ Much   __ Some   __ None

32. Would you be interested in spending an additional year at the University (beyond your degree) even if there was no possibility of obtaining a further degree or other formal recognition of your additional work?
    ____ Yes
    ____ No

33. Would you say that the lives of university graduates are generally characterised by worry and emotional tension by comparison with people living in their traditional societies? *(Mark one.)*
    ____ Much more strain and tension
    ____ More strain and tension
    ____ About the same, though the tensions are different
    ____ Less strain and tension

34. Out of the following, mark the *two* mottoes which you like best.
    ____ God is generous, man isn't
    ____ Cry for life, not for things
    ____ Fortune favours the brave
    ____ One plus God is majority
    ____ Little by little

35. Which of the following are the best things about the Western developed countries? *(Choose three.)*
    ____ High standard of living
    ____ High standard of health
    ____ National unity
    ____ Political stability
    ____ Ability of the individual to determine what his life will be
    ____ Scientific and cultural achievements
    ____ Strength and dignity in relations with other countries

36. What was the single best feature of British colonialism in Nigeria?
    _____

37. What was the single worst feature of British colonialism in Nigeria?
    _____

38. Do you think that 10 or 15 years from now your closest friendships and social life will have any tendency to follow "ethnic" lines? *(Mark one.)*
    ____ Yes
    ____ No
    ____ Can't say

39. Which of the following would you be likely to choose? *(Mark one.)*
    ____ An exciting and well-paid job which would last only for two or three years
    ____ A job which was somewhat dull and gave only an average salary, but which offered an assured career.

40. Do you agree or disagree with the following statement: "The sacrifice of present generations for future generations is a choice which must be made if rapid economic development is to be achieved."
    ____ Agree
    ____ Disagree

APPENDIX 2: THE QUESTIONNAIRES 187

41. Number the following in order of importance for a developing country.
    ____ Stable government
    ____ Rapid economic development
    ____ Democratic freedom
    ____ National unity
    ____ Honest and public spirited government leaders
    ____ National dignity and an independent foreign policy

42. What proportion of Europeans do you think are racially prejudiced against Africans? *(Mark one.)*
    ____ All, whether they admit it or not
    ____ Most
    ____ About half
    ____ A minority

43. In what order is it realistic for African governments to conciliate the following groups, in order to stay in power? *(Number in order.)*
    ____ Educated elite groups
    ____ Traditional leaders
    ____ Town working classes
    ____ Peasants

44. Would you consider taking a higher paid job in a rural area before a lower paid one in a city or town? *(Mark one.)*
    ____ Yes
    ____ Yes, but for a limited period only
    ____ No

45. What proportion of civil servants in most African countries are capable of putting national interests ahead of their own interests and family loyalties? *(Mark one.)*
    ____ Almost all
    ____ Most, but by no means all
    ____ Relatively few

46. Do you think that a university student should feel duty bound to leave the university and sacrifice his degree if his family badly needed him at home?
    ____ Yes ____ No ____ Not sure
    Do you think that most students would do so?
    ____ Yes ____ No ____ Not sure

47. Do you think that people in your home community tend to give more or less respect to university graduates than the accomplishment really deserves? *(Mark one.)*
    ____ More
    ____ Less
    ____ About what it deserves

48. How would you rate your University years in terms of your personal happiness? *(Mark one.)*
    ____ Best years of my life
    ____ Worst years of my life
    ____ Average
    ____ A little better than average
    ____ A little worse than average

49. What do you think are the most important sources of worry or strain in the lives of most university students? *(Pick three.)*
    ____ Competition with other students for high marks
    ____ Worry about employment after graduation
    ____ Worry about failure or low degree classification
    ____ Relations with opposite sex
    ____ Antagonistic relations with other students
    ____ Jealousy or antagonism within family at home
    ____ Other kinds of family problems
    ____ Relations with ABU teachers
    ____ Worry about fees

50. How would you rate ABU teachers in general with respect to the interest they take in students as individuals? *(Mark one.)*
    ____ Very good
    ____ Good
    ____ Medium
    ____ Poor
    ____ Very bad

51. Do you think that student enrolment in Nigerian universities should be expanded even if this means lowering entrance standards?
    ____ Yes
    ____ No

52. Which would you *condemn* most strongly? *(Mark one.)*
    ____ A civil servant who follows the law strictly and thereby causes some hardship to the public
    ____ A civil servant who "bends" the law and thereby helps the public

53. Would you want your daughters to get a university education?
    ____ Yes
    ____ No
    ____ Not sure
54. Do you think the syllabuses of Nigerian universities should undergo major revision to make them less "Western" and more "Nigerian"?
    ____ Yes
    ____ No
55. Do you think that most students tend to form their closest friendships among students from the same area of Nigeria?
    ____ Yes
    ____ No
56. Do you worry about the possibility that you might fail in your studies or get a degree classification lower than your proper ability? *(Mark one.)*
    ____ Very much
    ____ Some
    ____ Not at all
57. Which of Nigeria's former regions have you visited? *(Mark the ones you have visited.)*
    ____ West   ____ Mid-West   ____ East
58. How many of Nigeria's twelve states have you visited? (Include visits made to areas concerned during your lifetime; i.e., not just those made since the creation of the states.)
    ____ (Insert number.)
59. Do you think that ethnic loyalties as a divisive factor in Nigerian life will be less important twenty years from now? *(Mark one.)*
    ____ Much less important
    ____ Less important, but still a factor to be reckoned with
    ____ About the same
60. If someone said to you that you neither spoke English perfectly nor your own language perfectly would you agree or disagree?
    ____ Agree   ____ Disagree
61. How well do you consider you know the traditions of your own people? *(Mark one.)*
    ____ Very well
    ____ Well
    ____ Not very well

APPENDIX 2: THE QUESTIONNAIRES

62. List the three ethnic groups with which you feel your own group has most affinity; list in order of closeness.

    _____
    _____
    _____

63. What do you think are the most common sources of worry and strain among civil servants who are university graduates? *(Number in order.)*
    - ____ Relations with politicians
    - ____ Slow professional advancement
    - ____ Lack of security in job
    - ____ Inadequate salary
    - ____ Relatives who need help
    - ____ Lack of personal fulfilment in job
    - ____ Problems with wife or wives and children

64. Do you expect ever again to live (as opposed to visit) in your home community?
    - ____ Yes
    - ____ No
    - ____ Not sure

65. When most students are confronted with situations of extreme personal difficulty, in whom do you think they generally place the most trust? *(Number in order.)*
    - ____ Wife
    - ____ Mother
    - ____ Father
    - ____ Uncle
    - ____ Brother
    - ____ Sister
    - ____ Friend

66. Do you think that people in your family and home community pay more attention to your opinions and advice as a result of your university education? *(Check one answer.)*
    - ____ Much more
    - ____ More
    - ____ About the same as before
    - ____ Less

APPENDIX 2: THE QUESTIONNAIRES   191

67. How would you rate the opportunities for getting ahead which are open to people getting their degrees now, in comparison with those who graduated ten years ago? *(Mark one answer.)*
    ____ Better   ____ Worse
    ____ About the same ____ Much worse

68. How well do you consider that you speak your own language? *(Mark one.)*
    ____ Very well
    ____ Well
    ____ Not very well

69. In what order would you list the qualities you look for in a job? *(Number in order.)*
    ____ Security
    ____ High salary
    ____ Status in the community
    ____ Personal fulfilment and maximum use of talents
    ____ Usefulness to the community

70. Which do you think is better for a developing country (if the choice has to be made)?
    ____ An authoritarian government with a strong commitment to economic development
    ____ A democratic government closely connected with the masses but not so committed to economic development

71. What motivates developed countries to offer aid to underdeveloped ones? *(Number in order.)*
    ____ Sincere desire to help
    ____ Political advantage
    ____ Economic advantage

72. Do you think that the generation of university graduates which is emerging from the universities now has a more national outlook than those of ten years or more ago? *(Mark one.)*
    ____ More national in outlook
    ____ Less national in outlook
    ____ About the same

73. Should the standard of living of Nigeria's civil servants be revised downward to be closer to that of the "masses"?
    ____ Yes
    ____ No

74. Do you feel that you personally will be able to make a significant contribution to Nigeria's future?
    ____ Yes
    ____ No
    ____ Can't say
    ____ Some contribution, but not a very significant one

75. What attitudes do you think most university-educated Nigerians have towards Westerners and Western culture? *(Check as many answers as seem to you appropriate.)*
    ____ Respect   ____ Envy
    ____ Contempt   ____ Avoidance
    ____ Imitation   ____ Ambivalence
    ____ Hostility   Others *(Write in:)* _____

76. What attitudes do you think most non-educated Nigerians have towards Europeans and European culture? *(Check as many answers as seem to you appropriate.)*
    ____ Respect   ____ Fear
    ____ Contempt   ____ Inability to understand
    ____ Imitation   ____ Ambivalence
    ____ Envy   ____ Suspicion
                             Other *(Write in:)* _____

77. If someone said that "University education makes one a different person", would you agree or disagree?
    ____ Agree
    ____ Disagree

78. Rate the following as problems of most African countries. *(Number in order of preference.)*
    ____ Ethnic and regional loyalties, as opposed to national ones
    ____ Lack of educated administrators and technicians
    ____ Corruption among politicians
    ____ Corruption among civil servants
    ____ Interference and exploitation by developed countries
    ____ Lack of tolerance and fair play among political activists

79. Do you think that independence came too soon for most African countries? *(Mark one.)*
    ____ Too soon
    ____ Too late
    ____ About right

80. Do you think it likely that you will later take up a career in politics? *(Mark one).*
    - ____ Very likely
    - ____ Possibly
    - ____ No
    - ____ Can't say

QUESTIONNAIRE II

Personal Background

We will appreciate it if you will provide the following information, none of which will effect the anonymity of the survey. (Do not write your name on this form). Either fill in the blanks provided, or mark with a tick the appropriate alternatives.

1. Age: _____
2. Sex: ____ Male
       ____ Female
3. First language _____
4. Home State: _____
5. Marital status: ____ Married
                   ____ Not married
6. What is your present year at the university?
    - ____ Prelim year
    - ____ Basic Studies
    - ____ Part I
    - ____ Part II
    - ____ Part III
    - ____ Other *(write in)* _____
7. Indicate (by marking the appropriate alternative) what kind of primary and post-primary school you attended:

    Primary
    - ____ Government Primary
    - ____ Voluntary Agency Primary
    - ____ Other *(write in):*
    _____

    Secondary:
    - ____ Government Secondary
    - ____ Voluntary Agency Secondary
    - ____ Government TTC (ATC)
    - ____ Other *(write in):*
    _____

8. What is your religion?
   - ____ Islam
   - ____ Christian (indicate denomination: _____)
   - ____ Traditional, animist
   - ____ Agnostic, atheist

9. What is your father's *primary* occupation? (If your father is not now living, indicate his occupation before his death)
   _____

10. Please estimate your father's average annual income:
    - ____ Subsistence farmer
    - ____ Less than £50
    - ____ £50-200
    - ____ £200-400
    - ____ £400-600
    - ____ £600-1,000
    - ____ £1,000-2,000
    - ____ More than £2,000

11. Please indicate the level of education of your parents:

    Father:
    - ____ None (illiterate)
    - ____ Adult (literacy training)
    - ____ Partial primary
    - ____ Full primary
    - ____ Partial secondary
    - ____ Full secondary
    - ____ TTC
    - ____ Middle School
    - ____ Technical course
    - ____ University
    - ____ Islamic (Arabic)

    Mother:
    - ____ None (illiterate)
    - ____ Adult (literacy training)
    - ____ Partial primary
    - ____ Full primary
    - ____ Partial secondary
    - ____ Full secondary
    - ____ TTC
    - ____ Middle School
    - ____ Technical course
    - ____ University
    - ____ Islamic (Arabic)

12. If you have held a full-time job *before coming to the university* please indicate its nature: *(Do not include long vacation jobs)*
    _____

    How many years did you work full-time before you came to the university?
    - ____ Less than 1 year
    - ____ 1-2 years
    - ____ 3-5 years
    - ____ More than 5 years

13. What is your major subject at the university (or, if you have not yet chosen one, which is most likely)?
    _____

14. What career do you expect to go into after graduating from the university?
    ____ Federal government
    ____ State government
    ____ Teaching
    ____ Military or police
    ____ Industry, commerce, banks (large scale)
    ____ Professions (specify _____)
    ____ Other (specify _____)

Opinion Survey

15. Do you favour using one Nigerian language as a national language of the country? *(Mark one.)*
    ____ Yes
    ____ No

    If you *do* favour using a Nigerian language, which *one* do you suggest?
    _____

16. At what level of education do you think you began to think in national (Nigerian) terms? *(Mark one.)*
    ____ Primary
    ____ Secondary
    ____ University
    ____ Can't say

17. What is the most essential element of politics in Nigeria? *(Number in order of importance)*
    ____ Ideology
    ____ Amenities
    ____ Ethnicity
    ____ Political personalities

18. Which groups have the strongest sense of nationalism in Nigeria? *(Number in order)*
    ____ Senior civil servants
    ____ University students
    ____ Secondary school students
    ____ Military officers
    ____ Farmers
    ____ Town workers
    ____ Businessmen

APPENDIX 2: THE QUESTIONNAIRES

19. Do you agree or disagree with the following statement: 'On balance, colonization in Africa brought more advantages than disadvantages'?
    _____ Agree
    _____ Disagree

20. Do politicians primarily create tribalism, or primarily make use of already existing sentiments? *(Mark one.)*
    _____ Create it
    _____ Use existing sentiments

21. In Nigerian elections, what do you think contributed most to a politician's ability to gain support from people? *(Number in order of importance)*
    _____ Ideology
    _____ Ethnicity
    _____ Amenities for local communities
    _____ Traditional connexions
    _____ Personal wealth
    _____ National reputation

22. What were the greatest weaknesses of the first Nigerian Republic? *(Choose three)*

    _____ Ethnic bitternesses
    _____ Lack of ideology
    _____ Poor calibre of politicians
    _____ Constitutional balance between the regions
    _____ Financial corruption
    _____ Failure to promote rapid economic growth
    _____ Unrestrained use of power against opponents
    _____ Failure to retain sympathy of educated elite groups

23. Which do you think is most likely to protect your interests? *(Mark one)*
    _____ Federal government
    _____ State government
    _____ No opinion

APPENDIX 2: THE QUESTIONNAIRES   197

24. In most African countries, which occupational groups do you think have made the most positive contribution to the society? *(Number in order)*
    ____ Political leaders
    ____ Military officers
    ____ Senior civil servants
    ____ Businessmen
    ____ Technicians and professionals (doctors, engineers, etc.)
    ____ Students

25. Do you think that the politics of the future in Nigeria will be better or worse than the politics of the first Republic? *(Mark one)*
    ____ Better
    ____ About the same
    ____ Worse

26. Which of the following policies would you most approve for an African country to follow? *(Mark three)*
    ____ Exercise greater control over resident foreigners
    ____ Leave groupings like the Commonwealth
    ____ Maintain the existing type of relations with the West
    ____ Carry on tougher negotiations about commodity prices
    ____ Create closer relations with non-Western powers
    ____ Subscribe to an African high command
    ____ Offer support to African liberation movements
    ____ Join regional groupings in Africa

27. Should the new (12) states have the same or less powers than the former regions? *(Mark one)*
    ____ More
    ____ About the same
    ____ Less

28. To secure greater political unity and faster economic growth what kind of powers would you be willing to let government have over its citizens? *(Mark one)*
    ____ Absolute control
    ____ Very strong controls
    ____ Medium controls (as in Nigeria at present)
    ____ Weak controls and let citizens get on with the job themselves

APPENDIX 2: THE QUESTIONNAIRES

29. If you were asked to reckon your own sense of social identity in what order would you place the following? *(Number in order of importance)*
    ____ Identification with Africa
    ____ Identification with Nigeria
    ____ Identification with home community
    ____ Identification with home state
    ____ Identification with ethnic group

30. If you were to become a politician, at which level would you most like to participate? *(Mark one)*
    ____ Federal
    ____ State

31. What most determines the success of political systems? *(Choose one)*
    ____ Good constitutional arrangements and structures
    ____ Able and upright leaders

32. Which one of the following statements do you most agree with? *(Mark one)*
    ____ 'The Third World countries are poor because they have been and are exploited by the developed countries'
    ____ 'The Third World countries are poor because they are underdeveloped' (i.e., lack structures, skills and resources)

33. Which do you think are most essential if a political system is to be called "democratic"? *(Number in order)*
    ____ Constitutional structures respecting the balance of power
    ____ Honest government in the interests of the people
    ____ Competing politicians and political parties
    ____ Maintenance of civil liberties
    ____ Free press

34. What are the most important forces in economic development? *(Number in order of importance)*
    ____ Farming communities that accept innovation
    ____ Able politicians
    ____ Businessmen with initiative
    ____ Civil servants committed to the public good
    ____ Educated persons who help their own communities

APPENDIX 2: THE QUESTIONNAIRES   199

35. In what order do you consider the following political objectives desirable in Nigeria? *(Number in order)*
    ____ Endeavours to set up countrywide political parties
    ____ Endeavours to change state boundaries or set up new states
    ____ Reducing the gap between the rich and the poor
    ____ Reducing the disparity between the towns and the countryside
    ____ Closing the gap in educational development between different areas

36. A number of groups in Nigerian society are sometimes described as exploited and/or suffering. For which do you have the most sympathy? *(Number in order of most sympathy)*
    ____ Teachers (primary level)
    ____ Urban industrial workers
    ____ Farmers
    ____ Urban unemployed
    ____ Low-level clerical, messengers, etc.

37. Why are expatriates often disliked? *(Number in order)*
    ____ Carriers of a foreign culture
    ____ Arrogance
    ____ Insensitivity and misunderstanding of local customs
    ____ Unfairly privileged position
    ____ Seen as representatives of exploiting countries
    ____ Unwillingness to train Nigerian replacements

38. To which objectives should government give its most immediate attention? *(Number in order)*
    ____ Establishing government ownership of large-scale enterprises
    ____ Planning economic growth
    ____ Indigenising private business
    ____ Distributing benefits equitably in the country

39. Do you feel that you are as much a member of your home community as men and women your age who have not had education and who reside there permanently? *(Mark one)*
    ____ Yes
    ____ No
    ____ Can't say

40. What factors help a graduate to get ahead quickly in his career? *(Mark the three most important)*
    - ____ His academic qualifications
    - ____ Hard work
    - ____ Ethnicity
    - ____ Friends
    - ____ Family connexions
    - ____ Luck
    - ____ Seniority
    - ____ Competence
    - ____ Paying exaggerated respect to superiors
    - ____ State of origin

41. How would you describe your father's position in his own community with regard to the following?

    Wealth: ____ Above average ____ Average ____ Below average

    Education: ____ Above average ____ Average ____ Below average

    Traditional status or role: ____ High ____ Average ____ Low

    Progressive attitude: ____ More than average ____ Average ____ Less than average

42. When military rule ends in 1976, what kinds of political leaders would you like to emerge? *(Number in order)*
    - ____ Participants moved by ideology
    - ____ Members of the former political parties
    - ____ A new set of political participants
    - ____ Champions of community rights
    - ____ Military officers who run for public office
    - ____ Politicians more educated than those in the past

APPENDIX 2: THE QUESTIONNAIRES   201

43. If you were asked to make changes in local government in your areas, what would you most opt for? *(Choose three)*
    ____ Giving more powers to local authorities
    ____ Improving the clerical and technical skills of local authority employees
    ____ Amalgamating local authority areas
    ____ Breaking local authority areas up into smaller units
    ____ Reducing the powers of chiefs
    ____ Increasing tax powers of local authorities
    ____ Taking away tax powers from local authorities
    ____ Leaving more of the money they collect with local authorities
    ____ Taking away from entrenched local authority bureaucrats
    ____ Putting local government more under the control of state governments

44. In most Federal systems elsewhere in the world, either the Federal Government gets more powerful at the expense of the states, or the states get more powerful at the expense of the Federal government. Assuming that one or other has to happen, which would you prefer in the Nigerian case? *(Mark one)*
    ____ States have more power
    ____ Federal government have more power

45. What level of government is most important in bringing about economic development? *(Mark one)*
    ____ Local community
    ____ State
    ____ Federal

46. When you start working, for whom would you prefer to work? *(Number in order of preference)*
    ____ Government administration
    ____ Large private enterprise
    ____ Small private enterprise
    ____ Have own enterprise

QUESTIONNAIRE III

Personal Background

We will appreciate it if you will provide the following information, none of which will affect the anonymity of the survey. (Do not write your name on this form). Either fill in the blanks provided, or mark the appropriate alternatives.

1. Age: _____
2. Sex: _____ Male
   _____ Female
3. Home State _____
4. First Language _____

5. What is your present year at the university?
   _____ Prelim year
   _____ Basic Studies
   _____ Part I
   _____ Part II
   _____ Part III
   _____ Other (write in) _____

6. What is your religion?
   _____ Islam
   _____ Christian
   _____ Neither or other

7. What is your father's *primary* occupation? (If your father is not now living, indicate his occupation before his death)
   _____

8. Please estimate your father's average annual income (in Naira):
   _____ Subsistence farmer   _____ N800-2,000
   _____ Less than N400   _____ N2,000-4,000
   _____ N400-800   _____ More than N4,000

9. What is your major subject at the university (or, if you have not yet chosen one, which is most likely)?
   _____

APPENDIX 2: THE QUESTIONNAIRES 203

Opinion Survey

10. Which do you think is generally worse for a country?
    ____ Very strong government
    ____ Very weak government

11. If you had to choose, which do you think is preferable? *(Mark one.)*
    ____ Faster economic growth which creates inequalities between areas now, but which promises to make every area richer some time in the future.
    ____ Slower overall economic growth in which benefits are more evenly spread among different areas.

12. Many people assume that the masses of the people are not able to choose rationally in elections for national office. If one assumes that that is true, which of the following do you think is best? *(Mark one.)*
    ____ Nothing to suggest; in a democratic system we must take the risk of letting the people choose.
    ____ Finding some form of indirect election so that the final electors are sensible and informed.
    ____ A group of technocrats (able, skilled, and upright men) be permitted to rule without democratic participation.

13. Do you think that national unity in Nigeria is less or greater now than at the time of independence? *(Mark one.)*
    ____ Greater unity now
    ____ About the same
    ____ Greater unity at the time of independence

14. Under what control should the police be? *(Mark one.)*
    ____ Federal, state *and* local control
    ____ Federal control *only*
    ____ Federal *and* state control
    ____ State *and* local control
    ____ State control *only*

15. Should present generations be made to sacrifice for future generations so as to achieve rapid economic development? *(Mark one.)*
    ____ Yes   ____ No

16. How would you compare the following as elements in your own social identity (sense of belonging to social categories)?
    Nigerian identity is stronger than home state identity
    ____ Yes ____ No
    African identity is stronger than Nigerian identity
    ____ Yes ____ No
    Home community identity is stronger than ethnic identity
    ____ Yes ____ No
    Nigerian identity is stronger than ethnic identity
    ____ Yes ____ No
    Home community identity is stronger than Nigerian identity
    ____ Yes ____ No

17. If an unjust law or ruling were issued by the government, do you think that you and like-minded elites would have a chance of getting it changed or revoked? *(Mark one.)*
    ____ A good chance
    ____ Some chance
    ____ None

18. Which is more important in a developing country? (Mark *one* out of each pair of alternatives)
    ____ Economic development
    ____ Freedom
    ____ Economic development
    ____ Political stability
    ____ Economic development
    ____ National unity
    ____ Economic development
    ____ Democratic form of government
    ____ Economic development
    ____ Law and order in the society

19. Which of the institutions with which Nigeria began independence do you think continue to have value for Nigeria as an independent country? (Mark *one* alternative in the case of each system.)

System			
System of public administration	_ Much	_ Some	_ None
System of electoral democracy	_ Much	_ Some	_ None
Economic system	_ Much	_ Some	_ None
Educational system	_ Much	_ Some	_ None
System of modern law	_ Much	_ Some	_ None

20. Below are listed several pairs of things that are normally valued as objects of government policy. In each pair, mark the *one* that you consider *more* valuable or important.

    ____ Rapid economic indigenisation
    ____ Rapid economic growth

    ____ Keeping up with the demand for jobs for qualified graduates
    ____ Rapid economic growth

    ____ Expanding education rapidly
    ____ Expanding industrial capacity

    ____ Keeping up with the demand for jobs for qualified graduates
    ____ Raising the standard of living of the farmers

    ____ Urban amenities
    ____ Rural amenities

    ____ Law and order and political stability
    ____ Restructuring society to bring social justice

    ____ Democracy
    ____ Political stability

    ____ Democracy
    ____ National unity

    ____ Creating a strong national culture
    ____ Creating a strong national economy

    ____ Agricultural development
    ____ Industrialization

21. Should the incomes of Nigeria's elites be slashed (i.e., reduced by one-third or more) in order to narrow the gap between them and the common people?
    ____ Yes   ____ No

22. Of which possibility do people tend to be more afraid? *(Mark one.)*
    ____ That government will amass too much power
    ____ That government will be dominated by groups other than those they identify with

23. At what level of government do you think that democracy is most necessary in Nigeria *(Mark one.)*
    ____ Local government level
    ____ State level
    ____ Federal level

APPENDIX 2: THE QUESTIONNAIRES

24. If a leadership was inspirational, upright and efficient, do you think that it could overcome the inertia, selfishness and divisions that exist in Nigerian society, or would these problems resist in this generation the best leadership efforts? *(Mark one.)*
    ____ Leadership could overcome the problems
    ____ Problems would mostly remain, no matter how good the leadership

25. Do you think it is *possible* to transform Nigerian society as thoroughly as the Chinese Communists seem to have transformed their society? *(Mark one.)*
    ____ It is possible to transform Nigerian society thus
    ____ It is not possible to transform Nigerian society thus
    Whether or not you think it is possible, do you think it is *desirable*? *(Mark one.)*
    ____ Yes ____ No

26. In relations between ethnic groups what causes more harm? Mark *one* alternative in each case:
    ____ Distrust of one another based on mutual ignorance of traditions
    ____ Competition between elite members for jobs
    ____ Uneven development of different groups
    ____ Different historical, social and religious traditions
    ____ Antagonisms deliberately fostered through politics
    ____ Fears of being dominated by other groups
    ____ Divisions between groups created by foreign influences
    ____ Weakness of overall sense of national identity and solidarity

27. Which is more important in a developing country? Mark *one* alternative in each case:
    ____ Overcoming poverty
    ____ Overcoming ignorance
    ____ Governing elite elected in free and fair elections
    ____ Competent governing elite
    ____ Competence in managing public affairs
    ____ Integrity in managing public affairs

APPENDIX 2: THE QUESTIONNAIRES

QUESTIONNAIRE IV

Personal Background

We will appreciate it if you will provide the following information, none of which will affect the anonymity of the survey. (Do not write your name on this form). Either fill in the blanks provided, or mark the appropriate alternatives.

1. Age: ____
2. Sex: ____ Male
   ____ Female
3. Home State: _____
4. First language: _____

5. What is your present year at the university?
   ____ Prelim year
   ____ Part I
   ____ Part II
   ____ Part III
   ____ Other (write in) _____

6. What is your religion?
   ____ Christian
   ____ Muslim
   ____ Neither or other

7. What is your father's *primary* occupation? (If your father is not now living, indicate his occupation before his death)
   _____

8. Please estimate your father's average annual income (in Naira):
   ____ Subsistence farmer   ____ N800-2,000
   ____ Less than N400   ____ N2,000-4,000
   ____ N400-800   ____ More than N4,000

9. What is your major subject at the university (or, if you have not yet chosen one, which is most likely)?
   _____

Opinion Survey

10. If you had to choose, which do you think is preferable? *(Mark one.)*
    ____ Faster economic growth which creates inequalities between areas now, but which promises to make every area richer some time in the future
    ____ Slower overall economic growth in which benefits are more evenly spread among different areas

APPENDIX 2: THE QUESTIONNAIRES

11. Many people assume that the masses of the people are not able to choose rationally in elections for national office. If one assumes that that is true, which of the following do you think is best? *(Mark one.)*
    ____ Nothing to suggest; in a democratic system we must take the risk of letting the people choose
    ____ Finding some form of indirect election so that the final electors are sensible and informed
    ____ A group of technocrats (able, skilled, and upright men) be permitted to rule without democratic participation

12. Should present generations be made to sacrifice for future generations so as to achieve rapid economic development? *(Mark one.)*
    ____ Yes   ____ No

13. How would you compare the following as elements in your own social identity (sense of belonging to social categories)?
    Nigerian identity is stronger than home state identity
    ____ Yes   ____ No
    African identity is stronger than Nigerian identity
    ____ Yes   ____ No
    Home community identity is stronger than ethnic identity
    ____ Yes   ____ No
    Nigerian identity is stronger than ethnic identity
    ____ Yes   ____ No
    Home community identity is stronger than Nigerian identity
    ____ Yes   ____ No

14. Which is *more* important in a developing country? (Mark *one* out of each pair of alternatives)
    ____ Economic development
    ____ Freedom
    ____ Economic development
    ____ National unity
    ____ Economic development
    ____ Political stability
    ____ Economic development
    ____ Democratic form of government
    ____ Economic development
    ____ Law and order in society

15. Which of the institutions with which Nigeria began independence do you think continue to have value for Nigeria as an independent country? (Mark *one* alternative in the case of each system)

System of public administration	__ Much	__ Some	__ None
System of electoral democracy	__ Much	__ Some	__ None
Economic system	__ Much	__ Some	__ None
Educational system	__ Much	__ Some	__ None
System of modern law	__ Much	__ Some	__ None

16. Below are listed several pairs of things that are normally valued as objects of government policy. In each pair, mark the one that you consider *more* valuable or important.

    _____ Rapid economic indigenisation
    _____ Rapid economic growth

    _____ Keeping up with the demand for jobs for qualified graduates
    _____ Rapid economic growth

    _____ Expanding education rapidly
    _____ Expanding industrial capacity

    _____ Keeping up with the demand for jobs for qualified graduates
    _____ Raising the standard of living of the farmers

    _____ Urban amenities
    _____ Rural amenities

    _____ Law and order and political stability
    _____ Restructuring society to bring social justice

    _____ Democracy
    _____ Political stability

    _____ Creating a strong national culture
    _____ Creating a strong national economy

    _____ Agricultural development
    _____ Industrialization

    _____ Democracy
    _____ National unity

17. Should the incomes of Nigeria's elites be slashed (i.e., reduced by one-third or more) in order to narrow the gap between them and the common people?
    _____ Yes   _____ No

18. If a leadership were inspirational, upright and efficient, do you think that it could overcome the inertia, selfishness and divisions that exist in Nigerian society, or would these problems resist in this generation the best leadership efforts? *(Mark one.)*
    ____ Leadership could overcome the problems
    ____ Problems would mostly remain, no matter how good the leadership

19. Do you think it is *possible* to transform Nigerian society as thoroughly as the Chinese Communists seem to have transformed their society? *(Mark one.)*
    ____ It is possible to transform Nigerian society thus
    ____ It is not possible to transform Nigerian society thus

    Whether or not you think it is possible, do you think it is *desirable*? *(Mark one.)*
    ____ Yes   ____ No

20. In relations between ethnic groups what causes more harm? Mark *one* alternative in each case:
    ____ Distrust of one another based on mutual ignorance of traditions
    ____ Competition between elite members for jobs
    ____ Uneven development of different groups
    ____ Different historical, social and religious traditions
    ____ Divisions between groups created by foreign influences
    ____ Weakness of overall sense of national identity and solidarity

21. Which is more important in a developing country? Mark *one* alternative in each pair:
    ____ Overcoming poverty
    ____ Overcoming ignorance

    ____ Governing elite elected in free and fair elections
    ____ Competent governing elite

    ____ Competence in managing public affairs
    ____ Integrity in managing public affairs

22. Do you favour using one Nigerian language as a national language of the country? *(Mark one.)*
    ____ Yes   ____ No
    If you *do* favour using a Nigerian language, which *one* do you suggest?
    _____

APPENDIX 2: THE QUESTIONNAIRES 211

23. At what level of education do you think you began to think in national (Nigerian) terms? *(Mark one.)*
    - ____ Primary
    - ____ Secondary
    - ____ University
    - ____ Can't say

24. After transition to civilian rule in Nigeria, what factors do you think will most influence the majority of voters? *(Number in order of importance)*
    - ____ Ideology
    - ____ Amenities
    - ____ Ethnicity
    - ____ Political personalities

25. Do you agree or disagree with the following statement: 'On balance, colonization in Africa brought more advantages than disadvantages'?
    - ____ Agree
    - ____ Disagree

26. What were the greatest weaknesses of the first Nigerian Republic? *(Choose three.)*
    - ____ Ethnic bitternesses
    - ____ Lack of ideology
    - ____ Poor calibre of politicians
    - ____ One region too large
    - ____ Financial corruption
    - ____ Failure to promote rapid economic growth
    - ____ Unrestrained use of power against opponents
    - ____ Failure to retain sympathy of educated elite groups

27. Which do you think is most likely to protect your interests? *(Mark one)*
    - ____ Federal government
    - ____ State government
    - ____ No opinion

28. Do you think that the politics of the future in Nigeria will be better or worse than the politics of the first Republic? *(Mark one)*
    - ____ Better
    - ____ About the same
    - ____ Worse

29. Should the new (12) states have the same or less powers than the former regions? *(Mark one)*
    - ____ More
    - ____ About the same
    - ____ Less

30. To secure greater political unity and faster economic growth what kind of powers would you be willing to let government have over its citizens? *(Mark one)*
    - ____ Absolute control
    - ____ Very strong controls
    - ____ Medium controls (as in Nigeria at present)
    - ____ Weak controls and let citizens get on with the job themselves

31. Which one of the following statements do you most agree with? *(Mark one)*
    - ____ 'The Third World countries are poor because they have been and are exploited by the developed countries'
    - ____ 'The Third World countries are poor because they are underdeveloped (i.e., lack structures, skills and resources)

32. What are the most important forces in economic development? *(Number in order of importance)*
    - ____ Farming communities that accept innovation
    - ____ Able politicians
    - ____ Businessmen with initiative
    - ____ Civil servants committed to the public good
    - ____ Educated persons who help their own communities

33. Which of the following political objectives do you consider the *most* desirable in Nigeria? *(Mark one)*
    - ____ Reducing the gap between the rich people and the poor people
    - ____ Reducing the disparity between the towns and the countryside
    - ____ Closing the gap in development between different areas

34. A number of groups in Nigerian society are sometimes described as exploited and/or suffering. For which do you have the most sympathy? *(Number in order of most sympathy)*
    - ____ Teachers (primary level)
    - ____ Urban industrial workers
    - ____ Farmers
    - ____ Urban unemployed
    - ____ Low-level clerical, messengers, etc.

35. Do you feel that you are as much a member of your home community as men and women your age who have not had education and who reside there permanently? *(Mark one)*
    ____ Yes
    ____ No
    ____ Can't say

36. When military rule ends in 1976, what kinds of political leaders would you like to emerge? *(Number in order)*
    ____ Participants moved by ideology
    ____ Members of the former political parties
    ____ A new set of political participants
    ____ Champions of community rights
    ____ Military officers who run for public office
    ____ Politicians more educated than those in the past

37. What level of government is most important in bringing about economic development? *(Mark one)*
    ____ Local community
    ____ State
    ____ Federal

38. When you start working, for whom would you prefer to work? *(Number in order of preference)*
    ____ Government administration
    ____ Large private enterprise
    ____ Small private enterprise
    ____ Have own enterprise

QUESTIONNAIRE V

Personal Background

We will appreciate it if you will provide the following information, none of which will affect the anonymity of the survey. (Do not write your name on this form). Either fill in the blanks provided, or mark the appropriate alternatives.

1. Age:_____
2. Sex: _____Male
    _____Female
3. Home State:_____
4. First language:_____

5. What is your present year at the university?
   ____ Prelim year
   ____ Part I
   ____ Part II
   ____ Part III
   ____ Other (write in)_____

6. What is your religion?
   ____ Christian
   ____ Muslim
   ____ Neither or other

7. What is your father's *primary* occupation? (If your father is not now living, indicate his occupation before his death)
   _____

8. Please estimate your father's average annual income (in Naira):
   ____ Subsistence farmer   ____ N800-2000
   ____ Less than N400   ____ N2000-4000
   ____ N400-800   ____ More than N4000

9. What is your major subject at the university (or, if you have not yet chosen one, which is most likely)?
   _____

Opinion Survey

10. How fast do you expect that Nigeria's economic development will progress in the next twenty years? *(Check one)*
    ____ Very rapidly
    ____ Rapidly
    ____ Moderate speed
    ____ Slowly

11. Does your education tend to reduce the understanding between you and your parents and other members of your immediate family?
    ____ Yes
    ____ No

12. Do you think that in filling jobs requiring university degrees there tends to be too much emphasis placed on the place of origin of applicants?
    ____ Yes
    ____ No

13. Do you agree or disagree with the following statement: "The masses in African countries are not yet capable of making rational choices in elections for national political offices."
    _____ Agree
    _____ Disagree
14. Which are most important for a developing country? *(Choose three)*
    _____ National unity and patriotism
    _____ Efficient civil service
    _____ Abundant economic resources
    _____ Integrity in all ranks of society
    _____ Respect for authority
    _____ Modernizing and technical skills
15. Which three *non*-African countries do you admire most?
    _____
    _____
    _____
16. Which three African countries do you admire most?
    _____
    _____
    _____
17. List in order of importance the groups which most influence opinion in your home community. *(Number in order of importance)*
    _____ Secondary and university graduates
    _____ Middle level groups (clerks, traders, small contractors, etc.)
    _____ Traditional leaders
18. Would you prefer a job in your home state to one in a different part of the country? *(Mark one answer)*
    _____ Yes
    _____ No
19. Do you think that in general authoritarian governments dominated by public servants are better able to bring about rapid economic development than democratic governments dominated by politicians?
    _____ Yes
    _____ No
20. Suppose you wished to express feelings of affection to someone; would you prefer to do it in English or in your first language?
    _____ English
    _____ First language

21. Which of the following skills are most important for a developing country? *(Number in order of importance)*
    - ____ Political skills
    - ____ Administrative skills
    - ____ Technical skills (engineers, doctors, etc.)
    - ____ Business and entrepreneurial skills

22. Number the following values in order of importance:
    - ____ Equality
    - ____ Law and order
    - ____ Freedom
    - ____ Economic growth

23. How should a government act about ethnic loyalties? *(Check one)*
    - ____ Ignore them
    - ____ Abolish them
    - ____ Conciliate them

24. Which is the better way to bring about major social changes which are bound to come about sooner or later?
    - ____ Rapid change, which "gets it over with", but at the cost of some disruption of the lives of individuals and groups
    - ____ Evolutionary change, which is less disruptive but moves slower

25. Do you think that a university student should feel duty bound to leave the university and sacrifice his degree if his family badly needed him at home?
    ____ Yes   ____ No   ____ Not sure
    Do you think most students *would* do so?
    ____ Yes   ____ No   ____ Not sure

26. Do you think that people in your home community tend to give more or less respect to university graduates than the accomplishment really deserves? *(Mark one)*
    - ____ More
    - ____ Less
    - ____ About what it deserves

27. How would you rate your university years in terms of your personal happiness? *(Mark one)*
    - ____ Best years of my life
    - ____ Worst years of my life
    - ____ Average
    - ____ A little better than average
    - ____ A little worse than average

28. What do you think are the most important sources of worry or strain in the lives of most university students? *(Pick three)*
    - ____ Competition with other students for high marks
    - ____ Worry about employment after graduation
    - ____ Worry about failure or low degree classification
    - ____ Relations with opposite sex
    - ____ Antagonistic relations with other students
    - ____ Jealousy or antagonism within family at home
    - ____ Other kinds of family problems
    - ____ Relations with teachers
    - ____ Worry about fees

29. How would you rate your university teachers in general with respect to the interest they take in students as individuals? *(Mark one)*
    - ____ Very good
    - ____ Good
    - ____ Medium
    - ____ Poor
    - ____ Very bad

30. Do you think that student enrolment in Nigerian universities should be expanded even if this means lowering entrance standards?
    - ____ Yes
    - ____ No

31. Do you worry about the possibility that you might fail in your studies or get a degree classification lower than your proper ability? *(Mark one)*
    - ____ Very much
    - ____ Some
    - ____ Not at all

32. If someone said to you that you neither spoke English perfectly nor your own language perfectly would you agree or disagree?
    - ____ Agree
    - ____ Disagree

33. How well do you consider you know the traditions of your own people? *(Mark one)*
    - ____ Very well
    - ____ Well
    - ____ Not very well

34. Do you expect ever again to live (as opposed to visit) in your home community?
    ___ Yes
    ___ No
    ___ Not sure

35. Do you think that people in your family and home community pay more attention to your opinions and advice as a result of your university education? *(Check one answer)*
    ___ Much more
    ___ More
    ___ More
    ___ About the same as before
    ___ Less

36. How would you rate the opportunities for getting ahead which are open to people getting their degrees now, in comparison with those who graduated ten years ago? *(Mark one answer)*
    ___ Better
    ___ About the same
    ___ Worse
    ___ Much worse

37. How well do you consider that you speak your own language? *(Mark one)*
    ___ Very well
    ___ Well
    ___ Not very well

38. In what order would you list the qualities you look for in a job? *(Number in order)*
    ___ Security
    ___ High salary
    ___ Status in the community
    ___ Personal fulfilment and maximum use of talents
    ___ Usefulness to the community

39. Do you think that the generation of university graduates which is emerging from the universities now has a more national outlook than those of ten years or more ago? *(Mark one)*
    ___ More national in outlook
    ___ Less national in outlook
    ___ About the same

40. Do you feel that you personally will be able to make a significant contribution to Nigeria's future?
    ____ Yes
    ____ No
    ____ Can't say
    ____ Some contribution, but not a very significant one

41. Rate the following as problems of most African countries. *(Number in order of importance)*
    ____ Ethnic and regional loyalties, as opposed to national ones
    ____ Lack of educated administrators and technicians
    ____ Corruption among politicians
    ____ Corruption among civil sevants
    ____ Interference and exploitation by developed countries
    ____ Lack of tolerance and fair play among political activists

42. Do you think it likely that you will later take up a career in politics? *(Mark one)*
    ____ Very likely
    ____ Possibly
    ____ No
    ____ Can't say

43. If you had to choose, which do you think is preferable? *(Mark one)*
    ____ Faster economic growth which creates inequalities between areas now, but which promises to make every area richer some time in the future
    ____ Slower overall economic growth in which benefits are more evenly spread among different areas

44. Many people assume that the masses of the people are not able to choose rationally in elections for national office. If one assumes that that is true, which of the following do you think is best? *(Mark one)*
    ____ Nothing to suggest; in a democratic system we must take the risk of letting the people choose
    ____ Finding some form of indirect election so that the final electors are sensible and informed
    ____ A group of technocrats (able, skilled, and upright men) be permitted to rule without democratic participation

45. Should present generations be made to sacrifice for future generations so as to achieve rapid economic development? *(Mark one)*
    ____ Yes
    ____ No

APPENDIX 2: THE QUESTIONNAIRES

46. How would you compare the following as elements in your own social identity (sense of belonging to social categories?

    African identity is stronger than Nigerian identity
    ___ Yes ___ No
    Home community identity is stronger than ethnic identity
    ___ Yes ___ No
    Nigerian identity is stronger than home state identity
    ___ Yes ___ No
    Nigerian identity is stronger than ethnic identity
    ___ Yes ___ No
    Home community identity is stronger than Nigerian identity
    ___ Yes ___ No

47. Which is *more* important in a developing country? *(Mark one out of each pair of alternatives)*

    ___ Economic development
    ___ Freedom

    ___ Economic development
    ___ National unity

    ___ Economic development
    ___ Political stability

    ___ Economic development
    ___ Democratic form of government

    ___ Economic development
    ___ Law and order in society

48. Which of the institutions with which Nigeria began independence do you think continue to have value for Nigeria as an independent country? *(Mark one alternative in the case of each system)*

System of public administration	___Much	___Some	___None
System of electoral democracy	___Much	___Some	___None
Economic system	___Much	___Some	___None
Educational system	___Much	___Some	___None
System of modern law	___Much	___Some	___None

APPENDIX 2: THE QUESTIONNAIRES   221

49. Below are listed several pairs of things that are normally valued as objects of government policy. In each pair, mark the one that you consider *more* valuable or important.

    ____ Rapid economic indigenisation
    ____ Rapid economic growth

    ____ Keeping up with the demand for jobs for qualified graduates
    ____ Rapid economic growth

    ____ Expanding education rapidly
    ____ Expanding industrial capacity

    ____ Keeping up with the demand for jobs for qualified graduates
    ____ Raising the standard of living of the farmers

    ____ Urban amenities
    ____ Rural amenities

    ____ Law and order and political stability
    ____ Restructuring society to bring social justice

    ____ Democracy
    ____ Political stability

    ____ Creating a strong national culture
    ____ Creating a strong national economy

    ____ Agricultural development
    ____ Industrialization

    ____ Democracy
    ____ National unity

50. Should the incomes of Nigeria's elites be slashed (i.e., reduced by one-third or more) in order to narrow the gap between them and the common people?

    ____ Yes
    ____ No

51. If a leadership were inspirational, upright and efficient, do you think that it could overcome the inertia, selfishness and divisions that exist in Nigerian society, or would these problems resist in this generation the best leadership efforts? *(Mark one)*

    ____ Leadership could overcome the problems
    ____ Problems would mostly remain, no matter how good the leadership

APPENDIX 2: THE QUESTIONNAIRES

52. Do you think it is *possible* to transform Nigerian society as thoroughly as the Chinese Communists seem to have transformed their society? *(Mark one)*
    ____ It is possible to transform Nigerian society thus
    ____ It is not possible to transform Nigerian society thus
    Whether or not you think it is possible, do you think it is *desirable?* *(Mark one)*
    ____ Yes
    ____ No

53. In relations between ethnic groups what causes more harm? *(Mark one alternative in each pair:)*
    ____ Distrust of one another based on mutual ignorance of traditions
    ____ Competition between elite members for jobs

    ____ Uneven development of different groups
    ____ Different historical, social and religious traditions

    ____ Divisions between groups created by foreign influences
    ____ Weakness of overall sense of national identity and solidarity

54. Which is more important in a developing country? *(Mark one alternative in each pair:)*
    ____ Overcoming poverty
    ____ Overcoming ignorance

    ____ Governing elite elected in free and fair elections
    ____ Competent governing elite

    ____ Competence in managing public affairs
    ____ Integrity in managing public affairs

55. Do you favour using one Nigerian language as a national language of the country? *(Mark one)*
    ____ Yes   ____ No
    If you *do* favour using a Nigerian language, which *one* do you suggest? _____

56. After transition to civilian rule in Nigeria, what factors do you think will most influence the majority of voters? *(Number in order of importance)*
    ____ Ideology
    ____ Amenities
    ____ Ethnicity
    ____ Political personalities

APPENDIX 2: THE QUESTIONNAIRES   223

57. Do you agree or disagree with the following statement: 'On balance, colonization in Africa brought more advantages than disadvantages'?
    ____ Agree
    ____ Disagree

58. Which of the following political objectives do you consider the *most* desirable in Nigeria? *(Mark one)*
    ____ Reducing the gap between the rich people and the poor people
    ____ Reducing the disparity between the towns and the countryside
    ____ Closing the gap in development between different areas

59. A number of groups in Nigerian society are sometimes described as exploited and/or suffering. For which do you have the most sympathy? *(Number in order of most sympathy)*
    ____ Teachers (primary level)
    ____ Urban industrial workers
    ____ Farmers
    ____ Urban unemployed
    ____ Low-level clerical, messengers, etc.

60. Do you feel that you are as much a member of your home community as men and women your age who have not had education and who reside there permanently? *(Mark one)*
    ____ Yes
    ____ No
    ____ Can't say

61. When you start working, for whom would you prefer to work? *(Number in order of preference)*
    ____ Government administration
    ____ Large private enterprise
    ____ Small private enterprise
    ____ Have own enterprise

62. Which one of the following statements do you most agree with? *(Mark one)*
    ____ 'The Third World countries are poor because they have been and are exploited by the developed countries'
    ____ 'The Third World countries are poor because they are underdeveloped' (i.e., lack structures, skills and resources)

63. How satisfied are you with what your own career prospects are likely to be after graduation?
    ____ Very satisfied
    ____ Satisfied
    ____ Somewhat dissatisfied
    ____ Very dissatisfied

64. Would you say that the lives of university graduates are generally characterized by worry and emotional tension by comparison with people living in their traditional societies? *(Mark one)*
    ____ Much more strain and tension
    ____ More strain and tension
    ____ About the same, though the tensions are different
    ____ Less strain and tension

65. Would you want your daughters to get a university education?
    ____ Yes
    ____ No
    ____ Not sure

66. In most Federal systems elsewhere in the world, either the Federal Government gets more powerful at the expense of the states, or the states get more powerful at the expense of the Federal government. Assuming that one or the other has to happen, which would you prefer in the Nigerian case? *(Mark one)*
    ____ States have more power
    ____ Federal government have more power

67. Do you think that the politics of the future in Nigeria will be better or worse than the politics of the first Republic? *(Mark one)*
    ____ Better
    ____ About the same
    ____ Worse

68. Which do you think is generally worse for a country?
    ____ Very strong government
    ____ Very weak government